Enterprise Database in a Client/Server Environment

Michael Gorman

A Wiley–QED Publication

John Wiley & Sons, Inc.

New York • Chichester • Brisbane • Toronto • Singapore

Designations used by companies to distinguish their products are often claimed as trademarks. In all instances where John Wiley & Sons, Inc. is aware of a claim, the product names appear in initial capital or all capital letters. Readers, however, should contact the appropriate companies for more complete information regarding trademarks and registration.

This text is printed on acid-free paper.

This publication is designed to provide accurate and authoritative information in regard to the subject matter covered. It is sold with the understanding that the publisher is not engaged in rendering legal, accounting, or other professional services. If legal advice or other expert assistance is required, the services of a competent professional person should be sought. FROM A DECLARATION OF PRINCIPLES JOINTLY ADOPTED BY A COMMITTEE OF THE AMERICAN BAR ASSOCIATION AND A COMMITTEE OF PUBLISHERS.

ISBN 0 471-52164-7

Printed in the United States of America

10 9 8 7 6 5 4 3 2 1

Enterprise Database in a Client/Server Environment

Table of Contents

PREFACE

Enterprise database is not a weekend's work. It takes years. And, if any of the pundits are correct, having the right information *ahead of time* is the competitive edge. There are a number of studies showing that the real cost of information systems, maintenance, is about 75 percent of the total information systems expense. Thus, a two million dollar development project has a maintenance cost of about six million dollars, for a total price of eight million dollars. If the information systems business is to be removed as a roadblock to progress, information systems maintenance must become a fraction of development costs rather than a multiple.

This book contains strategies that make maintenance and evolution of enterprise-wide database systems efficient, cost-effective, quick, and correct. Now that's a big claim! This book is a direct consequence of a series of projects started in the early 1970s. The first full use of the contained methodologies was accomplished in 1985 when a U.S. Army General said: *OK, now that you've built two logistics systems in three years, build ten in one year! And, reduce the cost at each increment!* The mission was accomplished! Two *factories* were designed and built. The first was the *specification factory*, and the second was the *software factory*. For the first system of the ten, the estimates were 125 percent of time and cost of a custom system. That was because of the necessary factory and tool building. The actual costs ran 85 percent, and the project was completed early. The second increment was pegged at 40 percent. It came in at 20 percent, and also early. The remaining systems were estimated at 20 percent, but cost 10 percent. In all cases, the systems were ready before the data was!

The real test was maintenance. Because the specification factory was repository-based, and because the software factory was a direct consequence of the specification factory, changes were immediately traceable. Changes in fundamental formulas that predicted the availability of a weapons systems based on maintenance records were immediately able to be traced through the specification, and then located in the actual software factory's inventory. Once the software module was found and changed, generation of the production system versions was automatic. Changes that took months in the formerly custom-designed and custom-programmed versions now took a week for all the versions. The costs were so reduced that the two custom-created systems were replaced for less than one cycle of maintenance! Not only was the design and development accelerated, maintenance was reduced to a fraction of its former costs! In short, mission accomplished!

Database is a philosophy of quality organization, planning, and management. Enterprises that embrace database can research the past, control the present, and plan the future. Achieving database has never been easy. It requires a quality organization with carefully crafted policies and procedures. Designed well, these business policies and procedures become database objects that can be deployed throughout the organization in a client/server fashion to maximize sharing and consistency while minimizing data hoarding and irregularity.

The products of policy analysis form the foundation of database. Since to have database is to be organized, the essence of organizational quality is high caliber policy analysis. Database is merely an implementation strategy for policies and procedures. Database data are the executed policies, and the rules by which data is stored are the execution constraints imposed by the procedures. Hence, database is the direct effect of executed policies and procedures.

Over the years, database has concentrated on the policy component of policies and procedures. Recently, advances in DBMS technology have enabled the inclusion of both policies and procedures into database. The common implementation mechanism for the procedures component, that is, constraints (column and table), assertions and triggers are the result of ANSI database standard activities (specifically X3H2 and its family of SQL standards). Collectively, the data structures along with the sets of constraints, assertions, and triggers enable complete and comprehensive implementations of an enterprise's policies and procedures.

In today's parlance, a lucid *policy-procedure* pair is called a business object. The goal of business object analysis is to enable quality DBMS object design, that is, the definition of both the data structure and the data structure transformations that:

- Installs a new business object in the database
- Transforms a business object from one coherent state to another
- Removes an object from the database

How do you know that a business object is completely defined? How do you know the boundaries of a business object. When is there only one business object and not two? When are business objects nested? The answers to all these questions are found not by researching technology, but by thoroughly researching coherently crafted business policies and procedures.

Quality database begins with correctly formulated business policies and procedures. Database is merely their automation vehicle. Database deployment is merely a strategy for organization deployment. Quality begets quality, conversely...

Client/server is an implementation alternative for database deployment. Instead of having all the DBMS objects (data structures and methods) resident on a mainframe, they are distributed; some objects reside on the client, some on the server. It is not even required that all implementations within a corporation be implemented in the same manner.

The essential component of client server is the discrete packaging (from design through implementation) of database components so that they can be distributed throughout the different client/server alternatives.

This book is all about the creation of maintainable, client/server database applications for the entire enterprise by describing the essential models, methodology, and tools essential for its success. The essential models are: mission, data, database processes, information systems, business events, business functions, organization, implemented data, implemented information systems, and security. Each is precisely defined so that business object integrity is preserved, while at the same time preserving the maximum set of alternatives for business object deployment in today's client/server environments.

This book embraces the belief that the set correct specifications of enterprise database are very independent from how and where database is implemented. Thus, there may be multiple, concurrently executing, yet controlled sets of client/server implementations for the same specification

This book asserts that for a given set of business missions, and set of policies and procedures, there is one and only one set of correct database objects (data structures and methods (assertions, triggers and stored procedures).

Further, this book supports the notion that there may be multiple functional styles for carrying out a business's policies and procedures. There may even have to be different configurations of information systems supporting the different styles. Regardless of the style or information system configuration, the policies and procedures that are executed through the insertion, modification, and/or deletion of business objects are nonredundantly specified thus are implemented without the possibility of conflict.

This book is part of a total methodology. It defines the client/server paradigm that maximizes reuse and minimizes redundancies. It presents the essentials for planning client/server database projects, and presents practical, easy to follow guidelines for distributing the database and process models.

The second part, *Implementing Enterprise Database in a Client/Server Environment* contains detailed, step-by-step techniques to design, develop, and implement client/server database. Included in the second part are project planning guidelines, estimating mechanisms, and experience honed metrics. It also contains a complete schema for repository, and tested questionnaires for repository and distributed DBMS selection and evaluation. The second part is available from the QED Publishing Group for $125.00. Call them at 617-237-5656.

In short, this book defines the critical components of achieving high-quality, enterprise-wide client/server database; while no book can ever guarantee success, following the dictums of this methodology will certainly prevent failure.

ACKNOWLEDGEMENTS

I would like to acknowledge the help of those who made this book possible. Foremost there is my family, all of whom showed great understanding during the time it took to finish the book. Special thanks go to my son, Matthew, who spent many hours editing, and to my daughter, Elizabeth, who helped with final page make-up.

This book would have been impossible without help along the way from the late Matt Flavin. Matt pioneered many of the information engineering concepts that are credited to others.

Thanks also go to the *uncompensated co-conspirators* and their companies of the techniques and strategies contained in this book developed over the past 18 years through database project experience. In this group are Dick Fiddleman of the Council of Great City Schools; Ted Ziehe, Don Flannagan, and Dick Clikeman of MRI; John Roby of Defense Logistics; the late Matt Flavin and Andre Jezierski (whose pin-stripes kept everything lined up) of Yourdon; Art Chisholm, Bill Borst, Dan Prall, Larry Watkins, Scott Steele, George Harding, Jim Wells, and Eugene Lambert from DuPont; Ranga Rangarajan, Lee Bushnell and Janet Bollier of the Bank of America; David Anderson and Bob Evans of PECO; Perry Roubie and Sam O'Neal of CSC; Ed Peters and Bill Bronstein of Hershey; Dick Root and Ken Laszczych of Freddie Mac; Don Stewart and John Herge of CEXEC; Dick Zins, Jerry Moss, and all the GLAMIS crew from CBSI; Harry Merrifield of Paradigm; Joe *Flash* Callahan and Dick O'Neil of Grumman Data Systems; Hal Boylan and Eileen Clark of SRA; John Summers, Mike Goldman, Twyla Courtot, Linda Chambless, Stan Hopkins, Dagmar Bogan of MITRE/McLean; Vince Ventrone, Jim Valentine, Bob Pancotti, Carol Burher, Beth Wolfset, and Christine Georgelis from MITRE/Bedford; and finally to Hal Stull, the most uncompensated of them all!

This book's art was created on an Intel '486 machine with the *Arts & Letters Editor*, a truly commendable product from Computer Support Corporation, Dallas, Texas.

Finally, I am grateful to the staff at QED, especially Beth Roberts for her constructive editing and book formatting suggestions.

PART I

INTRODUCTION

Chapter 1, Introduction, presents the problems common in database applications, presents an appropriate enterprise database development paradigm, and describes the target environment for enterprise database.

1

CLIENT/SERVER MODEL

Today, enterprise database is deployed on distributed, heterogeneous hardware and systems software environments.[1] The hardware platforms are both multiple-vendor and multi-tiered, with different architectures. Included, for example, are mainframe terminals such as IBM 3270s, desktop computers such as MAC/PCs and IBM/PCs, servers such as SUN and DEC, and finally, mainframes, which are most commonly IBM or IBM-compatible. The heterogeneous systems software commonly includes operating systems such as MVS, VM/CMS, VMS, Unix, MAC/OS, and MS/DOS. DBMSs are often considered systems software and include IBM's DB/2, Datacom/DB, IDMS, Oracle, Sybase, and Adabas. In short, most businesses have embraced some form of downsizing, decentralization, and distributed processing.

1.1 Return to the Past?

To be sure, downsizing, decentralization, and distributed processing are the three newest *silver bullets*. These silver bullets are supposed to kill the *three monsters*:

- Centralized management information system (MIS)[2] inertia
- Impersonalized systems
- Big brother control

If we only had our own systems and data, we'd show 'em, is the MIS users' battle cry!

But, that's what we all had before centralized MIS, and the battle cry *then* was for centralized MIS so we could achieve economy of scale and scope, nonredundancy of data, and a single version of the truth (versus data chaos).

If we are not careful, today's new silver bullets are going to kill the present, leaving us only the past, which consisted of redundancy, conflicting semantics, and endless versions of the truth.

Figure 1.1 provides a set of data-oriented critical questions and answers to frame this issue. Semantics are the rules for meaning and usage. Figure 1.1 contrasts whether semantics are defined in a centralized or ad hoc manner. Data

---

[1] Enterprise in this book means a business, company, establishment, or industry.

[2] MIS, in this book, means any organized, data intensive system that provides current and historical information to assist in decision making, planning, and management of the enterprise.

3

Questions regarding data distribution effects	Semantic Control			
	Centralized		Decentralized	
	Data Storage Control			
	Centralized	Decentralized	Centralized	Decentralized
Is data able to be shared among sites?	yes	yes	no	no
Is concurrent processing of the same data possible?	yes	maybe	no	no
Are common or corporate reports possible?	yes	yes	no	no
Can there be an overbearing "big brother" feeling?	yes	maybe	no	no
Is there local control and ownership?	no	maybe	yes	yes
Does there need to be common data standards & policies?	yes	yes	no	no
Can local data requirements be satisfied?	maybe	yes	maybe	yes

Figure 1.1.   The effects of centralization and decentralization of semantics and data.

storage is the actual physical location of data. In most MISs that means databases. The key discriminator is whether there is either centralized data storage or distributed databases. The questions are those critical to large, multiple-site organizational MISs. The far right column represents the possible answers when an organization has fully embraced the three silver bullets, that is, decentralized semantics and decentralized data storage control. These answers are clearly undesirable. The far left column of answers represents the complete inverse of the silver bullets, that is, centralized semantics and centralized data storage. While the answers in the leftmost column are the most desirable, they have the negative effect of fostering the MIS environments of the three monsters. Of the two remaining columns, the better answers are in column 2.

A similar set of critical questions and answers regarding programs and systems is contained in Figure 1.2. Again, the least desirable is column 4, the most desirable is column 1, but the only one achievable without embracing the three monsters is column 2.

Why are the three silver bullets bearing down on us? The answer is due to the advances of technology, the lack of rapid MIS development, and the extreme maintenance backlog of the centralized MIS organization.

In regard to technology, today's desktop PC is a 50 MHz 80486, with 8 to 12 megabytes of memory and a 15 millisecond, 300 megabyte hard drive with a total

Questions regarding system distribution effects	Development Control			
	Centralized		Decentralized	
	Execution Location			
	Centralized	Decentralized	Centralized	Decentralized
Is the same program able to be shared among sites?	yes	yes	no	no
Is concurrent processing of the same data possible?	yes	maybe	no	no
Are common or corporate reports guaranteed?	yes	maybe	no	no
Can there be an overbearing "big brother" feeling?	yes	maybe	no	no
Is there local control and ownership?	no	maybe	yes	yes
Does there need to be common processing standards & practices?	yes	yes	no	no
Can local processing requirements be satisfied?	maybe	yes	maybe	yes

Figure 1.2.   The effects of centralization and decentralization of systems development.

cost under $4000. By any measure, that's a large, multi-million-dollar mainframe from the mid-1970's.

With respect to programmer productivity, PC application development environments such as dBASE IV, CLARION, and MAGEC and PC DBMSs such as Focus, Oracle, and Informix can produce entire applications in less than a week. In contrast, large division-wide or enterprise-wide MISs take scores of meetings, millions of dollars, and long waits. At the end of the wait, which is commonly from months to years, the delivered systems are often irrelevant and contain critical bugs.

A critical problem resulting from the seemingly endless delays in large-scale MIS development, deployment, and maintenance is MIS's lack of responsiveness to changing business requirements. Stories are rampant throughout the MIS industry about businesses' inability to make strategic changes because MISs cannot accommodate the proposed changes. Stories are also common about the extreme costs associated with making the simplest changes. The most common stories relate to the nine-digit zip code, and the upcoming change of century. Some organizations, having multiple campuses and buildings, found it not cost-effective to change the office numbers because they could not find all the computer file locations and program variables where office numbers are used.

In summary, because of today's technology, sophisticated systems can be efficiently operated on PCs, and because of productivity tools, these systems are practical and cost-effective to create. And, in reaction to the three monsters, the temptation of the PC and the do-it-yourself MISs is overwhelming. If we succumb to the temptation, however, the whirlwind we will reap is cited in column 4 of Figures 1.1 and 1.2.

We cannot however, dodge the silver bullets, because either they are already here, or because the cost savings derived from them are too overpowering. Therefore, the best set of characteristics we can achieve is seen in column 2 of these two figures. Set into a single list, the desired characteristics for any modern MIS are listed in Figure 1.3.

Because database and centralized semantics are so critical, the term *MIS*, which is not fully descriptive, is replaced with *enterprise database*. The focus of enterprise database is the complete set of business data and systems necessary to achieve effective business planning, control, and management.

1.2 Target Database Environment

Figure 1.4 depicts an overall enterprise database environment. Depicted are three broad classes of databases: operational, warehouse, and specialized study. In general, operational databases store data about the day-to-day operation of the corporation, and they are quite volatile but nonredundant. Warehouse databases, in contrast, store data that is primarily derived, historical, and may be replications

1.	Data: centralized semantic *control* with decentralized data storage
	Data that is able to be consistently understood by multiple sites
	Controlled, concurrent processing of nonredundant data
	Single versions of *truth* in reports
	A feeling that individual needs are reflected in data values and usages
	Appropriate local control and ownership of data
	Common standards for definition and practice
	Accommodation of local data storage requirements
2.	Process: centralized development *control* with decentralized execution control
	Programs that are able to be developed locally and distributed as necessary
	Processes that are able to access data in different locations
	Common report formats and meanings
	A feeling that individual processing scenarios and user interfaces are accommodated
	Control over the localized integrity requirements
	The deployment of standard, cost-effective programming practices that can be locally used
	Satisfaction of the local processing needs

Figure 1.3.   Desired characteristics of an enterprise database environment.

of derived data stored in different contexts.[3] [4] Specialized study databases contain temporal data supporting ad hoc, special needs. Each set of databases is presumed

---

[3] Ron Ross defines warehouse to be a structured database that stores consolidated data for decision support from production-level files or databases.

[4] Bill Inmon defines warehouse to be a collection of integrated, subject-oriented databases designed to support the decision support function, where each unit of data is relevant to some moment in time. The data warehouse thus contains atomic and lightly summarized data.

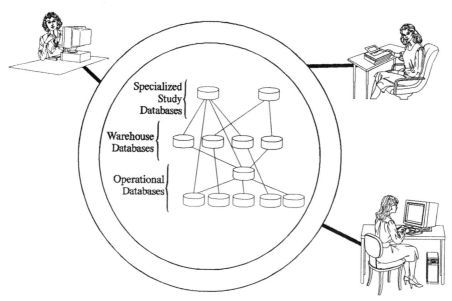

Figure 1.4   Overall enterprise database environment for client/server.

to be operated by an appropriate set of application software.

Surrounding this data architecture diagram is a server-based set of software that functions as a set of data collection systems and also sets of report templates that obtain centrally stored data for use by the end user.

As data collection systems, this software captures all operational data. This outer ring is essentially an automation of all data collection forms for all the various functional areas. If the collected data is entirely new, for example, a new employee, then the automated form cannot be pre-filled. If however, the data is a travel request for an existing employee, then upon entry of an employee number, basic employee information populates the form. Then the remainder of the travel request is populated by the data entry person. When the travel request is printed, all the data is printed. But, when the travel request is stored, only the new data is stored along with the employee number.

As report templates, these mini-programs can be a structured set of SQL-based queries that travels around the enterprise database environment obtaining selected data. Once obtained, the data might automatically load into PC-based databases and/or spreadsheets.

The goal of the enterprise-wide data entry system is to ensure that data, once entered, is clean and never needs to be re-edited or revalidated.

Once a specific set of data is entered, it resides on one server. If an application is distributed, the total set of data is distributed and resides on multiple servers. For a centralized application, the data would reside on one server. Figure 1.4 illustrates the various databases serving the enterprise-wide data collection systems.

Data, once collected, serves several distinct types of operational database applications. One type, external, involves building new data. For example, a travel system creates new data for employee travel/trips. Accounts payable stores newly received invoices and prepares newly created payments. A new-employee application generates new-employee records, new benefit selections, and the like. Other examples are order processing and inventory control.

Another type of application predominately uses existing data as the basis for revisions of data. For example, a personnel evaluation ranking application uses existing employee data, which upon analysis by employee evaluators creates a new ranking for each employee. In this application, relevant personnel data is copied down from the human resources server to a department server for those employees being ranked. A report on each employee is produced that is sufficient for the ranking process. After ranking, only the employee-ids and the new ranking information are moved back to the human resources server as update transactions.

A third type of example of an operational database application would draw down all employee numbers, names, departments, office locations, mail-stops, e-mail addresses, and telephone numbers to create various telephone books. These phone books might be printed, or be available and updated throughout the corporation on servers on a monthly or weekly basis.

A fourth type of an application is the creation of a corporation's general ledger. In virtually all cases, all the business data for a general ledger already exists on other types of business transactions. Examples include payables and receivables, as well as asset depreciations. Summary transactions representing these operational transactions are created from their operational databases and are applied against the ending balances from a prior accounting period to create balances for the new accounting period. This type of internal operational application creates a hierarchy between the ending balance and the transactions that are the basis for the new closing balance. There is also a relationship between an accounts payable summary transaction and the various supporting detail data stored on an accounts payable server. A key issue to be resolved is whether accounts payable is operated through a centralized server or a distributed one. If there are sufficient controls to prevent payment of duplicate invoices, a distributed environment would be allowable.

A final example of an operational application would be e-mail. It would depend on the existence of an online telephone book and a number of different mail servers.

While all five types of operational databases deal with day-to-day data, the fourth example would be considered a warehouse database because it consists entirely of derived data, and once an accounting period is closed, it is historic. In short, the demarcation line between operational and warehouse can be fuzzy. In addition, the e-mail system, given that it receives technical reports, abstracts, and articles for storage and distribution to employees, could also be an operational application.

Warehouse databases generally represent a corporation's long-term memory. Included for example, would be all travel expenses by employee, by project, and by location. Obviously, the data is redundant. In addition, the quantity, type, and style of warehouse databases is largely dependent on the corporation's management prerogatives. In contrast, the set of operational databases is largely independent of management prerogative as they are fundamental to all business.

Other examples of warehouse databases would be all financial records earlier than a current year, all closed-out project documentation, the automated aspects of a technical library, records of all long-term assets, and long-range trends of income, expenses, and contracts.

Human resources databases can be either all operational or part operational and part warehouse. Clearly, all complete personnel records for retired and former employees could be stored in the warehouse. So too could all the data from existing employees that is not considered *current*. For example, noncurrent data could include all but the last salary review, position history, and details about education. In this example, then, there would have to be a relationship between the two database types.

A most critical aspect of a warehouse database is that allied databases are all synchronized with respect to granularity and/or time. For example, if a set of context-dependent financial databases were available to project managers, they would all have the same *as-of* date. Thus all salary actions, personnel hire and termination actions, project labor expenses, and other direct cost expenses would be as of a certain date so that budgets and trends could be accurately tracked. Then, when the next wave of operational data is moved into the warehouse, all the as-of dates would be advanced.

The centralization or distribution strategy for warehouse databases depends on its contexts. For example, a human resources warehouse needs only be as centralized as the human resources department that serves it. Project information might be distributed down to the department *owning* the projects. A contractor vendor history warehouse database might be centralized for the whole corporation along with the price lists and contract terms and conditions.

Specialized study databases are as their name implies. The data contents of a specialized study database is obtained from either operational or warehouse databases. One special study might be to contrast employee rankings with years of service to ascertain if there is a decline in employee value beyond a certain age, or if the rankings decline more on one type of project than another. The critical aspect of a specialized study database is that after a fixed time, it disappears.

1.3 A New Paradigm

Business systems of the past were founded on functional decomposition. Essentially, the steps were to:

- Identify and define the business functions

- Discover the data and build database designs

- Create software systems to load, update, and report on the accomplishment of business functions

This three-large-step process was a second-generation approach to systems development. It replaced a first-generation, two-step approach, which essentially was to:

- Identify and define the business function

- Build a business system of processes and their necessary data to accomplish the business function

The first-generation approach, popular until the late 1970s, was doomed from the start because it did not recognize that data was inherently independent of process. The first generation resulted in redundant data definitions and conflicting semantics. The second generation, while a distinct improvement over the first, was also unacceptable because it does not deal with two very large issues:

- The mission of the business
- The three silver bullets

First, by its very definition, functional analysis undertakes to understand and to formalize a business's functions; that is, what a business is doing. What, however, a business is doing can be very different from a business's mission. A mission of a business, in contrast, is a statement of its goals and objectives. Seldom are the business's functions coincident with its goals. In addition to a scoping difference, functional analysis often leads to a restatement of how things are currently performed. Thus, systems built on a foundation that results from functional analysis seldom produces anything but new wrappings for old packages.

Second, the three silver bullets—downsizing, decentralization, and distributed processing—require:

- Multiple and possibly different implementation strategies for main-frames, mini-computers or servers, and PCs for essentially the same business system's functionality

- Distributed yet semantically integrated databases, where data is stored, transformed, restored, and then downloaded while maintaining consistency and uniform semantics

- Single, point-of-entry editing of all data, with the presumption that once data is *inside*, it is clean

- Report writing supporting data access (from whatever source) that can be interrelated and then reported without consistency and semantics conflicts

Figure 1.5 illustrates this type of environment. End user access is through PCs, in this example, Apple/MACs, IBM/PCs, or clones operating through X-Windows

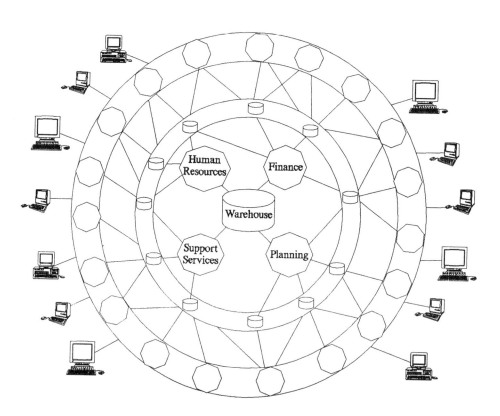

Figure 1.5.   Distributed information systems architecture for enterprise database.

access to minicomputers/servers of different types through networking. The servers may offer CASE, DBMSs, e-mail, specialized databases, local administrative data, and the like. Some of the servers can represent the processing and the data for corporate-wide functions such as personnel and finance. Connecting all the servers is an appropriate set of telecommunications hardware and software. Finally, at the core of this hardware networking topology are the mainframes that offer very large and fast processing for corporate-wide batch jobs, database archiving, and the like. Some organizations have found that the servers are so powerful and so comprehensive in their capabilities that mainframes are not needed at all.

The growth of this hardware was inside out—first mainframes, then servers/minicomputers, and finally PCs. If these collections of hardware cannot intercommunicate and work with each other, then redundancy, conflicting semantics, and endless versions of the truth will be upon us again. It is critical that the total suite of hardware devices be viewed as logical divisions of one physical environment.

Figure 1.6 illustrates a physically distributed environment as if it were seamless. The PCs (IBM, clones, and MACs), when they require services beyond their own domain, interact with the ring of data collection/report-template software systems. These systems typically operate from servers and when the data is collected and validated, it resides on the next inner ring of databases. These databases can function as transaction resources for centralized processing systems (Human Resources, Finance, Support Services, Planning, etc.). Of course, these four sets of systems are really subdivided into many subsystems. At the center of this database environment is the warehouse database in which longitudinal data is commonly stored.

The outside ring of software systems can also retrieve data that may have been placed there by the centralized processing systems, the server-based systems, or finally by the outermost ring of data collection/report-template systems.

The paradigm defined in this book:

- Utilizes the advance engendered in the second paradigm generation, that is, the independent discovery of data

- Embraces the requirements for downsizing, decentralization, and distributed processing

- Involves the business's mission and other critical models about the business that must be discovered and interrelated with the traditional data and process models

Collectively, this can establish enterprise database environments that enhance the ability of business executives to analyze the past, understand the present, and presage the future.

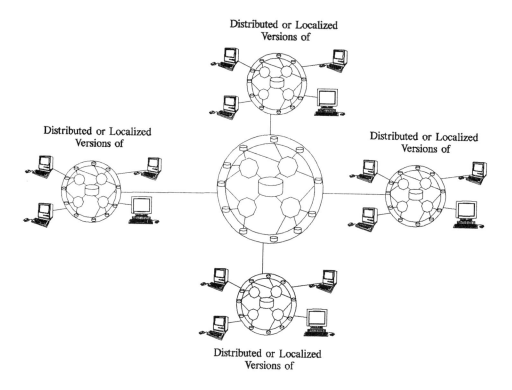

Figure 1.6. Distributed hardware, software, and data network.

The critical business models that must be emulated and then interrelated to arrive at a comprehensive enterprise database specification are:

- Mission
- Data
- Database process
- Information systems
- Business event
- Business function
- Organization
- Implemented data model
- Implemented information systems model
- Security model

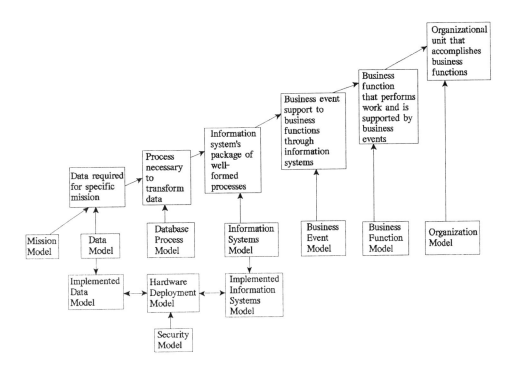

Figure 1.7.   Meta-models critical to successful enterprise client/server database.

Figure 1.7 depicts the interaction of these ten models, which are described in detail in Chapters 4 through 13. The first seven models as well as security represent the complete specification of enterprise database. The last three models represent all the different implementations of enterprise database.

The *mission* model hierarchically defines the goals and objectives the enterprise is attempting to achieve. For a large enterprise, the mission model can occupy from 25 to 35 pages of text in addition to the hierarchical diagrams. Because the business's mission is defined, it includes what should be the enterprise's goals and objectives rather than what the business is now doing, or who is doing it, or how it is done. Describing only what is being done (traditional functional analysis), who is doing it, and how it is being done only shines up tarnished functionality.

The *data* model defines the data that is required to accomplish the enterprise's mission. Each data model describes the data required by the lowest levels of the mission hierarchy. To eliminate the naturally occurring redundancy, the data models must be defined into a repository. The resultant data model is fully attributed and is in *third normal form* (see Appendix 1, The Glossary).

The *database process* model defines the set of database processes required to transform the third normal form data model tables. Included in the database processes are those that add, delete, and modify the basic table rows, and also those that control the relationships between and among rows of the same and different tables (referential integrity). The database process model is restricted to those database processes that maintain the data model's integrity. Included database processes beyond the normal set of row adds, deletes, and modifies would be all data edits and validations, computation of all derived columns, the complete specification of all referential integrity and associated referential actions, and the execution of other defined business rules. An example of a business rule that a database process would enforce might be that the total amount of payroll deductions cannot exceed 50 percent of the gross pay.

The *information systems* model defines collections of business processes that accomplish atomic (i.e., single purpose) business activities. A business system might accomplish the hiring of an employee, providing an employee a raise, or producing a list of all current employees for a particular business department. Each business system accomplishes a specific activity that the business is currently performing. Each business system must be complete. Thus, when an error occurs, the complete business transaction must be rolled back. For example, when the business system accomplishes the hiring of an employee, an error that prevents the allocation of the benefits to the employee might by management decree be declared to be an employee hiring error, precipitating a rollback of the entire transaction. That of course does not mean an automatic employee firing; it merely signifies that the hiring processes must be restarted from the beginning and reprocessed until completion is successful.

The *business event* model defines the events that require information systems' services during the accomplishment of business functions. An example of a business event might be the monthly financial closing. Another business event might be *project opening, project close-out,* or *client proposal development.* Each event can hierarchically decompose into subordinate business events, each of which references an information for services. In this case, the collective result of all the information systems execution satisfies the requirements of the referencing business function. One business event might be hiring plan development that would be necessary if a business contract is accepted by a client. The business event, hiring plan development, might include the execution of an information system that takes a snapshot of the current staff and creates several, multiple-year staff projections that are based on current trends in hiring, promotions, and attrition.

The *business function* model identifies the set of activities that accomplish one or more aspects of a business's activities. A business function might be to accomplish human resources' candidate recruitment, application processing, or the complete human resources function that would naturally include both candidate recruitment and application processing. A business function, once hierarchically defined, might require the use of various information systems in response to certain business events identified in the business function hierarchy. For example, in the human resources function of obtaining sufficient staff for a new contract, the business event, hiring plan development, has to be accomplished. The business event, in turn, causes the execution of the information system described above.

The final enterprise database specification model is about the business's organization. The *organization* model is hierarchical. At each level of the organizational model, the specific business functions to be performed are identified. One organization could be dedicated to the accomplishment of one entire class of business functions. For example, a human resources unit might be charged with all the HR functions. In another organization, a given project might be responsible for finding, interviewing, and recommending hiring. Then the HR organization would accomplish the final steps of benefits choice, employee records establishment, and the like.

The unique features of this new paradigm are:

- Each model, and each component within each model, is defined nonredundantly. Mission is defined once. So too is data, process, business system, business function, event, and organization. Because of the nonredundant definition, more time can be spent on each to ensure that it is correctly designed, and when executed, accomplished, or entered, is accomplished in a uniform manner. Because of nonredundancy, maintenance and evolution can be nonredundant; accomplished once, accomplished everywhere, with 100 percent certainty.

- Each model is related to the appropriate other models through many-to-many relationships. Thus, for example, multiple aspects of a business's mission may involve the same data; a process that is defined for editing and validating a date is defined once and executes against all dates the same way. Different subordinate business organizations can be designed to react to different collections of business events.

- Several of the models provide automatic cross-checks to ensure completeness and a high degree of quality.

Each of the above seven models represents a nonredundant specification of enterprise database that is ultimately accomplished manually, or through automation. The implementation of enterprise database is represented in the final three models:

- Implemented data model
- Implemented information systems model
- Security model

Automation may be accomplished through commercial, off-the-shelf packages (COTS), through custom programming, or through software generation. Once the systems are implemented, they must operate on computer platforms that consume resources and that transmit data. There are thus three versions of several of the models: specification, implementation, and operation. The models that exist in three forms are:

- Data
- Database process
- Information systems

Each of these models must be defined in all three forms to then provide a full exposition of the enterprise models, their implementation, and their operation. Implemented database processes either become automated facilities of the DBMS (e.g., ANSI/SQL triggers) or part of the information system's capability. Various configurations of implemented and operational enterprise models will provide different performance characteristics, depending on the centralization or decentralization of the computing resource, the type and kind of data transmission, and the centralization or decentralization of the organization using the resource.

The complete set of ten models (both specification and implementation) in this enterprise database development paradigm provides modelers the ability to simulate new business organization and deployment strategies.

A very important question arises from Figure 1.7. Is its left to right order the sequence in which enterprise database is specified? Or built? The answer is partially yes, but mainly no. The mission, data, and database process models are generally built first, and in that sequence. Thereafter, business functions are selected and developed. As these are detailed to the point of requiring automation, business events that trigger information system execution are discovered and detailed. Whenever possible, business systems are designed nonredundantly and with sufficient business function independence that they can be used across multiple business functions. The build sequence generally follows the design sequence.

Enterprise database, as manifest by reports from a repository designed according to the meta-schema identified in Chapters 4 through 10 is best understood by starting either at the apex of the mission or at business function hierarchies.

1.4 The Enterprise Database Specification

From the 1970s through the mid-1980s, the goal of MIS was to consolidate and centralize the data and the processes to reduce redundancy and control conflicts in semantics that arose during the 1960s. These redundancies and conflicts in semantics resulted from the multitude of small computers that existed at each company site. During that time frame, telecommunications was in a preconception stage. The computers, while not physically small, were small with respect to the throughput and capacity of computers of today.

Today, in the 1990s, the trend is to move away from centralized MIS for the reasons just cited in the leftmost columns of Figures 1.1 and 1.2. While the reasons for the move are important, the move itself is made possible in no small measure because of the advances in ANSI and ISO standards that address both standard data access (SQL) and data communications (OSI).

In short, the 1970s and 1980s were in reaction to the 1960s and the 1990s are in reaction to the 1970s and 1980s. In addition to mode shifts, there has been a tremendous increase in data and the diversity of data processing applications. While this might lead to the conclusion that the very nature of business systems has changed, today, as in the past, there is a core set of business processes that have remained fundamentally the same, for example, personnel, payroll, budgeting, and finance. What has changed are the requirements for online processing, ad hoc query, and sophisticated enterprise modeling. These requirements used to be humanly handled by crisis computer runs, perusing thousand-page listings, and endless hours at the desktop adding machines. Today, these three requirements must be incorporated into the systems as fundamental capabilities.

In the business systems of the 1960s, the specifications of the automated aspects of the business systems were typewritten and supplemented by hand-drawn diagrams. In the systems of the 1970s-1980s, all this documentation was redone. The rationale was that the documentation, being an alternate form of the actual system's design, had to be redone because the system design was being redone. In addition, there was an advance in documentation technology: word processing.

However, in the documentation of the 1960s, 1970s and 1980s, scant attention was paid to the development of an enterprise model as an independent component. An enterprise model is the formal definition of the enterprise's mission, its data, and processes necessary to carry out the mission, independent of the method or technique employed to accomplish the missions. The enterprise model was almost never created because the end users and the system requirements developers were almost always the same people. After all, why did they need a document telling them what they already knew, and, wouldn't this document be just a clone of the system's documentation? In short, if the subject of building an enterprise model was ever raised, its development was quickly deemed to be a waste of scarce resources.

The downside of not having the independent enterprise model is that when the business was redone, the actual data processing personnel—who had changed—did not know the applications. Consequently, the enterprise's mission and the corresponding data and process requirements had to be gathered for a second time.

Now it's the 1990s, and the systems of today have to be completely redesigned—again. The systems have to be redesigned to handle both DBMS and online processing. These systems also have to be redesigned to support requirements for reporting flexible and enterprise modeling. As in the 1970s and 1980s, the enterprise model does not exist. Thus it has to be captured for the third time.

A critical difference between today's systems and the systems of yesterday is that end users are not limited to the system requirements provider. Rather, the end user is anyone who has a need-to-know and who has access. A second difference in today's systems is that the form and structure of yesterday's documentation is almost useless. Today, enterprise systems are rarely custom coded. Instead, they are either generated through automated software builders, or they are COTS (commercial off-the-shelf) packages.[5] In either case, internal systems' documentation is irrelevant to the end user.

Today when specialized systems that use enterprise data are created, the requirements provider, knowing both the available enterprise data and the required processes, can quickly hypothesize a system and generate it. But where does knowledge of the available enterprise data and processes come from? In short, the answer is the enterprise model. The enterprise model contains all the necessary information to provide the online end user the knowledge necessary to obtain the relevant data and to understand the rules under which the data was created and is updated. By coincidence, the enterprise model is also the same information that must be gathered—for the third time—to then become the requirements for COTS selection or the *input data* for the software generation. Finally, after 30 years, the enterprise model is formally documented.

Tomorrow's systems, that is, those of the years 2000-2010, have to be responsive to end user needs. To successfully meet end user needs for flexibility and to accommodate the three silver bullets, information system development paradigms have to be created. A prerequisite to their effective use is the availability of an online enterprise model that, unlike today, is a thoroughly integrated, active component of the automated information system.

A very real difference between the prior two generations of information systems and today's third generation is that the enterprise model is formally captured and stored, and is actively made available for end user access. In prior generations, the enterprise model merely had to be understood to facilitate its transformation to a highly structured set of computer files, programs, and systems. Documented was the computer-transformed information system, not the business model. Today, because of COTS and generators, documenting the computer-transformed information system is unnecessary.

A key benefit resulting from the capture of the enterprise model is its availability to all authorized users. It can be updated to reflect new and/or evolving requirements and, once updated, new versions of information systems can be quickly generated.

---

[5] COTS has a far-ranging meaning. For example, a word processing package such as WordPerfect requires almost no parameter setting and specialization prior to its use. Other COTS packages can require *tens of thousands* of hours of work before they can be effectively used. In this book, COTS refers more to the latter than to the former.

1.5 The Enterprise Model

The importance of the enterprise model cannot be overstated. Because most organizations did not build an enterprise model in the 1960s, information systems had to be rediscovered in the 1970s, again in the 1980s, and now again in the 1990s. Given that essential business functions have not changed since the 1960s, why rediscover them every ten years?

While enterprise models cannot ensure success, MIS modernization will almost certainly fail without them. The extra cost for the enterprise model? It's negative! With enterprise models, the overall cost of information systems will be reduced, and their schedules will accelerate!

The enterprise model represents the enterprise's operational strategy and policy through which different organizations can research the past, operate and control the present, and plan for the future. While every business already has a default enterprise model (the current state), its enterprise model is not consistent, reliable, documented, or understood. Redundant and inconsistent processes and data cannot be discovered; thus they cannot be eliminated and/or resolved. For example, can a CUSTOMER_ORDER be placed by more than one SALESPERSON? When a programmer encodes the flexibility but a high-level manager says no, who's really implementing policy?

Without an enterprise model, data and process consistency, reliability, and currentness is seldom achieved. For example, why are there recurring manual data collections to obtain employee names, addresses, home telephone numbers, and emergency names? Why does a quick review of the current personnel file show that some zip codes, area codes, and other parts of an address are not recorded? Why do code tables abound, and why are some irreparably broken? Why, when historical reports are run against archive versions of databases, do newly created departments take on the historical cost data of defunct departments? Without an enterprise model we have only questions. With an enterprise model we cannot avoid asking *and* answering these questions with *both* questions and answers being recorded as policy definition and execution controls.

The information systems development process, which has traditionally been accomplished through individual applications, causes the creation of redundant and conflicting data collection, storage, and reporting components. Complexity, redundancy, and semantic disconnects are rampant. Interfaces are delicate and unstable as reports from one application are inputs to another.

The enterprise model affects information systems development by allowing COTS procurement, software generation, or custom development to proceed from known requirements to stable database designs, robust interfaces, and nonredundant data collections. Unfortunately, many current requirements are developed without knowing their true effect on existing environments. *Many COTS projects fail not because of COTS, but because requirements are vague, deliverables are underspecified, and progress controls are almost nonexistent.*

With an enterprise model, information systems projects begin with work breakdown structures (WBSs) that are drawn from the repository and that *learn* through their use. These WBSs help build reliable, repeatable, experience-based project plans. Integral to each project are updates to the enterprise model. As an information system is procured (in-house or COTS) and set into production, enterprise model changes and project accomplishment experiences are also placed into production in a lockstep manner.

Any information systems project (COTS, generation, or custom) must spring from a correct set of requirements that, when accomplished, have a predetermined effect on the business. It is not sufficient, however, to include just the data and process model requirements from the enterprise model in a request for proposal (RFP) from a COTS vendor.

> *To buy a COTS via untested requirements can waste hundreds of thousands of dollars and tens of thousands of staff hours. Underspecified RFPs provide COTS vendors easy money because vagueness allows extreme response flexibility. Contracts based on responses to vague requirements are virtually unenforceable.*

RFP requirements must first be validated through prototyping. RFPs, squarely founded on quality enterprise model requirements, provide vendors a clearer and more articulated problem from which valid proposals can be developed. And, once proposals are delivered, evaluators can select a COTS package with the confidence that the answers relate to correct, implementable requirements. In short, through the enterprise model *and* prototyping, COTS success is virtually ensured.

The enterprise model is the specification of the methods, policy, and strategy by which an organization conducts its business, independent of any automation consideration. Thus the enterprise model is independent of any information system's development organization. The enterprise model guides all information systems infusion (COTS, generation, custom) and is thus critical to the accomplishment of all business missions.

The enterprise model is a most valuable asset. It must therefore be specified and maintained by high-level policy makers, not the policy implementers (i.e., programmers). Specified nonredundantly, the enterprise model provides mechanisms for the organization, planning, and management of the very way business is conducted.

The enterprise model is thus the vehicle, that, implemented over time and through various projects, ensures the nonredundant, consistent, reliable, and integrated definition of data, processes, information systems, and the like.

1.6 The Effect of Client/Server

Client/server is not just another buzzword. It is potentially a dramatically more cost-effective way of accomplishing enterprise database. For the purposes of this book, client/server can go through any one of four stages:

- The distributed mainframe stage
- The intelligent data collector stage
- The downloading and subsequent processing stage
- The cooperative processing stage

The first stage is the distributed mainframe stage and is not much different from having centralized processing through a series of dumb terminals. The difference in today's mainframe processing is that one or a few centralized mainframes may be replaced with a series of specialized servers. The terminals, instead of being dedicated to just one mainframe, have the capability of choosing the server with which to interact. Still, complete processing is accomplished on the server. Screen formatting may be handled on the terminal, which is now called a client.

The second stage is the intelligent data collector stage. On the client, data is collected and possibly preprocessed as much as possible prior to being uploaded and then processed by the server. The client might have a subset of the personnel database and a set of valid projects. A time-card collection system might reside on the client, and time charges are completely entered and validated prior to server processing. This environment saves both communications cost and server processing. Once the validated time-cards are completed, a specialized client program would make contact with the server and upload the data as one fast batch. In this case, part of both the data model and the process model would have to be distributed.

The third stage of client/server evolution is when the client is employed to obtain data from the server. The level of sophistication here can range from the client's user having to know everything about how to request data to the client's user interacting with a program that in turn provides a specialized request. Once the server receives the request, the data is transmitted and stored as computer files in the client's machine. These files can then be manipulated by the client. For example, project earned-value statistics could be downloaded and stored in a spreadsheet package. Thereafter they could be turned into graphs, plots, and the like.

The fourth stage of client/server is true cooperative processing. In this scenario, both the client and the server would have to be quite sophisticated, possibly both having DBMSs. The client's user is creating, modifying, and developing reports from a thought-to-be client database, but in fact, some of the application is on the client machine and other parts are on the server. The location is both transparent and unknown to the user. All processing is automatically coordinated. No concern is ever raised about concurrency, timeliness, and so forth. Needless to say, this fourth stage is not yet here in the early 1990s. That's because communications speed is not fast enough, as well as because of the lack of sophisticated, open-systems architecture tool sets. Notwithstanding this, organizations are performing the other three stages of client/server.

The paradigm provided by this book enables these stages to be accomplished without having to redesign applications from scratch. That is because this book, if its precepts are followed, will cause information systems to be factored into their fundamental parts. These parts may have to be redistributed, but that's different from being redesigned. Also, with the tools now becoming available for complete software systems generation, regenerations and redeployments will become quick and efficient, cost-effective, and correct.

1.7 Environment and Strategy

The remainder of this book describes an environment and strategy to achieve enterprise database. Critical to this environment is the capture of the enterprise model and the implementation of the enterprise's memory: its data architectures. Once the data architectures are implemented in a sophisticated, generalized manner, software tools can be quickly and effectively deployed to create the necessary business systems to collect, update, and report critical business data.

The business systems can be implemented through a network of databases across different computing platforms. To make database a success, each must be carefully defined, deployed along with high-quality processing systems, and effectively utilized through high-level natural languages.

This book treats the three dimensions of enterprise database in Parts II and III. Repository, Part II, covered in Chapters 2 through 13, defines all the essential models and components within the models for storing the specification and the implementation of all the critical parts to achieve enterprise database.

Principles and Methodology, Part III, covered in Chapters 14 through 20, defines the database project environment, critical staff roles, database fundamentals, the make-buy-generate decision, quality work plan development, description of the critical enterprise database project work plans, and strategies for enterprise database tool (the repository and DBMS) selection.

Summary, Part IV, contains Chapter 21, which is a summary of the entire enterprise database effort.

Appendix 1 contains a glossary of terms and brief definitions of all the meta-entity types used in the repository. Appendix 2 provides a very high-level WBS for the enterprise database methodology. The actual WBS is over 100 pages. Appendix 3 presents the categories of questions that comprise the DBMS *yes/no* questionnaire. Appendix 4 presents the categories of questions that comprise the repository *yes/no* questionnaire. Each questionnaire contains about 4,000 questions. Appendix 5 presents the directions supplied to respondents of either the DBMS or repository questionnaires.

To be successful in repository, principles, methodology, and enterprise database is to be successful in database. To have database success is to be organized. And with an organized enterprise, the past can be researched, the present can be mastered, and plans for the future can be set into place.

PART II

REPOSITORY

Enterprise database is impossible without a repository. That is because enterprise database is implemented across the whole corporation on different hardware platforms, operating systems, programming languages, DBMSs, and COTS application packages such as spreadsheets, General Ledger, Procurement, Billing, and so forth.

If there is any chance of surviving the silver bullets, the environment portrayed in Figures 1.3 through 1.6 in Chapter 1 must be achieved. Since enterprise database takes years to implement and many different project teams working sometimes in parallel and sometimes serially, it is imperative that everybody work from the highest quality, integrated, and coordinated plan possible. And where do we find the plan and all its necessary supports? The repository. In support of repository,

Chapter 2, Metadata, defines metadata and explains why its definition, use, and management is essential to database success.

Chapter 3, Repository, The Metadata System, presents the keystone facility of the enterprise database environment, an information system that stores and manages all database systems specification, implementation, and maintenance.

Chapter 4, Mission Model, presents a detailed description of the mission description models.

Chapter 5, Data Model, details the repository components that comprise the specified data model and defines the intersections between it and the mission and process models.

Chapter 6, Database Process Model, presents detailed descriptions of the components making up the specified process model. Illustrated too are interactions between the specified data and information systems models.

Chapter 7, Information Systems Model, presents detailed descriptions about the components of the information systems model. Illustrated also are interactions between the specified process model and the business functions model.

Chapter 8, Business Event Model, describes the repository components that store specifications of the business events that occur over the business calendar. Also explained are interactions between the information systems model and the business function model.

Chapter 9, Business Function Model, describes the repository components needed to store the specifications of the various business functions that in turn result in the business events that trigger the execution of information systems. Illustrated as well are interactions between the business event model and the business organization model.

Chapter 10, Organization Model, presents detailed descriptions about the repository components that make up the business organization model. Illustrated as well are interactions between it and the business event model.

Chapter 11, Implemented Data Model, presents detailed descriptions about the repository components that make up the implementation of the data model that is specified within the data model (Chapter 5) and the database process model (Chapter 6). Illustrated as well are interactions between this model and the data and database process models.

Chapter 12, Implemented Systems Model, presents detailed descriptions about the repository components that make up the implementation of the various information systems that have been specified in the database process model and the information systems model. If the selected tool set is sophisticated enough, a great deal of discretion is allowed in determining the exact location of implemented processes, that is, client and server, and within each, application programs and DBMS. Illustrated as well are interactions between the implemented systems model and its associated repository models.

Chapter 13, Security Model, presents the reason why security is so critical in a client/server environment. Included with the description is the metamodel for holding necessary data for actually controlling and administering the client/server security. The security metamodel is based on the fundamental approach taken in ANSI/SQL, that is, that the view provides controls over both column and row access. The approach also includes the notion of Roles, an ANSI/SQL3 concept that has been made popular by Oracle Corporation.

2

METADATA

Metadata is the abstract representation or definition of individual enterprise database components. Thus any data that is a surrogate for something real is metadata. In enterprise database projects, therefore, all project specifications, project plans, database designs, data element definitions, programs designs, and so forth are metadata. As stated in Section 1.4 of Chapter 1, there have been significant advances in the collection, updating, and reporting of metadata. In high-quality enterprise database projects, all metadata must be collected, updated, and reported through computer-aided software engineering (CASE) environments. But, as this book shows, CASE cannot be restricted to just software; rather it must address the entire enterprise database environment.

Metadata exists one level higher than its corresponding *real* value instances. There may be multiple levels of metadata. Thus what metadata is to one level of real data may, in turn, be real data to its immediately preceding level of metadata.

For example, in an initial context, a schema for a particular database is metadata with respect to the real data stored in the database. But, in a repository system such as Oracle's CASE Dictionary (that is, a different context), the very same database schema becomes real data with respect to the repository's metadata that describes DBMS-managed schemas. In the first context, the schema's role is metadata while in the second context its role is transformed to real data. All of the business's metadata that describes individual application databases and subject area databases (collections of operational databases) must be defined and managed to have database success. *Metadata is the schematic and semantic translator for its stored enterprise memory.*

2.1 Metadata Systems

Metadata is commonly managed through a generalized commercially available data processing application called a repository management system. The American National Standards Institute's (ANSI) committee X3H4 has invented a standard for a repository and its host definition and manipulation system. The repository is called IRD (information resource dictionary) and system is called the IRDS (information resource dictionary system). The type of data stored in an IRD is called *metadata* because it is data *about* data rather than *real* data.

2.2 Repository Schema

Like a DBMS, the repository has the capability to define its own schema as well as to store and manipulate values represented by the metaschema.

Schemas consist of types and instances. A *type* is a named generalization for all its instances. For example, EMPLOYEE is a type and is a generalization for all living, breathing employees. At a higher level of abstraction, a DATA RECORD is also a type and represents a generalization of its instances: EMPLOYEE, HEALTH BENEFITS, SKILLS. Finally, at an even higher level of abstraction, the METAENTITY is a type that represents a generalization of its instances: DATA RECORD, DATA ELEMENT.

Real DBMSs have pairs (types and instances) with which we are all familiar. The types a DBMS can use to identify classes of instances are part of the DBMS's fundamental nature. For example, all DBMSs have the fundamental types: table and columns. Relational data model DBMSs do not possess the fundamental type: relationship. Network data model DBMSs possess several different types of relationships.

A DBMS can define instances to its types: data records (sometimes called entities or tables), data elements (sometimes called attributes), and relationships. An instance of a real DBMS data record type is EMPLOYEE. An instance of a real DBMS data element is EMPLOYEE NAME. Finally, an instance of a DBMS relationship is EMPLOYEE *bosses* EMPLOYEE, where *bosses* is the relationship between two different instances of EMPLOYEE.

A partial example of a defined DBMS schema might be:

```
DATA RECORD: EMPLOYEE
    DATA ELEMENT: EMPLOYEE ID
    DATA ELEMENT: EMPLOYEE BIRTH DATE

DATA RECORD: SKILLS
    DATA ELEMENT: SKILL NAME
    DATA ELEMENT: SKILL LEVEL

RELATIONSHIP: EMPLOYEE contains SKILLS
```

Once the DBMS schema is defined, an instance of the data record type, EMPLOYEE, is a specific living, breathing employee. An instance of a data element, EMPLOYEE NAME is Flash Callahan. Finally, an instance of a relationship, for example, EMPLOYEE bosses EMPLOYEE, is CALLAHAN bosses GORMAN. [6]

---

[6] Different DBMSs contain different types of relationships and different mechanisms of relationship implementations. The most common DBMS type today, relational (implemented through the SQL language) is very restricted as to the types and kinds of

2.3 Repository Capabilities

A repository that conforms to ANSI/IRDS, like a DBMS, contains two fundamental capabilities: it can define its own schema, and it can then store, update, and delete values represented by the defined schema.

With respect to meta-schema definition, the fundamental types possessed by an IRDS are: meta-entity, meta-attribute, and meta-relationship. A defined instance of a meta-entity type is TABLE. Another example is DATA ELEMENT. A defined instance example of a meta-attribute is TABLE NAME. Another example is DATA ELEMENT DEFINITION DATE. Finally, a defined instance of a meta-relationship is SUBDIVIDED INTO. Another example is CONTAINS.

A partial example of a defined meta-schema might be:

```
METAENTITY: TABLE
    METAATTRIBUTE: TABLE NAME
    METAATTRIBUTE: TABLE DEFINITION DATE

METAENTITY: DATA ELEMENT
    METAATTRIBUTE: DATA ELEMENT NAME
    METAATTRIBUTE: DATA ELEMENT DEFINITION
    METAATTRIBUTE: DATA ELEMENT DEFINITION DATE

METARELATIONSHIP: TABLE contains DATA ELEMENT

METARELATIONSHIP: DATA ELEMENT subdivided into DATA
ELEMENT
```

Once the meta-schema is defined, an instance of the meta-entity TABLE is EMPLOYEE. An example of an instance of the meta-attribute DATA ELEMENT NAME is EMPLOYEE FIRST NAME. Finally, an example of an instance of a meta-relationship DATA ELEMENT *subdivided into subordinate* DATA ELEMENT is EMPLOYEE FULL NAME subdivided into FIRST NAME, MIDDLE INITIAL, and LAST NAME.

The interrelationships of the various pairs and layers are depicted in Figure 2.1. An example is provided in Figure 2.2. The IRDS levels are represented by the named rows. The type of activity is represented by the named columns. Figures 2.1 and 2.2 are explained from upper right to lower left.

Each row except the first contains a pair of cells. The top row only has one item that represents the ingrained capabilities of the repository itself. That is, an

---

relationships. For a fuller treatment of relationships, read: *Database Management Systems: Understanding and Applying Database Technology*, published by QED Information Sciences, Inc., 1991.

ANSI/IRDS repository already comes with the ingrained capabilities of the fundamental types: ENTITY, RELATIONSHIP, and ATTRIBUTE.

The top row is the fundamental capability level, which can be used to generate the repository definition schema. The products of that generation are the data that is stored in the Repository Definition Database (Figure 2.1). In the example shown in Figure 2.2, the fundamental types are: entity, relationship, and attribute. These are used with the repository's fundamental capabilities to create instances of these fundamental types. The instances for the entity fundamental type are, for example, RECORD TYPE, DATA ITEM, and TABLE. A set of instances for the relationship fundamental type are: CONTAINS, BELONGS TO, and DEPENDS UPON. And, a set of instances for the attributes fundamental type are: DATA ELEMENT NAME, RELATIONSHIP NAME, and NUMBER OF DECIMAL PLACES.

These fundamental repository capabilities are used to generate instances; for example, the instances from Figure 2.2 for entity are: *record type, data item,* and *table*. These instances are in turn used by the repository as types for repository data loading and update. For example, the type RECORD TYPE is used to load an instance of record type: *employee*. The type DATA ITEM is used to load the instances *emp_name, emp_id,* and *depno*. The repository would then interact (directly or indirectly) with a DBMS and provide the DBMS with the data necessary for the DBMS to create instances for two of its types: TABLE and COLUMN DATA. An instance for TABLE is *employee*, and the instances for DATA ITEM are: *employee name, employee_id*, and *depno*.

Fundamental Level			Repository Definition Schema
Repository Definition Level		Repository Schema	Repository Definition Database
Repository Level	Application Schema	Repository Database	
Application Level	Application Database		
	Application Level Pair	Repository Level Pair	Repository Definition Pair

Figure 2.1.   Data levels and level pairs.

Fundamental Level			Fundamental Types: ENTITY RELATIONSHIP ATTRIBUTE
Repository Definition Level		Meta Types: RECORD TYPE DATA ITEM TABLE	Fundamental Type Instances: record type data item table
Repository Level	DBMS Schema Types: COL:EMP_NAME COL:EMP_ID COL:DEPTNO	Meta Type Instances: RT: employee DI: emp_name DI: emp_id DI: depno	
Application Level	DBMS Schema Instances: P. Shaw 525-88-2876 SQL Devel.		
	Application Level Pair	Repository Level Pair	Repository Definition Pair

Figure 2.2   Example of data levels and level pairs.

2.4 Repository Meta-Relationships

In a repository system, four distinctly different types of meta-relationships are able to be explicitly declared to be interrelated to the products defined in the repository. These are:

- One-to-many
- Recursion
- Many-to-many
- One-to-one

2.4.1 One-to-Many Relationships

The most common relationship is one-to-many. For example, *data record instance has many data record elements*. The relationship is hierarchical in nature. That is, for each owner instance, there can be one or more member instances.

Figure 2.3 depicts an IRDS owner-member relationship that exists in an IRDS between a data element's domain and the data element. For each data element there can be only one domain, while there may be many data elements governed by one domain.

2.4.2 Recursive Relationships

Recursive relationships are a special class of owner-member relationship in which the owner data record type and the member data record type are the same. A recursive relationship exists between one instance of a data record type and other instances from the same data record type. Over the years, recursive relationships have been known as nested relationships, looped relationships, and bill-of-materials relationships. When data record instances of a given data record type are

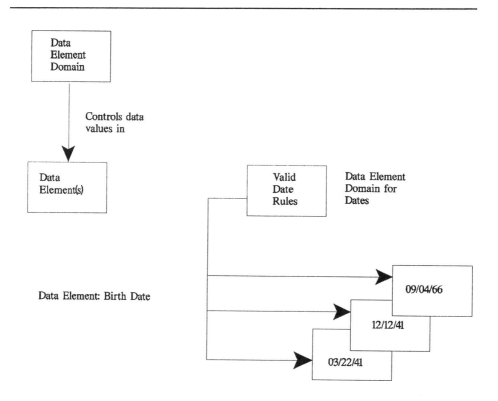

Figure 2.3.   One-to-many relationships between data element domain and data elements.

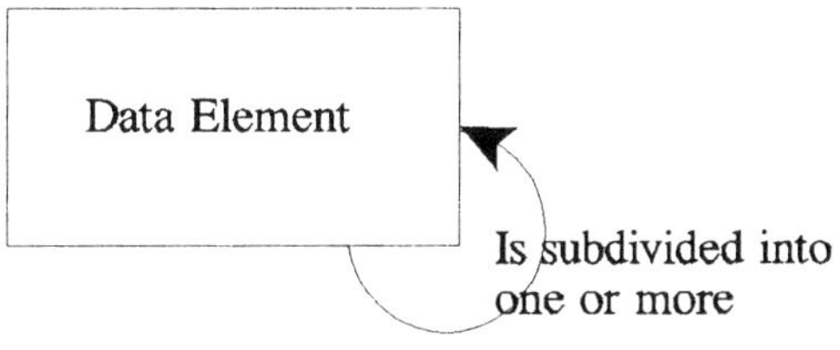

Figure 2.4. Recursive relationship between a data element and its compound components.

associated with other data records from the same data record type, the graphic symbol used to represent the relationship is a loop. Recursive relationships represent hierarchies of varying depths within one structure. Figure 2.4 presents a recursive relationship typically found in an IRDS. A meta-entity type, DATA ELEMENT, is defined in the IRDS as being both the subject and the object of the relationship IS DIVIDED INTO. For example, PART NUMBER might contain subordinate part numbers such as PRODUCT TYPE, MFG DIVISION, USE CLASSIFICATION, and the like. This book does not take a stand on the *correctness* of such breakdowns, just that they occur—all too frequently.

2.4.3 Many-to-Many Relationships

A common relationship type in a database is the many-to-many relationship. This relationship, like the one-to-many relationship, involves two different data record instances. The relationship, however, is one-to-many in BOTH directions. The first of the data record types is defined as the owner of the second, and the second of the data record types is defined as the owner of the first.

In an IRDS database application, the many-to-many relationship is very important. Figure 2.5 presents a many-to-many relationship. Instances of this many-to-many relationship are presented in Figure 2.6 and they show that the ZIP CODE data element is contained in the EMPLOYEE and COMPANY data record types, and the COMPANY data record type contains the CITY and ZIP CODE data elements.

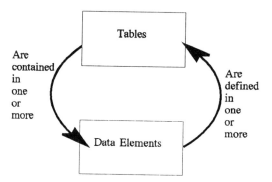

Figure 2.5. Direct many-to-many relationship between data elements and their containing tables.

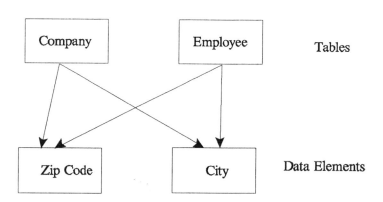

Figure 2.6. Many-to-many relationship (direct) between instances.

Examples of many-to-many relationships in an IRDS include:

- Policy governs many objects, and an object reflects many policies.

- A data record element is represented in many data record types, and a data record type represents the inclusion of many data record elements.

2.4.4 One-to-One Relationships

The one-to-one relationship is not often employed. It binds a single data record instance from one data record type to a single data record instance of another data record type. In an IRDS, an example is the relationship between a data record type and its primary key. For each data record type there exists one and only one primary key. Both DATA RECORD TYPE and PRIMARY KEY would be meta-entity types, and the relationship between instances of each would be one-to-one. A PRIMARY KEY meta-entity type could also have a one-to-many relationship between itself and the DATA ELEMENTs comprising its makeup, as would DATA RECORD TYPE and DATA ELEMENT.

An IRDS stores into its IRD data-about-data (sometimes called metadata) and data about processes (also called metadata) just like other dictionaries or CASE products. But unlike most commercially available CASE tools, an IRDS has the unique ability to completely *define* the metadata that is stored. Being able to completely conform the metadata schema is what is *required* for the environment described in this book.

2.5 Why Is a Repository Required?

The reason that a repository is absolutely necessary is that to achieve the requirements cited in Figure 1.3 in any practical, cost-effective way, the process of a system's specification, definition, generation, and maintenance must, to a great degree, be automatic. In short, to be successful we must have the systems definition productivity available on the PC, while at the same time have the rigor, shareability, and conformity that is supposed to be available through a centralized mainframe. Can this be achieved? Yes!

2.6 A Repository Q.E.D.

From late 1985 through 1987, the author, in conjunction with Computer Sciences Corporation's INFONET Division, the PECO Corporation, and the Information Analysis Corporation, used the techniques and methodologies described in this book to invent and deploy two types of factories: specification and software.

Achieved was the development and deployment of a generic U.S. Army MIS that was dispersed in many different forms throughout the world without sacrificing performance, consistency, or maintainability.

The first version, an operational but generic system, was estimated to cost 125 percent of a customized version. The second, 60 percent. The third and thereafter, 40 percent. When all the systems were delivered, the final price statistics were:

- First deployed system: 80 percent of the original estimate, a savings of 45 percent over the original estimate

- Second deployed system: 40 percent of the original estimate, a savings of 33 percent over the estimate (that was already pegged to save 40 percent)

- Third through tenth deployed system: 20 percent of the original estimate, a savings of 50 percent over the estimate (that was already pegged to save 60 percent)

Overall, if the projects were built the *old-fashioned way*, the work would have been ten times 100 percent, or 1000 percent. Because of the repository, the total for the three systems was 360 percent, or an average of 36 percent per system.

The environment employed a highly engineered, formally defined database project methodology against a very well-defined MIS product list. The metadata-database-system's (meta-base) database schema was specially created to contain and manipulate only the metadata products required by the database project methodology. Together, the methodology and metadata schema was specially tailored to fulfill the need of the Army MIS. Meta-base and repository are synonyms.

While the systems designers, functional experts in the Army MIS area, were creating the MIS design into the meta-base, data processing professionals were building a reusable software library of highly engineered, quality processing routines that were tailored to operate against standard database interfaces.

When the specification process was complete, a meta-base report writer produced the required database design (in the DBMS's schema language) and a required list of processing components from the reusable software library. In addition to a list of required modules, the meta-base report writer generated a process build sequence list that was read by the software library processor. Once run, complete application systems resulted.

Other meta-base programs produced user and systems documentation to fulfill contractual needs.

When the next version of the MIS was required, the process was repeated, using the specifications already contained in the meta-base as a template. If a requirement was a duplicate of one already present, the specification was merely tagged as being needed. If a new/unique requirement was encountered, that new specification was entered and stored in the meta-base. The new system's specification became the set of identified (reused) specifications and the new/revised specifications. The software for the second system was generated in a similar manner.

After about four versions of the MIS, fewer and fewer changes in either the specification or the software were needed to generate the newly required MIS version.

One of the largest benefits was in the area of maintenance. When the Army changed the required calculations for a certain formula, the meta-base, already containing a *where-used* list for the old formula, pinpointed the formula's exact location, first in the change to the specification and then in the software. Changes were incorporated quickly and correctly.

The Army MIS project resulted in ten different MIS versions. The environment contained a database project methodology, a specially designed repository, and a reusable software library. Altogether, the environment was used to rapidly produce high-quality, custom-tailored applications for the different application versions.

The Army MIS development environment's meta-base only contained a single metadata product list. That was because the only meta-products were the DBMS-based MIS. The environment also used only one methodology, designed especially for database projects. For complex projects, those that involve different types of hardware as well as different types of software, the development environment must necessarily be more sophisticated. In short, the environment must be capable of representing multiple product lists and supporting multiple methodologies. For these reasons, the environment control system must be an IRDS, because it alone can be completely conformed to meet the needs of the development environment. Chapter 18 discloses how to develop quality work plans, and Chapter 19 describes the process for selecting a sophisticated repository system.

3

REPOSITORY, THE METADATA SYSTEM

No one would ever question why a business needs it's finance books. Well, the repository is the business's information systems books. If you cannot run a good business without the former, you cannot run good information systems without the latter.

Figure 1.3 in Chapter 1 identifies the enterprise database client/server environment characteristics that must be achieved to ensure success. Vital to database success is control over semantics. The controls are mainly in the area of the definitions that form the basis of the interfaces to standard processes (e.g., computing net profit) and the standard data definitions (e.g., what does profit *mean*).

It is not necessary, however, to control the interfaces to the *end user*. Just how a data entry screen or report looks to different people is immaterial so long as the enforced semantics (rules of meaning and usage) are the same.

In the development of large data processing projects dealing with enterprise-wide, indispensable business functions, documentation of the design requirements and resulting information system specifications is seldom accomplished such that it is timely, accurate, or complete. That is disastrous for the following three reasons:

- Only the momentous facts that are remembered are recorded.

- As systems are specified, the lower-level design details are redundantly developed, often in conflicting manners.

- As system components are maintained, the efforts are crippled because of the undocumented business knowledge that is essential to understanding the component.

Amelioration of these three important problems starts with organizations adopting formal methods for performing analysis and design. Formal methods are only measurably productive and repeatable if they are very detailed and proceduralized. Such detail, however, dehumanizes knowledge workers, who, in turn, are certain to generate protests about being production workers on an assembly line, which, by the way, is worthwhile only when all of its products are the same. In contrast, to the production line, business information system designs are unique assemblies of large sets of components, many of which are similar in design.

Designing business information systems is not an activity for the production worker; rather, it is an activity for a knowledge worker. While there is clearly procedure to both activities, designing an information system requires individualized applications of creativity, human factors techniques, and rule making. Accordingly, requiring the robot-like use of a fully detailed methodology cannot result in responsive information system designs. Chapter 18, Work Plan Development, presents an approach for developing responsive, effective, and unique project work plans from standard sets of methodology tasks.

Building a business information system, once it is designed in sufficient detail, is largely a rote application of computer language coding. There are a number of quality and robust code generators that can use the metadata for a business information system design to produce computer code that is competitive in performance to a human coded application. There is, of course, no comparison between human coding costs and code generator costs.

To fully respond to the three problems cited above, knowledge workers should have the freedom to create their own analysis and design work products for data and processes within strictures dealing with format, time, quality, and resources. These work products must be placed into a repository. The repository, containing these products in fixed formats and sequences, can be accessed by code generators (both human and computerized) to build the business information system. If the generator is quick enough, a fully functional version of the business information system design can be live-tested a short time later. As design flaws[7] are found, the repository's metadata can be changed and the business information system regenerated. *In short, an interactive design process, in which the repository is the empowering component.*

Traditionally, it is not uncommon to expend 20 percent of a total systems development lifecycle on requirements and design. The remaining 80 percent is expended on building, testing, and documentation. Once implemented, 300 percent is spent over a system's lifecycle for changes, fixes, and evolutions, also in a 20/80 ratio. The overall total is 400 percent. If, with code generators, the 80 percent is reduced to effectively zero, then there must also be a profound reduction in the 300 percent systems lifecycle maintenance.

Needless to say, if the repository's meta-schema design is sufficient, the generated products can be complete and responsive to requirements. But if the repository's meta-schema design is insufficient, suboptimal business information systems result. Endemic in these suboptimal business information systems are, for example:

- The rechecking of prior processed data

- The redundant, inconsistent, incomplete, and wrong application of business rules

---

[7] There cannot be any coding flaws, as none was done.

- The excessive or unnecessary expenditure of testing, documentation, and maintenance resources

- The inefficient use of computing resources

3.1 Evolution of Repository Tools

A prerequisite to repeatability is the discipline of structured analysis used to analyze problems, opportunities, or activities in a rigorous manner. The goal of structured analysis is to create, through structured design, the specification of all the necessary components of a system (manual or automated) that can be implemented both quickly and accurately.

As applied to a large organization, structured analysis and design is used in a top-down fashion to look at the organization as a whole to obtain a better insight and an indepth understanding of the environment (existing systems, organizations, and technologies), the ultimate objective being to integrate these studied systems.

Over the past ten years a number of tools have been developed to help accomplish structured analysis and design. These tools have generally fallen into three categories:

- Data dictionary/directory tools
- Process analysis tools
- Computer-aided software engineering tools (CASE)

At first blush, each of these tools was heralded as being THE answer to the needs of structured analysis and design. Soon, the tools were determined to be just what their name implied—tools, each having both their own and then common shortcomings.

In the case of data dictionary system tools, these only allowed for the definition of the data component of a system. Data dictionary tools generally ignore the process side of a system's analysis and specification. Additionally, these tools usually do not have any method of graphical representation.

Process analysis tools are primarily used to record the definition of the process component of a system, but generally ignore the data dictionary (i.e., data modeling) component. Unlike data dictionary systems, however, these process analysis tools usually have a method of graphically depicting the processes. For some of the process tools, graphics is the only method of data entry, making it impossible, or nearly so, to port the specification to another tool.

In the case of CASE, a tool set which produces computer source language from process definitions, its data dictionary (i.e., data modeling) capabilities are still lacking.

Missing from nearly all the tools are three very important capabilities:

- Mission analysis
- Project management
- Specification sharing

Mission analysis is a necessary set of steps that precede both data and process modeling. Project management includes the ability to define, control, manage, and then historically review similar and different analysis projects. Specification sharing is a catchall phrase for the capabilities that allow different users of a structured analysis tool to employ another's already stored specifications in a nonredundant manner. The most effective way to share specifications is to have the *tool* built as a sophisticated, multiple-user data processing system.

Because of all the different types of information that need to be collected to perform complete structured analysis and design, the most logical choice for storing this data is a database. The ANSI X3H4 committee has developed a standard for this database and has developed a set of capabilities that must be present to support the database, called the Information Resource Dictionary (IRD) and the Information Resource Dictionary System (IRDS), respectively. This book calls the IRD a repository. The meta-schema necessary for enterprise database is presented through the models in Chapters 4 through 13.

In short, the form of a comprehensive tool sufficient to accomplish enterprise database is a well-developed repository, which combines the three tools cited above and supplies as well the three missing capabilities. A fully functional repository system:

- Permits the storage of critical business facts at the time they are identified and collected

- Permits business systems analysts to review existing business systems specifications, adopting those that apply, creating new ones when necessary, and identifying changes that may be needed

- Permits research into the design (specification), implementation, and operation of business systems to quickly identify components that have to change in order to respond to new or changed requirements

The metadata collected, stored, reported, and updated in a repository is not business data. Rather, repository data is the set of data definitions and processing rules pertaining to the capture of business data.

The business facts stored in a repository result from the proceduralized interaction and communication of the people striving to represent the integration of multiple missions, business data models, and business database process models that carry out these missions. The repository enables:

- The recording and then subsequent utilization of the knowledge and expertise of business analysts in the requirements determination and/or modification process

- The utilization of recorded business requirements by systems analysts, and by data and process administrators to design business systems, and to record these design specifications for subsequent implementation, or to aid in the ongoing evolutions of business systems

- The utilization of recorded design specifications by programmers and database administration staff to implement these business systems, and to record the implementation details of these business systems for subsequent use in the impact analyses critical for the timely evolution of business systems

If database projects are created in a quality way, a repository requires no new data collection efforts beyond those that have already been done. A repository does, however, change both the timing and the form of the collected metadata. Fully specified data processing projects have always required significant documentation. The repository makes this practical and cost-effective.

3.2 The Repository Purpose

The primary purpose of a repository is twofold:

- To provide a logically central repository for the collection and storage of data about past and present data processing projects, and the related information requirements of the enterprise

- To provide a common tool that facilitates the communication of business systems requirements between the various groups responsible for implementing those requirements

As the enterprise model evolves over time through individual projects that address one or more of the missions, a repository melds these changes into the overall enterprise model. Thus a repository always represents the current state of the enterprise, not the enterprise that was last documented.

As previously indicated, the documentation required for a database project is created (stored/retrieved/modified in a repository) during each of the phases of the data processing project. At the completion of each phase, the documentation (a repository's data representing the phase's deliverables) serves two purposes:

- It is testimony to what has just occurred.
- It is a proposal for the next phase of the project.

Since a repository contains all of the project documentation, any portion of it can be regenerated and/or changed on demand. The documentation contained in a repository then becomes a part of the normal work process of business analysts, systems analysts, data administrators, and database administrators in transforming business requirements into functional operational databases and further into an integrated database environment.

A repository works under the premise that the major business missions and functions of the enterprise are the driving force in the database project design. The activities within these missions drive the business, and the function's activities are represented in a repository's components. The relationships between these repository components tie the enterprise's data and processes together.

By using a repository, the requirements for each phase of a data processing project is communicated via a repository's standard reports, thus reducing the possibility of misinterpretation so prevalent in the more traditional methods of documentation. For example, there are currently seven types of data integrity rules within a repository. Each rule contains a standard grammar and solicits standard argument values. Reports from a repository can be obtained that print out these rules (detailing the rule, the associated columns, tables, and data elements) for review initially by the project staff, and then finally by appropriate quality control staff. Other reports can be produced enumerating the location within tables of the data elements. If a data element is to be represented in multiple tables, it becomes a likely candidate for one of the seven types of data integrity rules. If no rules are found, the project staff can determine why this is the case.

Without these types of standard specifications incorporation, standard reporting, and follow-on interactive updates, the entire process of quality system specification becomes almost impossible.

3.3 The Quality of a Repository

Typically, data processing systems are developed either through a process-intensive orientation or a data-intensive orientation. While each approach has its advocates, neither approach has been found to be complete. A quality repository's fundamental design is thus not biased toward either approach.

Rather, a repository is designed to store the products of data and process analysis. Furthermore, a repository provides the bridges for connecting data and process. Additionally, a repository stores both the specification components and the implementation components and the interconnections between these specification and implementation components of both the data and process approaches.

Notwithstanding a repository's breadth, depth, and interconnections, it is critical to state that the quality of the defined business data that is the system specification stored in a repository has nothing to do with the quality of a repository design. That is, if a faulty specification is stored in a repository, a repository cannot—by magic—determine this lack of quality and reject storing the data, while exhibiting messages of righteous indignation.

However the converse is not true. If a repository's design is faulty, then the comprehensiveness of the system design stored as metadata within a repository is limited. Therefore, every reasonable and practical attempt must be made to ensure that a repository's design is of a quality nature, and does not preclude technology advances that may arise in future repository versions.

For example, only normalized columns should exist within tables. While a repository stores data elements, tables, and the data elements associated with those tables, a repository itself *cannot know* whether the data elements assigned to the specific tables are in third normal form. Whether a collection of columns are in third normal form or not is a judgment that can only be made by a human analyst, possibly with the assistance of a computer program designed to assist the analyst. Such a computer program could examine the data elements from which a collection of different columns are derived and report that they are on different levels within a database hierarchy.

Likewise, while a repository stores various definitions of processes (database process and information system processes), a repository itself *cannot know* whether those processes are not in conflict. Again, whether a collection of processes are not in conflict is a judgment that can only be made by a human analyst, possibly with the assistance of a computer program designed to assist the analyst. A repository analysis program could, however, be written that examines all the view columns, which are in turn mapped to table columns, which are in turn mapped to data elements, which are in turn mapped to data element domains, and determines that the view columns are being combined in *illegal* ways, for example, arithmetically adding the view column EMPLOYEE_ID to EMPLOYEE START DATE.

While the enterprise database project methodology work breakdown structure calls for the definition of data elements in a nonderived format, and calls for the development of tables in third normal form, and finally calls for the detailed review of process specifications, neither the methodology nor a repository in and of themselves, can know whether any of those three principles have been followed. There must be a series of analysis programs supplementing the ADD, DELETE, or MODIFY functions of a repository to determine possible errors in quality design. These errors must then be reported for possible correction.

Even if a methodology has a task completion code box, and/or if the repository data update software is programmed to ask questions like *is this a derived data element*, the analyst could either lie or not know the correct answer. In short, neither a methodology nor a repository replaces quality work done by analysts and programmers.

As stated above, and in accord with the examples given, a repository can certainly be supplemented with processing software that assists in the presentation format of metadata or in the development of quality data and process specifications.

3.4 Passive and Active Repositories

There are two types of repository: active and passive. A *passive* repository is a computer system that is *available* for use whenever metadata is available. If metadata is available but is not stored in the repository, the repository cannot know of its existence. *In short, a passive repository is current if and only if it is used in a rigorous and disciplined way.*

An *active* repository is a computer system that is woven into the very fabric of the computer system's implementation and operational environment. Thus its use cannot be avoided. Every time a data processing activity that involves implementation and computer systems operation occurs, the repository is either automatically interrogated regarding the acceptability of the activity or it automatically receives information about the results of the activity.

An active repository implies that it can *stop* certain activities from occurring that are deemed unacceptable. From that point of view, a COBOL compiler is active. That is, it will not generate an executable program until the COBOL code passes certain *quality tests*.

A repository is analogously active if actions are not allowed upon the failure of certain rules. For the purposes of the repository, these *prohibited actions* fall into two categories: prevention of program execution, and preventing metadata storage, deletion, or update (guarding semantic integrity).

As an example of program execution prevention, if the repository contains a rule that states that all processes must be specified *and approved* before they are allowed into production, then an active repository would prevent the registration of the program (successful registration implies permission to begin execution) unless the repository contains the data necessary to validate that the program's process has been specified and approved. Approvals might only be performed by certain staff, upon presentation of certain types of evidence.

A passive repository enables the generation of a report listing the programs that have been approved, and possibly the programs that have not yet been approved. Such a report might be used to instruct staff not to allow certain programs into production. However, the paper listing in and of itself could not prevent an unapproved program from executing. Since the execution step by the program could not be prevented by the repository from occurring, the repository is operating in a passive role.

The second type of repository activeness, safeguarding semantic integrity, relates to the prevention of metadata storage until repository rules are honored. For example, if a DBMS data element were defined as CHAR X(40) but the corresponding data element were defined as NUMERIC 99v99, an active dictionary would prevent the DBMS data element definition from being stored. The passive repository, on the other hand, would only report the discrepancy or enable it to be found.

The execution-type activeness is currently available from within some DBMSs on behalf of its self-contained repository data for just the DBMS's database applications. Extending this type of activeness into the metadata that is related to the DBMS's integrated data dictionary can be accomplished through *user exits*.

The semantic integrity activeness can be placed into the repository at any time, and can be active for all repository users regardless of the technology of systems implementation. This integrity is specified through *rules* and the incorporation of processing-logic implications of the rules in the repository load/update programs.

A summary of the types of computing environments and the applicability of execution and semantics control is provided in Figure 3.1.

Given the *power* of an active repository, it would seem ridiculous to ever obtain a passive repository. However, the very power of an active repository is also its major drawback. For a repository to be active, it must be completely woven into the computing fabric. Missing from capture by an active repository are three sets of metadata:

- The metadata resulting from the specification of computer systems

- The metadata resulting from all activities that occur within the computing system that have not been *bound* into the repository's capture environment

- The metadata that is available on computing systems that are distributed

Most active repositories are fully integrated with a DBMS. For example, there is the catalogue with DB2, the integrated data dictionary (IDD) with IDMS, and ADA/DD with Adabas. Each of these DBMS-bound repositories is especially designed for the DBMS that is the repository's host. This means that if an organization has two different DBMSs on the same computer, there will likely be two different active repositories. And, when an organization moves from one computer to another, the repository and all its metadata will be left behind if the DBMS cannot also move.

A passive repository, in contrast, can be used to collect the three sets of metadata cited above. Furthermore, a passive repository can be completely independent of an installation's DBMS. This means that if an organization has two different DBMSs on the same computer, there could still only be one passive repository to hold the commonly used metadata. And, when an organization moves from one computer to another, if the repository was properly selected it too could *make the move*. Finally, a passive repository could reside on a node of a distributed environment, available for all to use.

To have a complete applications environment (specification, implementation, operation, and maintenance), therefore, an organization must capture all the available metadata, and that requires both one passive repository and one active repository for each DBMS. Such an environment is illustrated in Figure 3.2, which shows one passive repository and three active ones. This figure presumes that

Scope of Repository Control	Possible Type of Repository Control	
	Execution	Semantics
DBMS Schema	YES	YES
Non-DBMS files	NO *	YES
DBMS-related programs	YES	YES
Non-DBMS programs	NO *	YES
Minicomputer database	NO **	YES
PC database	NO **	YES
PC files	NO **	YES
PC programs	NO **	YES

Notes: (*) indicates that NO could be YES if brought under DBMS control.
            (**) indicates that NO could be YES if the repository is distributed.

Figure 3.1   Possible types of repository control.

there are three different DBMSs processing business information system data. Each DBMS would have its own active repository that could provide both execution and semantic controls. The passive repository would contain the location for the totality of all business semantics. It would be accessed and the appropriate set of semantics would be copied over into the active repository for execution enforcement.

The passive repository is needed to capture the metadata resulting from the specification of computer applications, and the metadata resulting from the *unbound* and distributed activities. Each active repository would be used to capture the metadata that results from the implementation and operation of DBMS-based data processing applications.

In terms of the total quantity of data stored by a passive and an active repository, a passive repository contains only about 20 percent of the data contained in an active repository. That is because the quantity of data needed to represent computer programs, schemas, views, and files and all the operational statistics generated about the use of those items far outnumbers the characters necessary to specify those same items. It is clear however, that nearly 100 percent of the data stored in a passive repository is *human*-generated, and is intended to survive well beyond any technology change, while nearly 100 percent of the data in an active repository is computer-generated, and would have to be regenerated when there is a technology change in any event.

A final observation concerning an active and a passive repository is that the data contained in an active repository is really the technology artifacts generated by data processing and should be under the control of a *database* administrator, while the data contained in a passive repository is the specifications of the business's rules, policies, and procedures that *must* be technology-independent and should be under the control of the *data* administrator along with the appropriate subject area administrators and application area administrators.

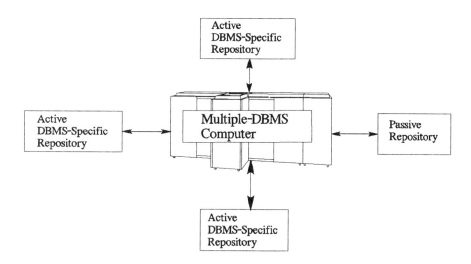

Figure 3.2   Active and passive repository environment for a multiple DBMS computer.

3.5 Repository Models

The overall enterprise business model consists of a discrete set of meta-models. These are illustrated in a simple way in Figure 3.3, and are:

- Mission
- Data model
- Database process
- Information systems
- Business event
- Business function
- Organization
- Implemented data
- Implemented information systems
- Security

In *every* database application, all these models are built *every time*. In most database applications, however, these ten models are neither formally defined nor accomplished in a methodical manner. This is unacceptable for any large database application because its long-term ability to be deployed and its maintenance depend on their very existence.

The mission model, independent of the other models, contains the information that defines the mission of the enterprise. For example, a mission of the enterprise is to pay its employees. Chapter 4 presents a description of the mission model.

The data model contains the information to properly reflect the data necessary to carry out the identified missions. The set of data is dependent on the predefined set of missions. For example, for a corporation to pay its employees, some of the required data includes salary structures, tax withholding tables, and time cards. The specification of data is dependent on mission but is independent of the remaining models. The relationship between data and mission is many-to-many. This means that the same data may be used for more than one aspect of a mission. Chapter 5 presents a description of the specified data model.

The database process model contains the information to properly reflect the necessary processes to transform the data that serves the mission, for example, the series of formulas for computing net pay. The processes are dependent on the set of data required by the mission. Note that the relationship between database process and data is not to data directly, but to the intersection of mission *and* data. That shows that a given database process may be employed multiple times for different intersections of mission *and* data. Because of this type of relationship, the processes are able to be defined nonredundantly. Chapter 6 presents a description of the database process model.

The information systems model represents the packaging of sets of database processes into systems. The relationship between software systems and the *necessary process to transform data* enables the incorporation of the same set of necessary

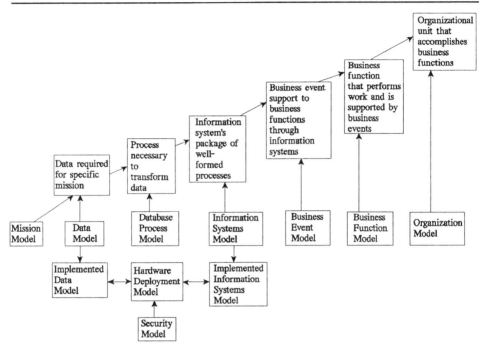

Figure 3.3. Meta-models critical to successful enterprise client/server database.

processes into programs, into subsystems, and then into systems. As each database process is unit-tested, it can be certified as correct. Collections of certified database processes, that is, programs, are thus easier to test. Chapter 7 presents a description of the information systems model.

The business event model represents the corporation calendar for critical events that require information systems support. The purpose of the event model is to know which information system has to execute at specific times or in response to specific enterprise events. For example, a payroll must be produced every other Friday, tax deposits must occur every 1/8th of a calendar quarter, and enterprise tax returns are due March 15. The relationship is many-to-many, enabling a single event to trigger the execution of multiple information systems, and a single information system could be triggered by multiple events. Chapter 8 presents a description of the business event model.

The business function model identifies the set of activities that perform an entire business function. There is a distinct difference between a mission and business function. The mission relates to hierarchical descriptions of the enterprise's goals and objectives. A mission might address the goals and objectives of a specific financial area, for example, the long-range financial planning aspects of purchasing, leasing, and/or renting enterprise assets. If an organization is not yet performing long-range financial planning, there would of course be no corresponding business function.

Once hierarchically defined, the automated aspects of business functions are accomplished through information systems. The interface between the information system and the business function is the business event. As the activities represented by the business function require information systems support, the appropriate event is recognized and the information systems support is provided to satisfy the event.

The relationship between business function and business event is many-to-many. Thus multiple business functions may require information services through the same event, and multiple business events may be required to service the needs of a single business function. Chapter 9 presents a description of the business function model.

The organization model represented in Figure 3.3, is the enterprise structure that exists and that carries out the various business functions. Since the relationship is also many-to-many, a given organization can respond to multiple functions, and a given function can be responded to by multiple organizations. Chapter 10 presents a description of the organization model.

The implemented data model, Chapter 11, defines and presents strategies for the proper and efficient client/server deployment of the data model, and depending on the DBMS, a significant amount of the database process model.

The implemented information systems model, Chapter 12, defines the four common configurations of client/server, and for each describes strategies for selecting the proper and efficient deployment. These alternatives range from the traditional mainframe and dumb terminal to the fully cooperative suite of clients and servers.

The security model Chapter 13, explains the reasons why database has caused the need for very sophisticated security. Also presented are the types and kinds of meta-information that must be collected to both fully define and then fully implement security.

These ten models and the intersections between these models are an oversimplification of the meta-models represented in the repository, and are an oversimplification of the relationships that exist among the various parts of the meta-models. With respect to active and passive repositories, the meta-models that are technology-dependent are the implemented data model, implemented information systems models, and some aspects of the security model.

The first seven models are in the passive repository, while the last three exist in active repositories. Figure 3.4 depicts the relationships among the models with respect to technology. The specified data model is transformed into the various DBMS schemas, becoming the implemented data models. Then, when the implemented data model is loaded by the DBMS and occupies physical space on disk drives, it becomes the operational data model. Thus, the data model exists first as specified, then as implemented, and finally as operational. In an analogous manner, the specified process model (database process and information systems) is transformed into the implemented process model (automated DBMS functions like triggers, and implemented information systems) and finally as an operational process model (computer jobs).

At the apex of these three layers of data and process models is the mission model. The mission model is related to both the specified data and process model. Interconnecting the data and process models at the first two levels (specified and implemented) are views. The word *view* is meant to be precise, mapping to a formally defined language, ANSI/SQL. Data integrity rules also intersect data and database process models because in most DBMSs, many of the data integrity rules can only be enforced through specially created processes. The interaction of the mission and the layers of data and process models is shown in Figure 3.4.

3.6 Passive Repository Components

The components of a passive repository include:

- Mission model
- Data model
- Database process model
- Project management model

Figure 3.5 identifies the models present in the passive repository. In this book, the process model is further subdivided into the database process model, the information systems model, and the business function model. These models (mission, data and database process) are those listed under the passive repository icon. The models present in an active repository are listed under the leftmost active repository icon.

While the project management model is not actually part of the enterprise business model, it is essential for tracking progress in MIS projects. The project management model consists of meta-entities in five areas:

- The project's PERT chart
- The estimates for accomplishing work
- The schedule for work progress
- The connections to the actual meta-product instances
- The actual time required to create meta-product instances

Collectively, these meta-entities enable real enterprise database project planning and management.

In any project, the mission model is essential because it defines the overall business of the enterprise which then acts as the scope boundaries for enterprise database applications. Specific aspects of the mission can be done in stages and/or phases.

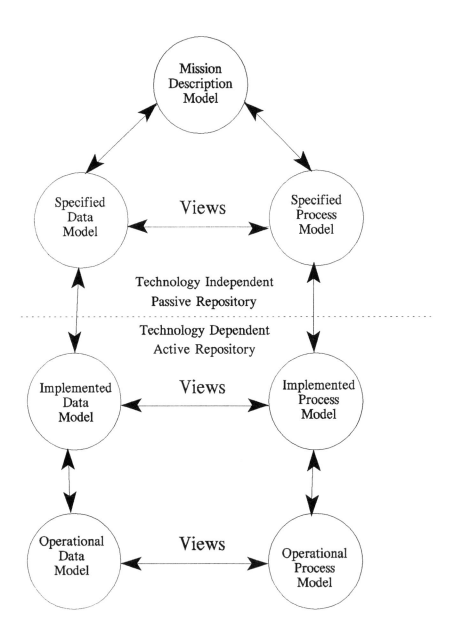

Figure 3.4   Interrelationship among meta-models.

The meta-entity clusters for the mission model are described in Chapter 4. Chapter 5 describes the meta-entities required for the data model. Chapter 6 describes meta-entities required for the database process model. Chapter 14 describes the meta-entities required for the project management model.

3.7 Active Repository Components

The components of an active repository are the implemented data and process models. The implemented data model contains DBMS schemas and views. The implemented process model is the implemented database process model and the implemented information systems model. The operation data and process models are outside the scope of this book.

The interaction of all these models was shown in Figure 3.4. The actual interface mechanism between the data and database process models on each level

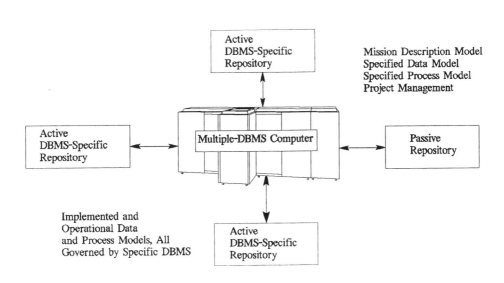

Figure 3.5   Allocation of meta-models to active and passive repositories.

is twofold: data integrity rules and views. The meta-entity clusters for the implemented data model are presented in Chapter 11. The meta-entities for the implemented process model, that is, the information systems model, are presented in Chapter 12.

3.7.1 Implemented Data

The implemented data model represents the transformation of the technology-independent data model into the specific instances of the DBMS schemas and DBMS views. For the most part, any DBMS's embedded repository contains all the necessary supports for this embedded data model. In ANSI/SQL-based DBMSs, these tables are called the schema information tables and are described both in quality books on ANSI/SQL and in the ANSI/SQL standard itself. In all other DBMSs, these tables are vendor-proprietary.

There are two main reasons for the creation and retention of both the specified data model and the implemented data model (DBMS schema and views). These are:

- Distributed database
- Performance-based designs

The scope of the data model in this book is enterprise-wide. For a large corporation, such a model likely contains 1000 to 2000 third normal form tables and, if loaded, would represent hundreds of millions of data rows. Such *monster* database structures were tried in the 1980s with failure almost always the outcome. The reasons for failure are many, but the most commonly observed are:

- Lack of decentralized control and ownership

- Lack of decentralized semantics tailoring

- Inability to create locally tailored reports

- Forced centralized standards for hardware and software

- Lack of computing power and software capabilities to handle a monster database

While overall computing power has dramatically increased, the increase has mainly been in the area of computation. *Data* processing power increases have not kept pace with the increases of CPU processing power. Thus even if all the other reasons were resolved, the lack of computing power would still be a problem. The only practical implementation technique for enterprise-wide databases is thus through decentralized processing. To achieve decentralized processing there are at least three alternatives:

- A distribution of the rows of an entire database schema. This means that the schema is the same everywhere but the rows are different.

- A distribution of the tables and their associated rows. This means that a centralized schema is partitioned to keep tables singly located in different places with all the appropriate rows.

- A distribution of both some of the tables and some of the rows. This means that there are disparate schema databases, multiply occurring, with unduplicated rows.

With any of these alternatives, if the dictums of Figure 1.3 in Chapter 1 are to be achieved, there must be a single, centralized definition of a single, enterprise-wide specified data model that consistently maps to the decentralized versions of the implemented data model.

Different computing platforms have varying performance characteristics. These differences, along with the intrinsic differences in performance of DBMSs, lead to implementing the same database data model differently. The specified data model might be created in third normal form with no derived data. To achieve acceptable performance, however, transformations of the data model may be required. Some of the transformations may be to create derived data, summary data, and specially duplicated columns that take the structure out of third normal form.

3.7.2 Implemented Information Systems

The implemented information systems represent the specific instances of systems, subsystems, and programs that accomplish the mission of the database and that interact with the DBMS. The meta-entity clusters representing information systems are first specified in Chapter 7, and after technology transformation they are represented in Chapter 12.

Because enterprise databases can be practically achieved only through distribution, so too are the information systems that perform the necessary data processing activities. Because the information systems are distributed, there are multiple information systems interacting with the same parts of a database. Some may be interactive, some batch, some on a mainframe, some on servers, and some on PCs. It is impossible for even sophisticated repositories to contain the specifications of all these different versions in an active manner. Because enterprise database is physically distributed, it is virtually assured that multiple DBMSs from one or more vendors will be involved. So while initially attractive, to extend a specific DBMS's repository to accommodate the needs of a passive repository is likely to result in an unacceptable technology dependance between that DBMS and the entire set of components within enterprise database.

3.7.3 Operational Data Model

The operational data model is the set of O/S files that represent the implemented database. The operational data model contains interrelationships between the other models. These files are under the control of the computer's operating systems and are thus outside the scope of this book.

3.7.4 Operational Process Model

The operational process model is the set of run-units that represent the implementation of the information systems. The operational process model contains interrelationships between the other models. These files are under the control of the computer's operating systems and are thus outside the scope of this book.

3.8 The Repository Environment

3.8.1 Using a Repository in a non-DBMS Environment

There is nothing inherent in the design of the repository that restricts its use to only database environments. Simply, the repository is a tool for rigorously specifying and enforcing the semantics for data and processes, and for storing the interrelationships among these semantics.

The repository could therefore be used to store the metadata for data processing applications that are not under the control of a DBMS. The very significant benefits of operating an application under the control of DBMS is addressed in DBMS books. The benefits derived from having a data processing application defined through the repository is quite independent from the benefits derived from having the application operate under the control of a DBMS.

3.8.2 Using Repository in Development, Testing, and Production Environments

An application (PC, minicomputer, or mainframe (DBMS or nonDBMS)) can exist in three different states: development, testing, or production. Thus there is a need for three or more repository databases: one for production, one or more for testing, and one or more for development.

For security and integrity reasons, the production repository database cannot ever have its specification or implementation components of its data or process models updated. These can only be replaced. Also, for these same reasons the test repository cannot ever have the specification data or process models updated. They are only to be replaced. And finally, in the development environment, all the repository component instances are able to be updated.

3.8.2.1 Development Environment Repository

The development repository is used for the initial specification of application business models (both data and process). To keep application business models from *bumping* into one another, a preliminary activity of *project registration* is accomplished. During this process, an application declares its *turf*. At that time, all record instances identified by the project are *owned* by the project and cannot be updated by another project. If there is conflict, then the managers of the two projects have to achieve a consensus definition of the repository component. This protected environment thus allows repository record occurrences to be updated easily via the online data entry/update subsystem as the nature of the business requirements evolves, while at the same time keeping tight control over interfering effects of other application development projects.

The development environment provides full reporting capabilities against all repository data. Upon completion of the specification of the application data model, appropriate groups determine the impact on the existing enterprise business model (data and process). Once all outstanding issues have been resolved and the application business model approved, the application can proceed through normal development phases.

3.8.2.2 Test Environment Repository

At certain intervals, or according to a certain schedule, components of development are ready to proceed to a testing phase (environment). At such time, the portions of the development repository that are ready to proceed into testing are migrated to the testing environment. The test environment repository is the *old* production repository as modified by the development activities that proceed into testing. Since formal testing is occurring, no metadata within the specified data and process models are allowed to be updated. Certain metadata in the implementation repository must necessarily be updated as required by the testing environment.

The users of the repository in the test environment are only those allowed to perform testing activities.

Access to the repository is read-only except as noted above. Once the modifications to the production systems have been acceptably tested, the test repository is moved into production.

3.8.2.3 Production Repository Environment

The production repository environment contains the version of the repository that reflects the current business requirements of the organization. No updates of the specified or implemented process and data models are allowed.

3.8.3 Using Repository in a Multiple-Tiered Environment

Figure 3.1 identified the different database environments and indicated the possible repository activeness. The question answered by each row is whether a rule that is *specified and implemented* in the repository is trapped when the rule is violated. An execution trap implies that some program that violates the rule is prohibited from executing. A semantics trap implies that some instance of metadata (specified or implemented) is prevented from being stored.

A method to have more YESes in the execution column is to require all files to be defined under the control of DBMS, which is not a bad idea for many more reasons than just control. Extending that to other mainframe programs would extend execution control to them as well.

The repository can also be present on middle and lower levels, or through the development of the repository on the PC itself. This is illustrated in Figure 3.6. In this environment a mid-level IRDS would provide metadata information about the databases within its sphere. In addition, the IRDS would *know* about the next higher-level IRDS and the set of *lower*-level IRDS.

If the repository is ported to middle and lower levels, procedures must exist for ensuring that the metadata catalogues are regularly exchanged among the levels.

3.8.4 Integration of Passive and Active Repository

In general, there are two alternatives for implementing the integration between a passive and an active repository:

- Extending the active DBMS-repository
- Standalone passive repository with *bridges*

Extending the DBMS-repository initially seems attractive for the following reasons. First, a vendor's DBMS-repository typically supports the majority of the implemented data and process models required by a repository. Second, the

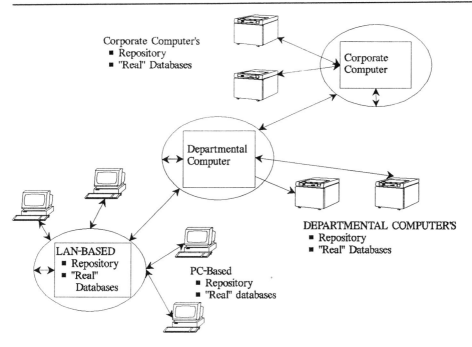

Corporate Computer's
- Repository
- "Real" Databases

Corporate
Computer

Departmental
Computer

DEPARTMENTAL COMPUTER'S
- Repository
- "Real" Databases

LAN-BASED
- Repository
- "Real"
  Databases

PC-Based
- Repository
- "Real" databases

Figure 3.6   Repository distributed by tier.

components not already present in the DBMS-repository can often be implemented through extensions to the vendor's own repository, that is, by defining the meta-entities and meta-relationships not already represented.

However there are two main drawbacks. First, it requires that an organization decide on the DBMS that it is going to use for its production applications, and that the same one be used for all production applications. Second, it means that in the event of a technology change, the DBMS-repositories would have to *move*, and that is seldom possible. So, while initially attractive, extending a DBMS's repository to accommodate the needs of a passive repository is likely to result in technology dependence.

The standalone repository alternative seems initially not to provide a mechanism to relate the data and process specification models to the actual data and process implementation models. This can be overcome by building a computerized bridge between the specification and implementation models. This *bridge* would have to be custom built, and would require sophisticated referential integrity to ensure that the active and passive repositories be correctly integrated. While development of this approach is fairly straightforward, and would lead to some data redundancy between these two independent repositories, it is preferred so as to maintain the portability of the passive specifications, and maintain the ability to have an active repository for production environments.

3.9 Who Is Responsible for a Repository?

3.9.1 The Parts of a Repository

As stated above, a repository is a database application that stores information about a business. The forms of the data in the repository are business data structures, business processes, and their interacting rules. The information content of a repository is the shared responsibility of the business systems analysts and data administrators primarily, and others secondarily.

Like all database applications, a repository is a computer software system that likely utilizes a DBMS. Thus it consists of a number of different parts. It has a logical database that contains the repository's schema and subschemas; a physical database that contains data files, indexes, relationships, and programs for data loading and update; an interrogation component for repository reports and analysis modules; and, finally, the repositories contain system control capabilities in support of backup and recovery, security and privacy, and so forth.

Since the repository is a database application, it also has data (business data structures and processes). The following section 3.9.2 identifies the nature of the repository data, and who is responsible for the data's gathering, storage, and long-term maintenance.

Finally, since every database application undergoes conceptual specification, implementation, and then ongoing maintenance, Section 3.9.3 identifies who is responsible for the repository data related to those phases.

3.9.2 Responsibility for Repository Components

Figure 3.7 identifies who is responsible for the content of the specification data and process components.

The logical database of the repository, that is, its schema or the meta-model, is the responsibility of the data administration group. They must be sensitive to input from other organizations since the principal beneficiaries of the repository are other organizations, not data administration. Data administration then is responsible for the correct and accurate definition of the repository's meta-model and the documentation of the repository, such as its user manuals, reference materials, and standard report specifications.

The physical database of the repository, that is, its storage structure, access strategy, development of data loading procedures and data update subsystems, and backup procedures are the responsibility of the database administration group. The database administration group must be sensitive to input from the data administration group and from other groups as these other groups are responsible

Repository Component	Organizational Responsibility
Mission description model	Senior business management
Specified data model	Subject area administrators and application area administrators
Specified process model	Subject area administrators and application area administrators
Implemented data model	Database administrators
Implemented process models	Individual project leaders for operational and warehouse projects
Operational data model	Computer operations
Operational process models	Computer operations

Figure 3.7. Repository development and administration responsibility.

for determining the schema, and for collecting, loading, and updating the data that is to be serviced by the repository.

The interrogation aspects of the repository have a shared responsibility. That is because the interrogation consists of both standard and ad hoc reports. The initial set of standard reports are to be specified by data administration and implemented by database administration. That is because there are already a large number of repository report specifications that can readily be implemented. Ad hoc reports are principally the responsibility of the users of the repository. In some cases the users will be data administration, sometimes database administration, and sometimes other development organizations.

The system control aspects of the repository are the responsibility of database administration. That is, they are responsible for the database's backups, recovery, physical reorganization, logical reorganization, security and privacy administration, and the like.

3.9.3 Responsibility for Repository Data

Repository data, that is, metadata, are the specifications, implementation details, and operational characteristics of enterprise database. The responsibility for the data within the repository falls into many groups, as depicted in Figure 3.7.

All data and processes exist from two viewpoints: projects and the enterprise. From the project viewpoint, the data and the processes from different projects can be in conflict. From the organization's point of view, that would be disastrous. To protect against that, both *database* administration and *process* administration groups need to review the output of individual projects to ensure there are no conflicts with the overall enterprise business model.

Enterprise database consists of both data models and process models. From the data model point of view, data administration is responsible for building the overall enterprise data model, and is therefore the group to determine the impact of a specific project's data model on the overall enterprise data model. Problems identified have to be resolved by those responsible for the overall business missions represented by the enterprise data model.

Analogously, there should be an analysis of the enterprise process model (especially the processes that define and maintain data integrity, and that perform basic data transformations) to determine the impact of a particular database application's required processes (data loading, update, and reporting) on the enterprise's overall process model.

Once the impacts of a particular database project against the overall enterprise model have been determined, a detailed specification and implementation strategy for a database project can begin. As the project is implemented, the repository data is modified to reflect the most current set of specifications and implementations of the global business model (data and processes).

Eventually, database projects become implemented. Once implemented, application maintenance begins, and new projects are started. The repository must store metadata from projects in different phases.

3.10 Repository Summary

The complete set of metadata maps onto the complete lifecycle of an application, that is, its:

- Specification
- Implementation
- Operation (and maintenance)

Passive repositories are effective only in environments that are well disciplined and well established. Few are. A passive repository can only effectively handle the metadata produced during the data processing application's specification. If good work habits and practice are in place, however, a passive repository can handle metadata produced during the data processing application's implementation and operation (and maintenance) activities. However, such habits and practice are much more difficult because there are likely to be many more implementation and operation teams than there are specification teams. Simply put, it is unlikely that a passive repository will *end up* containing sufficient metadata to control the complete lifecycle.

An active repository, in contrast, addresses the implementation and operation (and maintenance) phases in an active way, for those applications that are under the control of a DBMS. Implementers and operators (and maintainers) will be using the DBMS-repository without knowing it. It is therefore likely that the active repository will end up containing sufficient metadata to control the implementation and operation (and maintenance) phases.

In short, a complete and fully functional repository environment is one in which there is a passive repository that contains all the application's specification metadata, and then one (or more) active DBMS-based repositories that contain all the applications' implementation, operational, and maintenance metadata.

The following is a partial list of benefits attained through the use of a repository. A repository will:

- Assist top management in identifying the resources required to build an information system.

- Provide discipline and control for the design process.

- Provide a structured approach to conceptual design.

- Enhance the application development process through the utilization of prior work.

- Provide a management facility for monitoring database projects.

- Allow for the nonredundant storage of data definitions and business policies that produce greater consistency throughout the enterprise.

4

MISSION MODEL

The mission model consists of five major meta-entity types, which are:

- Mission description
- Database domain
- Object
- Business function
- Business term

Figure 4.1 presents a diagram that depicts the mission model meta-entity types. The relationship between all the meta-entity types is many-to-many. Because of

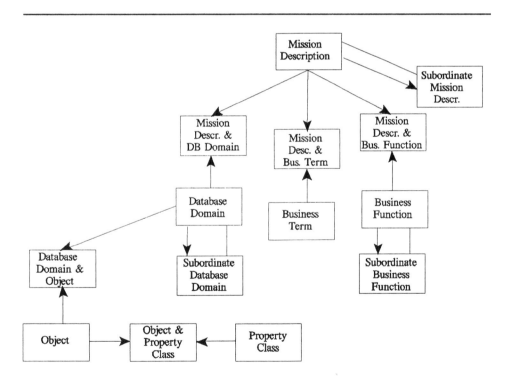

Figure 4.1.   Mission description meta-entity model.

the many-to-many relationship, database domains can be employed to accomplish many missions, and missions may share the use of multiple database domains. The database domains may, in turn, employ common objects, and an object may serve a shared use in multiple domains. Finally, the missions are accomplished through multiple business functions, and business functions are accomplished within multiple missions. The many-to-many relationships serve two purposes:

- They prevent the redundant specification of data and business functions.

- They promote the recognition that both data and business functions are shared in the accomplishment of the enterprise's missions.

Objects serve as the intersection between the mission and data models. Similarly, business functions, defined only at a high level in the mission model, serve as an intersection between the mission and fully developed business function model.

4.1 Mission Descriptions

The mission description meta-entity is recursive. This is shown through the relationships between it and the subordinate mission description meta-entity. There is a one-to-many relationship from mission description to subordinate mission description, but only a one-to-one relationship between the subordinate mission description and mission description. Similarly, business process and database domain are recursive.

The relationships between mission description and business term are many-to-many. This is shown via the two one-to-many relationships between mission description and business term to the intersecting meta-entity mission description and business term. Similarly, there are many-to-many relationships between:

- Mission description and database domain
- Database domain and object
- Mission description and business function

The final relationship is a one-to-many between property class and object.

A mission description meta-entity contains a textual description of the mission of the enterprise. Figure 4.2 contains the overall mission description for the Blades Steel Company. The description states the essential mission of Blades Steel. *Not specified nor described is how the mission is accomplished, nor who accomplishes the mission.* The mission is apolitical. The mission description is silent on these very contentious issues. Because the mission description is neutral, it can be set down and reviewed with a minimum of rancor and jockeying for position and power.

The Blades Steel Company, a specialty manufacturing company, designs, develops, markets, and distributes ice skate blades for both figure and hockey skating.

Blades Steel Company accomplishes sales and marketing, manufacturing, and distribution.

Marketing advertises and promotes the products through professional endorsements, competitions, and the like.

Sales manages regions and local salespersons within those regions.

Manufacturing researches, develops, and manufactures the various types of ice skate blades.

Distribution stocks and delivers blades to both boot makers and directly to custom skate builders.

Figure 4.2.   Example of mission description for Blades Steel Company.

The first paragraph sets down the overall business mission. The second paragraph identifies the three major subordinate missions. The third through the fifth paragraphs provide a high-level description of each of the subordinate missions.

Because the analyst determined that the subordinate mission description of marketing and sales was complex, it was further subdivided. This additional level of description is contained in Figure 4.3. Figure 4.3 was examined and it was then determined that three subordinate mission descriptions needed further explanation. These were: sales, marketing, and order processing. These three subordinate mission descriptions would then be described.

Figure 4.4 provides an overall graphic of all the mission descriptions. If the quantity of mission descriptions is large, the graphic may have to cover a number of pages. The quantity of levels on each page is usually limited to two levels on the first page and then three levels on subsequent pages.

The purpose of the mission description is to provide both a textual and graphic representation of the aim of the enterprise—in short, what the enterprise is all about. In addition to the words, there is the graphic. There should not be a subordinate mission description without a graphic box representing it.

It is not uncommon for a 500 million dollar business to have its mission description text and diagram fill about 30 pages and six pages, respectively. Once the mission descriptions are determined, high-level data and busineess function descriptions are created as a proof of correctness for the missions. Neither the data descriptions nor the business functions are more detailed than a high-level form. The set of meta-entity types for a complete data model is provided in Chapter 5. The set of meta-entity types for a business process model is presented in the chapter dealing with database processes (Chapter 6), information systems (Chapter 7), business events (Chapter 8), and business functions (Chapter 9).

- Identifies prospects and creates account profiles for sales strategy development

- Transforms prospects into clients after qualification

- Provides support of existing customers through sales support

- Accomplishes order taking and processing

- Effects shipments to customers

- Obtains information related to competitors for company products

- Works with home office and field personnel to maximize the acquisition of customers while minimizing costs and time

- Creates advertising programs and promotions so that the products are well known and supported

Figure 4.3.   Subordinate mission description example for sales and marketing.

4.2 Database Domains

Once the set of mission descriptions are determined, a description of the data required to carry out the missions is created and then diagrammed. Figure 4.5 contains two different database domains, one for sales, and another for marketing. In the event that a specific database domain describes complex sets of data, multiple levels of the database domain description may be required. In the case of marketing, the amount of data required to accomplish the mission is sufficiently complex to subdivide the database domain into two subordinate database domains: advertising and promotions. Diagrammatically, the database domain hierarchy is presented in Figure 4.6.

The subordinate domain for advertising is presented in Figure 4.7. This description enumerates the types and kinds of data required to carry out the mission of advertising.

Each subordinate database domain is examined to determine the names of the data. In this description, the names are:

- Products
- Advertising programs
- Regions
- Seasons

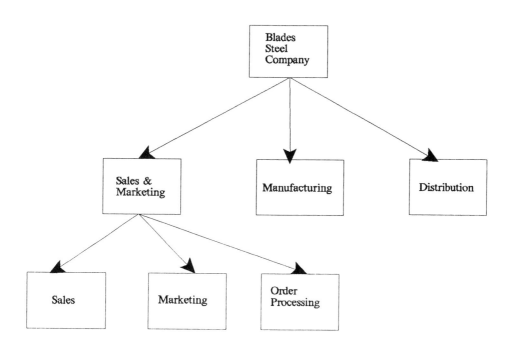

Figure 4.4   Mission hierarchy for Blades Steel Company.

In this example, the names of the seasons are actually data values, and these along with any others would become part of the database's data integrity rules for valid values. A diagramming technique created especially for data and the relationships among data is called entity-relationship diagramming. With this technique, the entities are drawn as rectangles and the relationships are drawn as diamonds. The name of the relationship is inside the diamond. An acceptable alternative of this technique is to just have lines between the entities and to have the lines named.

Figure 4.8 shows a database domain diagram for the subordinate database domain advertising. Figure 4.9 presents the description of the data required to support promotions. The graphic equivalent of the description is provided in Figure 4.10. Note in Figure 4.10 that n-ary (i.e., more than two-way) relationships are shown. The entity relationship diagramming technique shown here is not intended to be in third normal form. Rather, the diagramming technique is just supposed to depict the required entities and the relationships among the entities.

<u>DATABASE DOMAIN EXAMPLE: SALES</u>

Sales establishes, operates, and monitors the various sales offices throughout the country.

Sales takes in orders, monitors order processing, and tracks customer invoicing and payments.

<u>DATABASE DOMAIN EXAMPLE: MARKETING</u>

Marketing develops the various advertising and promotion campaigns that are to occur throughout the year for each product.

Figure 4.5.   Database domain examples for subordinate mission descriptions for sales and marketing.

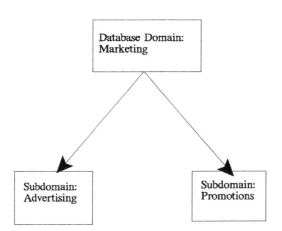

Figure 4.6.   Two database subdomains for Blades' marketing.

It is possible that some of the entities are merely data elements, while others are complex. For example, a skating professional may really be a person with multiple addresses and phone numbers. And, a dealer may be an organization with multiple locations, addresses, and phone numbers.

Advertising creates the multimedia advertising programs for each of the products.

Advertising programs are geared to specific seasons of the year, that is, back to school, Christmas, and summer skating.

Advertising programs are also geared to specific regions of the country.

Figure 4.7.   Database subdomain for advertising.

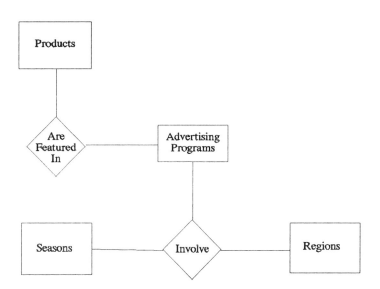

Figure 4.8.   Subdomain graphic for advertising.

The purpose of the database domain diagram is not to be precise and exacting but to be comprehensive. The goal is to have the reviewer say, that's just the right kind of data needed to satisfy the required mission description.

When all the entity relationship diagrams are created, siblings are combined. Entities that are named the same are not presumed to be the same. Analysis must show that to be true. If not, one or both of the entities must have their name and definition changed. As the sets of sibling diagrams are merged from lower to higher levels, the quantity of commonly named entities on different diagrams

---

Promotions obtains celebrity endorsements for each of the skating blade types.

Tours are created for each celebrity that takes them to local trade shows, and for presentation to skating professionals.

Films are created showing the professionals giving specific tips on how to achieve the very best results.

Promotions also creates sales contests for the local dealers of the various type of blades and for the boot manufacturers that employ the blades directly on the boots.

Figure 4.9.   Subdomain for promotion.

---

diminishes. Diagram merger becomes optional when the use analysis of a common entity is subject to update (add, delete, or modify) in one diagram and is only referenced (read) in another diagram. The set of entities that share common business policy for add, delete, and modify are generally all within the same subject area database.

At most half billion dollar businesses, there are about 60 or so significant areas within the mission description for which database domains and collateral entity relationship diagrams have been constructed. These 60 make up about ten subject area databases. Across all the entity relationship diagrams there are about 500-600 nonredundantly defined entities. The creation of entity relationship diagrams as a graphic expression of the database domains is the first step in creating the enterprise data model. The second step is object creation.

4.3 Objects

As stated in the preface, database is a philosophy of quality organization, planning, and management. Central to these organizational characteristics are carefully crafted policies and procedures. Designed well, these business policies and procedures become database objects that can be deployed throughout the organization in a client/server fashion to maximize sharing and consistency while minimizing data hoarding and irregularity.[8]

In today's parlance, a lucid *policy-procedure* pair is called a business object. The goal of business object analysis is to enable quality DBMS object design, that is, the definition of both the data structure and the data structure transformations that:

---

[8] A very early presentation on objects and their role in correct business policy formulation can be found in almost every chapter of *Fundamentals of Information Modeling*. Yourdon Press, New York, 1981.

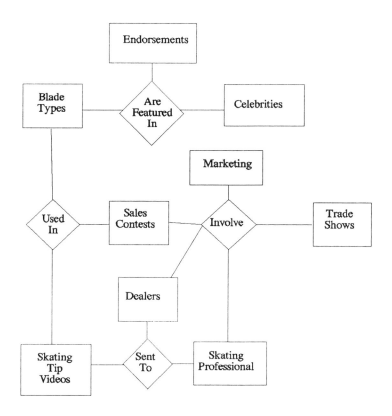

Figure 4.10. Subdomain graphic for promotions.

- Installs a new business object in the database

- Transforms a business object from one coherent state to another

- Removes an object from the database

Objects are found by researching business policies and procedures. The first step in object formation is to discover its data component, that is, through entity analysis. The set of entities in the entity-relationship diagrams are just noun phrases that represent persons (e.g., employee, contractor), places (address, region, district), or things (contract, purchase order, skill_information). These entities are represented at various levels of granularity. Some are *big* like EMPLOYEE, others are *smaller* like SKILL_INFORMATION, and some are data fields like ANNUAL_BONUS. If all the entities were detailed to the level of third normal form, the quantity of entities would be about 800-1200. As a single composite drawing, this massive amount of entities is unreviewable by managers. As a consequence, objects, which are entity collections that are policy-homogeneous with respect to data, are developed within the scope of a database domain. Diagrams are then developed for all the objects for procurement, for employees, for security plans, and the like. This narrowed review scope ensures that managers and functional experts agree as to the set of entities and the relationships that subsequently become the basis of the enterprise data architecture. Entities that are shared among database domains must be reviewed in common to ensure that they are really common.

When entities are in third normal form, they can be too detailed for effective functional manager review. To illustrate the problem, the following set of entities are all related to EMPLOYEE:

- Address
- Biographic_information
- Chosen_benefit
- Dependent
- Federal_tax_withholding
- Performance_review
- Professional_honor_society
- Project_assignment
- School_attended
- Skill_code
- State_tax_withholding

In this example, if the entity EMPLOYEE is represented solely by its third normal form entities, the word EMPLOYEE would not even appear. How then can a manager know if EMPLOYEE is represented at all, and if so, whether the relationships between EMPLOYEE and other major entities are properly reflected? To solve this problem, "super-entities" are created. These are more than just super-entities, though; they are actually objects. The reason they are objects is that their complete definition (through its set of related meta-entity types) includes both a data structure component and the associated set of rules and processes (methods). All entities within an object contain a key, one that distinguishes one object instance from another. For employee, the object's key is EMPLOYEE_ID, and that key is contained in every entity that is part of the EMPLOYEE object. The prime entity is the entity in which the only key is the object's key. Secondary object entities are those that have EMPLOYEE_ID as a foreign key. Entities that are shared between objects are those that contain multiple prime entity primary keys as the key of the shared entity.

To start the creation of objects, each entity from the entity relationship diagram is examined to determine if it is one of the following:

- An object

- A property class that describes a collection of data elements that are represented in the object

- A data element that is a partial descriptor of one or more of the property classes that comprise the data structure of the object

A property class is a collective representation of data elements that share the same purpose or intent, but always with respect to something else. For example, the ADDRESS property class can be inferred to represent:

- Street number
- Street name
- City
- State
- Zip

And the address property class is on behalf of an employee, or a customer, or some other object. In this case, the object's primary key (e.g., EMPLOYEE_ID or CUSTOMER_NUMBER) would be a foreign key that is also an integral component of the address's primary key. From this example, then, the data structure component of an object is the collection of the associated property classes. While each entity contains its own primary key, when the entity is considered within the context of an object, the entity additionally contains at least one other key: the object's primary key.

When all the entities are reviewed and classified as objects, property classes, or data elements, the set of objects within the business should be reduced to about 80. When these objects are grouped by subject area, each diagram becomes easily reviewable.

When each object is defined, the appropriate property classes are identified. Identified property classes serve two purposes. First, they are useful in helping explain the kinds of data represented by the object. Second, when the data elements are assigned to the object prior to the step of generating third normal form tables, the property classes become very large hints as to appropriate data elements.

It is neither necessary nor desirable to assign data elements to property classes. This is because the property class should be descriptive of the data of more than one object and infer different data elements. For example, the LIFE INSURANCE POLICY object and a PURCHASE ORDER object both have some very critical dates. If the appropriate property class, CRITICAL DATES, has data elements allocated to it, it would be useful to only one of the two entities. By not assigning data elements, the property class can be useful to both, serving as a suggestion of the kind of data elements that are appropriate.

NAME: CONTRACT

DEFINITION:

- A contract is an agreement between the company and the customer.
- A contract enables orders to be entered by a customer.
- A contract is PLACED by a salesperson.

PROPERTY CLASSES:

- Contract identification data
- Detailed orders information
- Pricing and cost data
- Summary order information
- Salesman contact activity
- Order payments received

Figure 4.11. Definition and applicable property classes for the contract object.

Figure 4.11 presents the data structure component of an object. The object is CONTRACT, and a bulleted form of a definition is provided. At the end of the figure is an enumeration of the property classes that represent the types/kinds of data elements that should be found when reviewing a fully attributed CONTRACT object. The method component of the object consists of the set of database processes (Chapter 6) that transform the object in appropriate ways.

Figure 4.12 presents a definition of a property class. The property class described is pricing and cost data. The description provides some insight into the types of data elements that are necessary for the object CONTRACT when it is completely designed to third normal form.

The collection of all objects interrelated by the most common relationships and organized by subject area becomes the high-level data model of the business. The data contained in the high-level data model is only that which is implied by the business's mission. Furthermore, no aspect of the mission is left unaddressed by the high-level data model.

Figure 4.13 presents a very simple object diagram for the objects required for a sales and marketing subject area. The diagram shows the basic objects and the relationships among the objects.

The data addressed by the high-level object data model is not restricted to just the data contained in a database. Some data may be outside the database and even outside data processing. The issues of inclusion are addressed when the implemented data models are designed and built.

PROPERTY CLASS: Pricing and Cost Data

DESCRIPTION: Pricing and cost data represents the data that provides information about the details of prices charged and the different types of additional costs that may be involved. Included in costing data are the rates for certain quantities of users, shipping and transportation costs, and any restocking fees if the material is returned.

Figure 4.12.   Definition for the pricing and cost data property class.

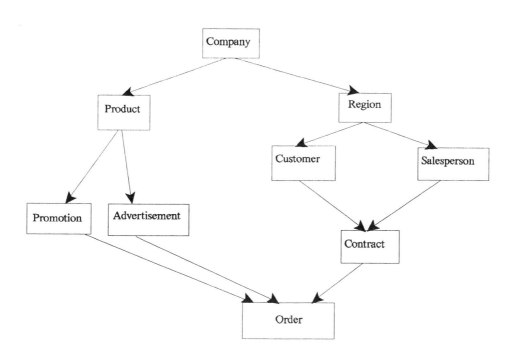

Figure 4.13.   Object diagram for Blades.

Object formation is not complete. It requires the discovery and binding of all the database processes that maintain object integrity. These database processes are presented in Chapter 6.

4.4 Business Function

The business function model represents the set of business functions necessary to carry out that set of the corporate missions deemed necessary by the enterprise managers. The data represented by the high-level data model, that is, the objects, should be the complete set needed by the missions. The set of objects needed by the business functions should map to at least a subset of the objects required by the missions. Any objects not needed by a business function can only imply that there are business functions not currently being performed. The business functions are detailed only to serve as a proof of correctness for the mission model. The objects are the data-intersections between the missions and the business functions, and thus serve as a proof of completeness.

Figure 4.14 illustrates the interaction among the mission, object, and business function models. The subordinate mission, marketing, is currently accomplished through the ACCOMPLISH MARKETING business function. This function consists of three sets of activities, PERFORM MARKET RESEARCH, CONDUCT ADVERTISING CAMPAIGNS, and EVALUATE MARKETING EFFECTIVENESS. The first, PERFORM MARKET RESEARCH, requires data from the high-level data model through some type of access to customers. Functional analysis would determine which functions require enterprise database support, and which do not.

The mission model is the *ideal* model and the business function is the *here and now* model. Thus there may be some data (objects) imputed by the mission model that are currently outside the scope of current business activities.

Because an activity is specified by the high-level business function model does not imply that the function is automated. Some functions and subordinate functions will remain manual forever. The issues of inclusion are addressed when the information systems models are designed and built.

4.5 Business Terms

Business terms are often unique to an organization. Some terms that are common throughout an industry are sometimes uniquely defined within organizations. It is necessary, therefore, that all business terms be defined and catalogued for ready access. Figure 4.15 contains a list of business terms that may be used throughout the business model. It is not uncommon that a business term is also a component of the business model. For example, in Figure 4.15, customer, account, location, and prospect may all be entity types. Sometimes, they may be data elements, as might be Serial_Number. Notwithstanding, these will likely appear within text that defines, for example, an entity, a relationship, or a process.

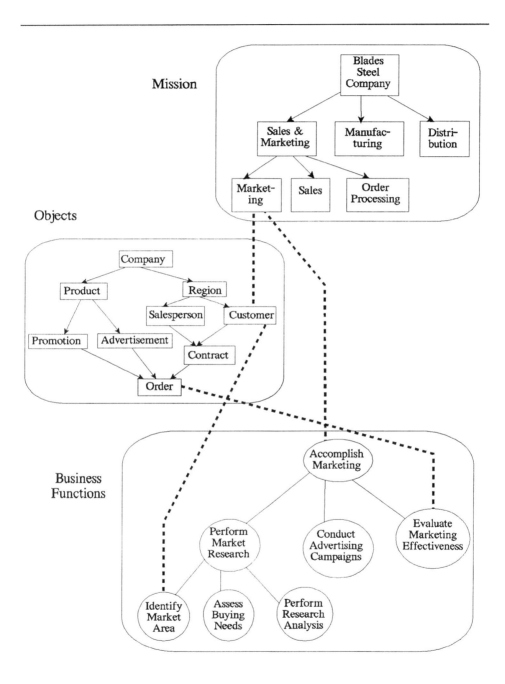

Figure 4.14. Mission, object, and business function interaction.

4.6 Mission Model Summary

The purpose of the mission model is fourfold:

- To clearly identify and describe, by means of the mission hierarchy, the mission of the business, that is, the overall business aim, purpose, goal, or calling. Once stated, it is subdivided into subordinate missions, each of which is described.

- To clearly set down, by means of an analysis of the types of data that can be inferred as required to achieve the mission, a high-level data model. The high-level data model serves to reinforce a reviewer's agreement that the mission analysts understand the organization's mission.

- To clearly illustrate, by means of exposition of *a* valid set of high-level functions, that the high-level data model can be used to achieve the goals and aims set down in the mission model.

- To clearly enable the outside reviewer, by means of the definitions of the business terms, to understand the various descriptions contained in the mission, data model, and process model.

Account:	Organization that has purchased merchandise from Blades Steel Company
Contact:	Person affiliated with an account of Blades
Contract:	Agreement between a customer and Blades that defines all inclusive service to include service cost and specified time
Delivery Date:	Month/day/year when ordered merchandise was shipped to account
Location:	Account address consisting only of city, state
Prospect:	Organization not purchasing product yet; a potential account
Serial Number:	Number that uniquely identifies the skate blade manufactured by Blades

Figure 4.15. Examples of business terms.

The mission hierarchy is different from the business function hierarchy. The mission is an *aim, goal, or objective to be achieved*. In contrast, a function is an *act, operation, or some type of work that is performed*. There may be more than one set of valid business functions that achieve the goals/aims set down in the missions. A mission may be achieved by one or more business functions. Furthermore, a business function may achieve one or more missions. Missions and business functions are different, but they are also related in a many-to-many fashion. Thus one business function accomplishes more than one mission, and it may take more than one business function to accomplish a mission.

A commonly heard criticism of information systems activities is that by the time they are done, they are irrelevant to current needs. Not only is this criticism valid, it is *the* justification for developing the mission model in the first place. The mission model is ideal-oriented, without regard to current business functions. The object model is based on the mission model, thus objects are also ideally oriented. It is common for missions and objects to be far ahead of both current automation and business activities. As business functions are accomplished and implemented through information systems, these new information systems will fit well into this ideal framework. And, as the years progress, the business function-based information system is able to expand into this ideal-oriented framework.

A concern sometimes raised in the development of a mission hierarchy is just how many levels are sufficient. While there is no fixed number of levels, there is a rather simple guideline: If one subordinate sibling mission infers the same data and/or the same processes as another subordinate sibling mission, then only one of the subordinate missions is needed.

A similar guideline is offered for the database domain hierarchy: if one subordinate sibling database domain contains the same entities as another subordinate sibling database domain, then only one of the subordinate database domains is needed.

Some branches of the business function hierarchies ultimately result in business events that then cause the execution of an information system to accomplish the data processing aspect of the business function. Clearly, detailing business functions down to that level is too detailed to be considered a high-level business function model. The quantity of levels is governed by two guidelines. First, the quantity of levels and associated business function descriptions should be sufficient for the reviewers to grasp that the mission is adequately represented. Second, the business function detailing cannot be detailed to the level of a module that affects a third normal form data model, because the third normal form data model does not yet exist.

The complete definition of the meta-entities comprising the mission description meta-model are contained in Appendix 1.

5

DATA MODEL

The data model is the set of meta-entities that represent the technology-independent specification of the data required to accomplish the enterprise mission. Implementation of the data model can be in whole or in part. Some parts may be implemented on only one computer while other parts may be distributed. The data model contains interrelationships between the mission and process models.

5.1 Basic Meta-Entities

Figure 5.1 presents an overall logical database diagram of the meta-entity types contained in the data model.[9] At the top left of Figure 5.1, the meta-entities comprising the intersection between the mission model and the data model are shown. These meta-entities are:

- Database domain and subordinate database domain

- Database domain and object, that is, the relationship between database domain and object

- Object, property class, and the relationship between object and property class (property class & object)

The relationship between the mission model and the data model is many-to-many. This recognizes that missions use common data and vice versa. For example, the mission description for the Blades Steel Company (Figure 4.2 in Chapter 4) contains three distinct areas:

- Sales and marketing
- Manufacturing
- Distribution

---

[9]   In this book, data models are represented as two-dimensional tables, that is, relational. If the DBMS of choice for implementation is relational, then the transformation is simple. If the DBMS is nonrelational, that is, network, hierarchical, or independent logical file, then the relational expression of the data model can be transformed in quick order.

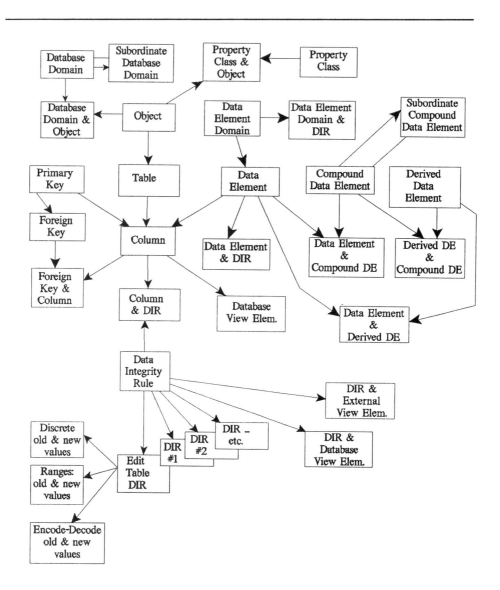

Figure 5.1.   Specified data model meta-entity types.

The corresponding data that supports these missions will certainly include products (ice skate blades). In sales and marketing, products are what is shown and sold. In manufacturing, product is what is made. And, in distribution, product is what goes to the local distributors and ultimately to the customers. Another common type of data is customer, which is used in both sales and marketing and also in distribution. By defining data nonredundantly, and then relating it to the appropriate missions, the first manifestation of shared data will materialize. It is critical to show that data is shared as soon as possible in any enterprise database project. Identification of shared data encourages group participation in data definition, forms design for data capture, and gives early return on investment for accelerated project accomplishment. Data definitions already present that are reused cannot help but save time as well as many different types of project efforts.

At the bottom right of Figure 5.1, the meta-entities comprising the intersection between the data model and the database process model are shown. These meta-entities are:

- Column & Database View Element
- DIR & Database View Element

Like the relationship between data and mission, some database processes can also be reused. They are reused differently, however. This book restricts the definition to database processes as those actions that act directly on the columns within tables across all rows, on rows, and on the relationships among rows from the same table and between tables.

If a data element is used in many different tables under different column names, for example, TELEPHONE_NUMBER, the database process by which it is edited can be employed many times. These database processes are defined nonredundantly; thus the relationship between database process and data is one-to-many. When data is subject to multiple types of edits, the relationship between the data and the associated database processes is one-to-many. Hence the overall relationship between data and database process is many-to-many. In the case where there are multiple database processes that edit the same data, there must be a "higher" database process that determines the action to be taken when one or both of the edit database processes fails. Thus, within database processes (Chapter 6), the hierarchical relationship also exits.

The remaining meta-entities contained in Figure 5.1 define the meta-model for the data model. There are four basic clusters of meta-entity types that serve to completely define:

- Data elements
- Tables
- Relationships (foreign keys)
- Data integrity rules

A *data element* is an atomic, primitive business fact. By *atomic*, we mean the fact is not compound or complex. Address is compound; state name is not. By *primitive*, we mean the fact is not derived. It is the result of a formula that would produce GRAND_TOTAL, for example. Figure 5.2 presents the definition for the data element CONTRACT_IDENTIFIER. This data element contains a name, a brief definition, and characteristics of the type of data represented by the data element,

---

NAME: CONTRACT_IDENTIFIER

DEFINITION: A contract number is a unique number assigned by accounting

TYPE: NUMERIC

PICTURE: 9(5)

Figure 5.2. Contract identification data element definition.

---

such as its picture, which shows CONTRACT_IDENTIFIER to be a five-position numeric.

A *table* is a collection of assigned data elements that represent the data required for a coherent business policy. The term table is used because it represents a specific two-dimensional data modeling technique. A table consists of a set of columns. A column is the specific allocation of a data element to a table. When tables are valued, they are said to contain rows of data. Each column within a row represents only one value.

In Figure 5.3, the table CONTRACT IDENTIFICATION is the collection of all data elements necessary to completely identify a contract. There may be multiple tables that collectively represent the data necessary for the object CONTRACT. The identification of the contract would have been accomplished in the mission description model. The data model meta-entities would define the necessary data structure for the object.

In addition to columns, a well-defined table has a primary key, which is a named collection of columns whose combined value is unique across all rows of the table. Tables do not exist in isolation from all other tables.

TABLE: Contract Identification

DESCRIPTION: The contract identification data record type contains data that identifies the contract between the company and its clients. The identification data elements include the contract number, the name of the client, its address, contract officer, and other identifying information.

Figure 5.3. Contract identification table definition.

CONTRACT_START_DATE

EMPLOYEE_PAY_RAISE_DATE

DEPENDENT_BIRTH_DATE

Figure 5.4.   Examples of columns.

Figure 5.4 presents a collection of data elements that have been allocated to a table. Note that in each, the data element name is prefixed by some indication of its context. The data element START_DATE is prefixed by CONTRACT, the data element PAY_RAISE_DATE is prefixed by EMPLOYEE, and the data element BIRTH_DATE is prefixed by DEPENDENT. In these examples, definitions are required only for the data elements and for the tables. When a complete definition of the table and its associated columns is presented, the table's definition is usually sufficient to explain the context for the contained data elements.

Relationships between tables in relational data models are represented as foreign keys. Figure 5.5 lists the CONTRACT_IDENTIFICATION table. The primary and foreign key statements are provided. The foreign key statement identifies the table that provides the primary key reference for the foreign key. The foreign key clause also states the actions that are to be taken when an attempt is made to insert, modify, or delete a CONTRACT_IDENTIFICATION row that violates a proposed required match between the value contained in SALESPERSON_OF_RECORD and one row from the SALESPERSON table.

Figure 5.6 provides a graphic of all the tables that are contained in the data model for the marketing database. As syntax, these 12 tables would be expressed as a series of figures like Figure 5.5. Each relationship in Figure 5.6, shown as a line and single-headed arrow between tables, is syntactically expressed as foreign key clauses of the form contained in Figure 5.5.

The final component of the data model is data integrity rules. These rules specify the integrity that must exist when no updating is taking place. For example, in Figure 5.7, the first example states that CONTRACT_END_DATE cannot be earlier than the CONTRACT_START_DATE. In this example, both columns are likely in the same table. In the second example, the TOTAL_ORDER_COST column represents the sum of the LINE_ITEM_ORDER_COST columns from the LINE_ITEM rows. The third example states that all the columns must be valued before the row is accepted for inclusion in the database.

DATA RECORD: CONTRACT_IDENTIFICATION

PRIMARY KEY IS CONTRACT_ID

FOREIGN KEY IS SALESPERSON_OF_RECORD REFERENCES SALESPERSON
    ON INSERT, REJECT
    ON MODIFY, SET NULL
    ON DELETE, SET NULL

DATA ELEMENTS ARE:

    CONTRACT_ID, TYPE IS INTEGER 9999999
    CONTRACT_NAME, TYPE IS CHARACTER 25
    CONTRACT_START_DATE, TYPE IS DATE
    CONTRACT_END_DATE, TYPE IS DATE
    SALESPERSON_OF_RECORD, TYPE IS INTEGER 999999
    TOTAL_CONTRACT_VALUE, TYPE IS MONEY 999,999.99

Figure 5.5.   Contract identification table and columns.

Collectively, these four meta-entity clusters,

- data elements,
- tables,
- relationships or foreign keys, and
- data integrity rules,

must have all their metadata defined and stored in the repository for the data model under design prior to the development of a corresponding database process model.

5.2 Data Element Meta-Entity Cluster

While data elements are the atomic facts to be represented in any data model, they are seldom simple. Take for example, a telephone number. To begin with, in the United States, the telephone number consists of two parts: exchange and number. But to uniquely define a telephone number in the United States, each <exchange + number> pair is prefixed by another number, the <area code>. Finally, to distinguish countries there is the country code. In short, the telephone number is not simple, but compound. To fully express compound data elements, additional meta-entities are required. Figure 5.8 illustrates the set of meta-entity types required to completely represent data elements. The basic meta-entities are:

- Column
- Compound data element
- Data element
- Data element domain
- Derived data element

The following meta-entities represent relationships among the basic ones:

- Column & data integrity rule
- Column & database view element
- Data element & compound data element
- Data element & data integrity rule
- Data element & derived data element
- Data element domain & data integrity rule
- Derived data element & compound data element
- Subordinate compound data element

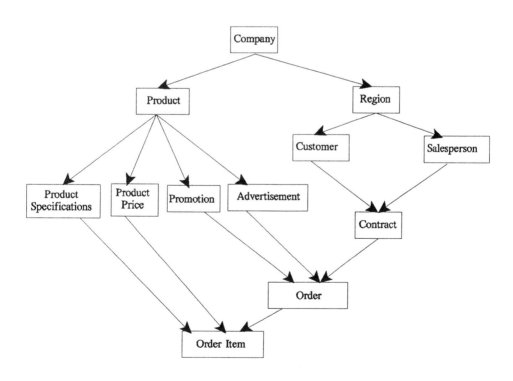

Figure 5.6.   Table diagram for Blades.

DATA INTEGRITY RULES

1.   CONTRACT_END_DATE GE CONTRACT_START_DATE

2.   TOTAL_ORDER_COST EQ SUM (LINE-ITEM-ORDER-COST)

3.   All columns must be valued before the row is stored.

Figure 5.7.   Data integrity rules.

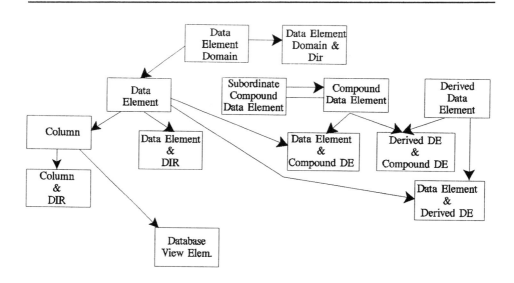

Figure 5.8.   Data element meta-entity cluster.

The purpose of the meta-entities presented in Figure 5.8 is to accurately and comprehensively represent the complexities surrounding the capture of data element names, definitions, and value semantics.

5.2.1 Data Element

The data element meta-entity represents the specification of the atomic fact—independent of its use whenever possible. Immediately connected to data element are two meta-entities: data element domain and column. Figure 5.2 provided an example of a fully defined data element. The complete set of data integrity rules that control the values and other types of editing are described in Section 5.5. The meta-entity that interrelates data element and data integrity rule was shown in Figure 5.1. The reason the editing and validation rules are not fully described under data elements is that data integrity rules must be specified nonredundantly. That way they can be specified once and referenced many times. Editing rules specified for money-type numerics can be referenced wherever employed, that is, SALARY, REMAINING_BALANCE, INVOICE_AMOUNT, and the like.

Data elements represent discrete instances of business data. Examples of business data are: SOCIAL SECURITY NUMBER, RECEIPT DATE, FIRST NAME, ADDRESS, REMAINING AMOUNT, and so forth. Data elements exhibit many characteristics, all of which must be known before a true understanding of the data element can be made.

There are a number of issues surrounding data elements, and to presume that a data element naming standard is a way to solve these issues is too trivial. In short, there is much more to a data element than just its name.

5.2.2 Data Element Domain

The data element domain meta-entity provides an overriding statement about the definition and the allowed set of values represented by a data element domain, and in turn, the allowed data values specification for data element and finally, the column. As with data elements and columns, the complete set of applicable editing and validation rules are specified within the data integrity rules.

Given that data element domains, data elements, and columns can each contain a set of data integrity rules, a problem arises when their restrictions are conflicting. Because of this distinct possibility, the repository system must contain sufficient processing logic to report conflicts. A conflict exists whenever a set of data integrity rules for a data element, with respect to the overriding data element domain, allows values outside the range of the data element. For example, if data element domain data integrity rules only allow the values A, Q, or M, but the data element data integrity rules allow the values A, Q, R, or M, there is a semantic conflict that must be reported and corrected.

Another attribute of a data element is its use context. For example, the data element REMAINING AMOUNT might be allowed to have negative values in some situations but not in others. In a checking account, for example, a negative REMAINING AMOUNT might be allowed, resulting in INTEREST being charged by the bank. In the case of a mortgage payoff, the amount to be paid is likely required to be exactly that which is due, since the REMAINING AMOUNT on a mortgage cannot be negative. After all, a negative balance on a mortgage conflicts with the very definition of mortgage. And, of course, if a REMAINING AMOUNT data element were part of an INVENTORY-ON-HAND data record, not only would negative numbers not be allowed, but fractions would also never be allowed. After all, what would be the meaning of 7.89 bolts?

5.2.3 Compound Data Element

Some data elements are not simple. That is, they do not represent a single value from a simple business policy. There are two different cases of complex data elements: compound data elements and derived data elements.

As an example, the data element PART_NUMBER may actually consist of multiple data elements such as YEAR_OF_MANUFACTURE, MONTH_OF_MANUFACTURE, and DIVISION. That is, the data element PART_NUMBER is really three different data elements that are themselves obscured. This obscurity is a problem because the real, underlying data is hidden from analysis and documentation. To eliminate this situation, the compound data element must first be entered into the compound data element meta-entity. Then, the real data elements must be entered as data elements. The relationship between the two meta-entities is provided by the relationship meta-entity: data element & compound data element. In the situation where a compound data element is itself compound, the meta-entity subordinate compound data element is provided to hierarchically decompose it.

Another type of data element is ADDRESS. This data element presents a whole different set of problems, least of which is its data type. ADDRESS does not represent a discrete value, but a set of *lower-level* data elements, each of which has a discrete value. Each of the lower-level data elements may be of a different data type. For example, ADDRESS is most likely composed of EFFECTIVE DATE, STREET NUMBER, STREET NAME, CITY, STATE, ZIP, and COUNTRY. Again, each of these data elements may have rules for the types of values, rules for specific ranges of legal values, and in the case of CITY and ZIP, have specific instances of legal values—in combination. In the case where the country was the United States, letters would be illegal in ZIP code, while in CANADA, an all-numeric ZIP code would be illegal. So, what would be the domain prefix of ADDRESS? The first data type, the mode data type, or the average (whatever that means). Of course, one solution would be to prohibit ADDRESS type of data elements. But that would be like throwing the baby out with the bath water!

5.2.4 Derived Data Element

A data element may be derived. For example, a candidate data element TOTAL_DEPARTMENT_SALARY may be derived from the summation of the values from the EMPLOYEE_SALARY data element that exists in the EMPLOYEE rows. The data element TOTAL_DEPARTMENT_SALARY is derived. To fully define this data element, its name is entered into the derived data element meta-entity. The data elements from which it is derived are entered in the data element meta-entity. Finally, the relationship and the computation rationale are entered in the relationship meta-entity data element & derived data element.

Figure 5.8 provided the meta-entity data structure to handle the case where a compound data element consists of one or more derived data elements. Such would be the case where PART_NUMBER applied to an assembly and was defined to also include the total weight of all contained subassemblies.

A final type of data element is REMAINING AMOUNT. This data element is obviously computed from some other source. Furthermore, it may have certain rules about its upper and lower limits (negative not allowed, for example). This data element is subjected to rounding rules for MONEY, and may be allowed to be operated upon in certain ways but not in others. For example, the SQUARE ROOT of REMAINING AMOUNT is not sensible, but the STANDARD DEVIATION of REMAINING AMOUNT (which involves square roots) may be. Again, identifying the data type as numeric would be misleading because not all arithmetic operations are permitted—sensibly.

The point to all of these examples is that data elements conform to certain rules of behavior, some of which are implied by their obvious data type and others of which are mistakenly implied by their data type. For example, a STREET NUMBER might lead one to believe that the type of value is numeric, except when the STREET NUMBER is 104A. SOCIAL SECURITY NUMBER is certainly numeric but does not participate in numerical calculations.

Some data elements of different types may be combined to yield legal results. For example, MOMENTUM is defined as FORCE times DISTANCE. Yet the square of force makes no sense, while the square of distance results in AREA.

5.2.5 Column

The column meta-entity represents the data element's use within the context of a table. Figure 5.4 contained three columns. All the columns represent dates with the table name as the first part of the column name. Most likely, the three columns relate to the three data elements: START_DATE, PAY_RAISE_DATE, and BIRTH_DATE.

Columns thus represent a contextual use of a data element. Some data elements may be represented multiple times and others only once. For example, if the data element is TELEPHONE_NUMBER, a column might be HOME_TELEPHONE_NUMBER, OFFICE_TELEPHONE_NUMBER, or CUSTOMER_TELEPHONE_NUMBER. In this case, OFFICE and HOME are name modifiers used to specify the data element's use within multiple columns.

Data elements, as columns, are employed within the context of a table. In the case of HOME_TELEPHONE_NUMBER and OFFICE_TELEPHONE_NUMBER the context might be the same EMPLOYEE table. Some data elements may be referenced many times across a set of tables, for example, EMPLOYEE_ID. In the case of EMPLOYEE_ID, many of its references are actually used as a foreign key. That makes its correct usage even more important, because if its editing or values are different the DBMS may not be able to correctly identify that the rows are in fact related.

Whenever a column has a specialized use within a table, a *religious war* is sure to break out as to whether the use should be reflected in the column's name. The war is, however, founded on an incorrect proposition, that the purpose of a data element name is to restate the data element's semantics rather than serve as a shorthand for its business definition. Given that there are plenty of other meta-attributes for specifying the various semantics, the data element name can be reserved to be just the common English name, and no more. The context name is contained in the table's name, and thus has no place being part of the column's name. The column's use is also just another meta-attribute, and so has no part in the data element's name.

As with data elements, the set of data integrity rules are nonredundantly defined. Figure 5.1 showed the meta-entity that interrelates column and data integrity rules.

5.2.6 Use Anomalies

SOCIAL SECURITY NUMBER is typically represented as a nine-digit number, but it is not arithmetic in nature. Consequently, it would be senseless to compute the average SOCIAL SECURITY NUMBER for a sampling of EMPLOYEEs. Additionally, there are legal and illegal values for SOCIAL SECURITY NUMBER. While its form is certainly numeric, SOCIAL SECURITY NUMBER is not numeric in the conventional sense. Thus to prefix SOCIAL SECURITY with its data type NUMERIC would be misleading as to its true nature, to say nothing of ruining a perfectly good name (NUMERIC SOCIAL SECURITY NUMBER), and taking up an additional eight character positions of the name.

RECEIPT DATE is another business data element that is also numeric. RECEIPT DATE has numeric qualities, legal and illegal values, and if properly stored can be used in some types of arithmetic logic. For example, a query might be constructed to print the DATE that is 15 days beyond a specific RECEIPT DATE. Multiplying two dates would make no sense. However, computing the standard deviation, average, or median number of days after an invoice was issued before it was paid would make sense. Such a calculation involves subtraction, summing, and square roots. Again, to say that RECEIPT DATE is a number is to mislead users as to allowable operations. To establish a data type called DATE is a good solution, but unless that is carefully thought out as to internal storage, the variety of external representations, and finally the problems caused by different time zones, and so forth is to again create a problem greater than that which existed originally. To prefix RECEIPT with the data type DATE begs the inclusion of the phrase " of, " which again causes the addition of four additional characters in the data element name with no real semantic value.

FIRST NAME is most probably an alphabetic data element. Its values are restricted to a combination of the instances of LETTERS, with the first letter being in UPPER CASE. In general, numbers would probably be an indication of an error, although not always. After all, there is C3PO and R2D2! Determining the real data element name here is difficult. After all, is NAME a part of the data element's name, or is it an indication of the type of data (character)? Thus the data element's name could be NAME, or FIRST, or FIRST NAME, or "NAME, FIRST." Depending on how that question is answered and presuming the domain to be CHARACTER leads to the following alternatives for first name:

- CHARACTER NAME
- CHARACTER FIRST
- CHARACTER FIRST NAME
- CHARACTER NAME FIRST

5.2.7 Data Element Summary

To fully understand data elements, it should be quite clear that their scope, intent, rules, and other types of metadata must be known. All these additional semantics (rules of meaning and usage) are represented in data element meta-attributes different from the data element's name. With that approach, the semantics can be expressed in a form that is appropriate for the subject data element.

An early solution to the representation of all data element semantics was to pack them all into the name space. While initially attractive, the initial solution, once all the appropriate semantics are known, becomes a nightmare because the name space is usually limited in length. The limitation, usually 32, then causes the creation of abbreviations, which are separated by underscores (_); taken to the extreme this can lead to 17 single letters with 15 interleaving underscores. The sheer weight of the Rosetta Stone to decode all this would certainly be a millstone around any user's neck. With the advent of repositories that follow the ANSI standards (ANSI/IRDS) all the data type, value editing characteristics, and all the other critical data element characteristics can be defined as separate meta-attributes to collectively represent the full semantics of the data element. In short, the necessity to overload the data element's name space is certainly no longer needed.

5.3 Tables

A table is an expression of business policy. While it is possible that only one table is needed to comprise the data structure component of an object, it is more likely that multiple tables are required to fully express an object's data structure. Figure 5.9 shows the meta-entities related to the complete definition of a table, which are:

- Column
- Primary key
- Table

The column meta-entity and its associated set of semantics is a specific, value-based implementation of part of the table's business policy. Collectively, the proper set of columns represents a coherent business policy statement. In addition to columns, a well-formed table contains a primary key that maps to one or more columns. The value of a table's primary key is unique across all rows.

Tables are derived through intensive data analysis. The first part of the data analysis is accomplished in the high-level enterprise data model project. This project is described in Chapter 19.

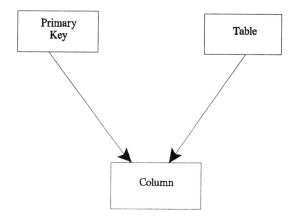

Figure 5.9.   Table meta-entity cluster.

5.4 Relationships

A relationship, like a table and a column, is the expression of a business policy that exists between tables.[10] Relationships between tables are represented through special columns called foreign keys. A *foreign key* is typically the primary key from another table that is allocated to the table as a way of expressing a one-to-many or a one-to-one relationship.

Tables can have one or more foreign keys. The meta-entities related to the complete definition of a table are illustrated in Figure 5.10 and are:

- Column
- Primary key
- Foreign key
- Foreign key & column

Relationships between tables are expressed through foreign keys. The relationship is most commonly one-to-many. In this case, the relationship means that there is one row in one table that is related to many (or possibly many) rows in the other tables. An example is that an EMPLOYEE has multiple DEPENDENTS. In the source table, the most common technique employed to express the relationship is to declare that the primary key of the EMPLOYEE table, that is, EMP_ID, is related to a column in the DEPENDENT's table, that is, PARENT_EMP_ID. Since the PARENT_EMP_ID is not a natural column of the dependent table, it is said to be a foreign key.

Two other relationship types are common. First, if the set of columns comprising the foreign key is required to be unique, the relationship between the tables is actually one-to-one. Second, if the table names of the one-to-many relationship are the same, the relationship is hierarchical, or recursive.

Whenever a relationship is sufficiently formal, it often requires multiple attributes to document its existence. To document these characteristics, the relationship is defined as a formal table with all the appropriate names, definitions, and primary and foreign keys. As tables, relationships lose their distinctive characteristics.

5.5 Data Integrity Rules

Simply put, a data integrity rule is a rule that, when executed, either restores integrity or tests whether integrity remains.

Traditionally, data integrity rules are an integral component of the computer programs associated with data processing applications. With the arrival of database,

---

[10] This book only presents binary relationships because the data modeling technique of the represented metadata representation is relational.

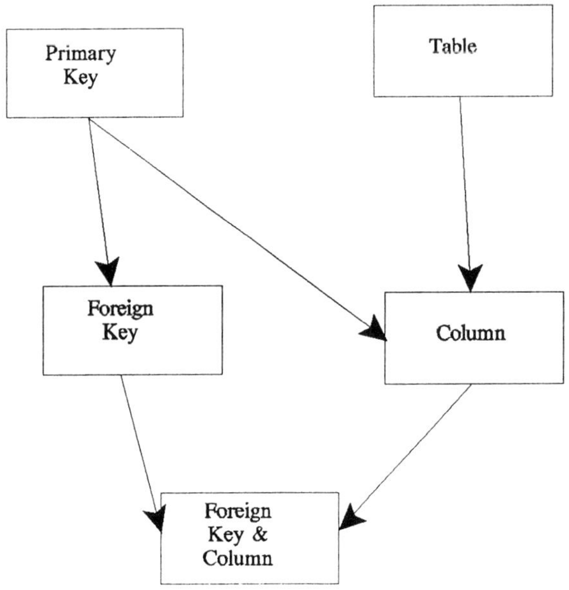

Figure 5.10. Relationships meta-entity cluster.

computer programs have become less and less the central focus of the data processing. Computer programs have been replaced with query statements, automatically generated screen programs, and entire programs that are only ten to twenty statements long. In addition to a complete change in program form, the quantity of opportunities for updating a DBMS table within a database environment has greatly increased. Because of these needs, data integrity rules must be centrally designed and made available in the repository.

If the rules are in the repository, a DBMS schema designer can know the integrity requirements for complete specification of table-based triggers and assertions and column-based validations. Figure 5.11 presents the complete set of meta-entity types for data integrity rules.

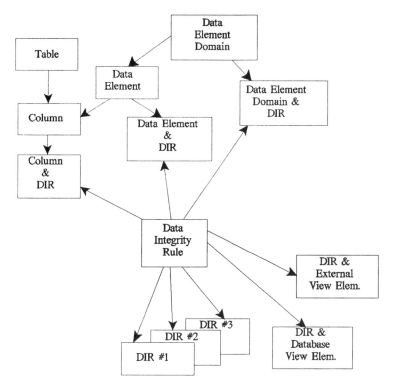

Figure 5.11. Data integrity rule meta-entity cluster.

The meta-entity types supporting data integrity rules are:

- Column
- Column & data integrity rule
- Column & database view element
- Data element
- Data element & data integrity rule
- Data element domain
- Data element domain & data integrity rule
- Data integrity rule
- Data integrity rule & database view element
- Table

5.5.1 Types of Data Integrity Rules

Columns, individually and in specific combinations within one or more tables, are governed by one or more data integrity rules. Seven common classes of data integrity rules are:

- Single table, single column
- Single table, multiple column
- Single table, single column, multiple row
- Single table, multiple column, single row derived data
- Single table, single column, multiple row derived data
- Multiple table derived data
- Multiple table, multiple column (referential integrity)

Each column might have one or more data integrity rules defined within the context of a table. A rule might be that the column cannot be blank (or NULL) whenever the row is stored or subsequently updated. There might be other rules that are related to valid values, invalid values, ranges of valid and invalid values, and the like.

Tables themselves also have data integrity rules, in that all the rules associated with all the columns are identified as belonging to the table.

5.5.2 Data Integrity Rule Specification

A modified Backus Naur form of notation is used to illustrate data integrity rules. To indicate a particular column of a particular table that was retrieved from the database according to a specific select clause, the following notation is utilized:

$$C ::= \text{column id}$$
$$T ::= \text{table type}$$
$$SCn ::= \text{select clause}$$

Thus C.T.SC1(i) is the i-th column (C) within the table (T) that is selected by the first select clause (SC). The number suffix on the SC denotes different select clauses. If different <table id number>s or different <column id>s are stored, then either different tables and/or different columns are employed in the rule.

For convenience, the term <column> is used as a shorthand way to denote a specific <column> within a specific <table>. Each data integrity rule type is illustrated through a definition, example, and a grammar.

5.5.3 Single Table, Single Column

Definition: A data table that contains the valid and invalid values for columns.

Example: BIRTH_DATE column must contain only valid dates.

The requirements for defining column data integrity rules are the identification of the column, and the identification of whether the editing rule is for valid/invalid discrete values or for valid/invalid value ranges. These rules are already defined in the repository under the category of edit tables. Included herein are the table structures for edit tables, illustrating the type of data needed to define column data integrity rules.

Column:	<column (i)>
Valid Values:	<value> [,<value>]...
Range Values:	<FROM <value> TO <value>>...
Encode-Decode Values:	<ENCODE <value> DECODE <value>>...

5.5.4 Single Table, Multiple Column

Definition: Columns that are related to each other in a way not covered by any third normal rule.

Example: There are two different columns, CONTRACT_START_DATE and CONTRACT_END_DATE, and the dates are related; the CONTRACT_END_DATE must certainly occur on or after the CONTRACT_START_DATE.

The requirements for defining this rule are the names of the two columns and the relational operator that exists between instances of the columns.

Column:	<column (i)>
Binary Operator:	<binary operator>
Column Name:	<column (j)>
<binary operator>s::=	¦Less than (LT) ¦Less than or equal to (LE) ¦Equal to (EQ) ¦Greater than or equal to (GE)

¦Greater than (GT)

Example: DEATH DATE GE BIRTH DATE

5.5.5 Single Table, Single Column, Multiple Row

Definition: An intra-table, single column, multiple row rule is one in which the rows from the same table are related to each other through the value instances of one column.

Example: Each CUSTOMER can have multiple CONTRACTS, but there is the rule that each CONTRACT_NUMBER's value must increase, thus installing a new contract with a CONTRACT_NUMBER that has a duplicate number or that is less than an installed number would be a violation of this rule.

The requirements for defining this rule are the name of the column to which the rule applies, the algebraic formula that governs the value of one instance of the column to the next, and the table selection clause that selects the records to which the rule applies.

  Column: <column (i)>

  Algebraic Formula: <formula>

  <formula>s::=   <C.T.SC1(i)>   <=>   <C.T.SC2(i)>   <formula operation>

  <formula operation>::=   programmable operation on the value of the column obtained from the second select clause before it is stored as the value of the column obtained from the first select clause.

  <select clause>::=   selection criteria for selecting the row upon which the <formula operation> is to be executed before the new row is stored.

Example: SELECT LAST CONTRACT,
CONTRACT_NUMBER (CONTRACT (CURRENT)) =
CONTRACT_NUMBER (CONTRACT (LAST)) + 1

5.5.6 Single Table, Multiple Column, Single Row Derived Data

Definition: An intra-table derived data rule is one in which the value of a column in one row of one table is the result of a calculation of one or more columns within the same row of the same table.

Example: The term of the contract in days is equal to the number of days between the end date of the contract and its start date.

The requirements for defining this rule are the names of the two columns and the relational operator that exists between instances of the columns.

Column: <column (i)>...

Algebraic Formula: <formula>

<formula>s::= <C.T.SC1(i)> <=> <C.T.SC1(j)> [<formula operation> <C.T.SC1(k)>]...

<formula operation>::= programmable operation on the value of <column (k)> obtained from the record selected before it is combined with the data value of <column (j)> from the same record before it is stored as the value of <column (i)> in that same row. This operation may iterate.

<select clause>::= selection criteria for selecting the row upon which the <formula operation> is to be executed before the new row is stored.

Example: TERM_OF_CONTRACT = CONTRACT_END_DATE - CONTRACT_START_DATE

5.5.7 Single Table, Single Column, Multiple Row Derived Data

Definition: A single table, single data element, multiple row derived data rule is one in which the value of a column within the next-to-be-stored row has been computed from a data value stored in the most-recently stored row. Relationally, a serial number concept must be operating to select the most immediately stored row.

Example: A table contains a column REMAINING_OBLIGATORY_AUTHORITY. The value stored in this column is to be the value stored in the same column of the preceding row minus the amount of the current CONTRACT's value.

The requirements for defining this rule are the name of the column to which the rule applies, and the algebraic formula that governs the value of the column of the most recent row.

Column: <column (i)>...

<formula >s::=   <C.T.SC1(i)>   <=>   <C.T.SC2(j)>   [<formula operation> <C.T.SC3(k)>]...

<formula operation >::=   programmable operation on the value of <column (k)> obtained from the record selected by the second select clause before it is combined with the data value of <column (j)> from the record obtained from the third select clause, before it is stored as the value of <column (i)> in the row selected by the first select clause. This operation may iterate.

<select clause> ::=   selection criteria for selecting the row upon which the <formula operation> is to be executed before the new row is stored.

Example: REMAINING_BALANCE   (CONTRACT   (current))   = REMAINING_BALANCE   (CONTRACT   (last))   - PURCHASE_ORDER_VALUE

5.5.8 Multiple Table Derived Data

Definition: A multiple table derived data rule is one in which the value of a column in one table is the result of a calculation on one or more instances of the same or different columns in other tables.

Example: DEPARTMENT table has a TOTAL CURRENT SALARYs column. The value of that column would be affected by the EMPLOYEEs associated with the DEPARTMENT. As an employee is hired, transferred, or terminated, the TOTAL CURRENT SALARY column would have to be modified accordingly.

The requirements for defining this rule are the names of the two columns and the relational operator that exists between instances of the columns.

Column: <column (i)>...

<formula>s::= <C.T.SC1(i)> <=> <C.T.SC2(j)> [<formula operation> <C.T.SC3(k)>]...

<formula operation> ::= programmable operation on the value of <column (k)> obtained from the a table type instance that was selected by the second select clause before it is combined with the data value of <column (j)> from possibly a different table type instance that was obtained from the third select clause, before it is stored as the value of <column (i)> in a table type instance of a type that may be different from either of the two other types that was obtained by the first select clause. This operation may iterate.

<select clause> ::= selection criteria for selecting the owner row, whose primary key is then used to select the member rows across which the <member record operation> is to be executed.

Example: SELECT DEPARTMENT WHERE DEPARTMENT_NAME EQ "ACCOUNTS_PAYABLE"

SELECT EMPLOYEE WHERE EMPLOYEE DEPARTMENT NUMBER EQUAL DEPARTMENT_DEPARTMENT_NUMBER

DEPARTMENT_SALARY = SUM (EMPLOYEE_SALARY)

5.5.9 Multiple Table, Multiple Column (Referential Integrity)

Definition: Referential integrity is a data integrity rule that is an extension of the single table, multiple column rule. Referential integrity involves multiple tables. Furthermore, the rule includes the specification of the automatic actions the DBMS is to undertake whenever an update is attempted that violates the rule.

Example: There is a CURRENT DEPARTMENT NUMBER column in the EMPLOYEE table. If an EMPLOYEE is transferred this field has to be updated with a DEPARTMENT NUMBER that is valid. The employee could not be transferred to a nonexistent department. Additionally, if a DEPARTMENT is dissolved, either the EMPLOYEEs must be "transferred" to a special nonexistent department (e.g., UNASSIGNED) or the EMPLOYEEs must be dissolved (probably an undesirable effect), or the dissolution of the DEPARTMENT must be disallowed. A referential integrity rule thus must not only specify the column basis for the referential integrity but also specify the operations effect of the rule (disallowed, dissolve, or NULL).

The requirements for defining this rule are the names of the two columns, one that acts as the primary key of the owner, and the other that acts as the foreign key in the member. Additionally, there is the requirement to state the actions that are to be taken whenever a referential integrity rule is violated. There are three actions possible:

- When the owner row is deleted, then the member row's foreign key is updated to a NULL value, or the member row is deleted, or the owner action is rejected.

- When the member's foreign key is updated to a nonexistent owner primary key value, then either the update is rejected or the value is set to a NULL value

- When a new member is inserted, but the value of the member's foreign key is a nonexistent owner primary key value, then either the insert is rejected, or the value is set to a NULL value.

```
OWNER TABLE IS <owner table name>
MEMBER TABLE IS <member table name>
CONSTRAINT IS <owner table primary key> EQUAL
    <member column name>
ON DELETE <member action>
ON MODIFY <member action>
ON INSERT <member action>
```

EXAMPLE:
```
OWNER TABLE IS employee
MEMBER TABLE IS dependent
CONSTRAINT IS emp.ssn EQUAL dep.emp.ssn
ON DELETE cascade
ON MODIFY reject
ON INSERT reject
```

6

DATABASE PROCESS MODEL

The database process model is manifest through a set of meta-entities that reflect the technology independent specification of database processes required to accomplish the transformation of the data determined necessary by the database's mission.

It is essential that the database process model be independently defined for two reasons:

- The database processes are the second half of objects.

- The database processes must be available to all appropriate information systems in a non-redundant fashion—available to all, captive by none.

Objects were first identified during the development of the mission model. In the data model, the objects were fully detailed—as to data. In this chapter, the second half objects is identified. Completely defined and deployed, the set of all business objects help to fulfill the promise of database: quality organization, planning, and management.

A business object is a carefully crafted policy and associated procedures. Implemented as database objects they can be deployed throughout the organization in a client/server fashion to maximize sharing and consistency while minimizing data hoarding and irregularity.

These database processes are subsequently allocated through views to one or more of the information systems meta-entity models (Chapter 7), in reaction to the business events (Chapter 8) that accomplish the automation aspects of various business functions (Chapter 9) by enterprise organization units (Chapter 10).

The database process model contains the interrelationships between it and:

- The data model through database view and the database view column

- The various information systems subordinate models (document, form, report, file, and screen) through external views and the external view elements

The purpose of the database process model is to specify the database processes that interact with views that in turn represent the interface to the database. The view contains the specification of the data interface to the database's tables, columns, and rows. In addition, the view contains the specification of the selection and relationship navigation.

109

6.1 Controlling Quantity of Update Interfaces

To control the quantity of update interfaces to resultant databases, a minimization rule should be enforced. The minimization rule restricts the interaction between database processes and databases to three: add, delete, and modify. Additionally, each add, delete, or modify deals with only one table and with only one row in the table. Under this minimization rule, if there is a 300-table database, the number of update database processes is 900. The database processes are thus defined in third normal form. Chapter 13 describes why achieving database process third normal form is important.

Two types of minimization rule violations are commonly found. The first occurs when each business system is defined to include its own update programs rather than use one or more of the fixed set of database process updates.

The second type of violation occurs when the one-table and one-row rule is relaxed to allow database changes to multiple rows in one command, or to more than one table by the update statement.

The first violation easily occurs when an information system is being implemented. It is not uncommon to have a quantity of data update programs five to ten times the quantity of database tables. Thus, for a 100-table database, there would be from 500 to 1000 database update programs. If each business program contains its own custom coding for database update, there would then be from 150-325 percent more update programs to design, debug, and document under this database update program scenario versus the restricted scenario.

The second violation occurs when database processes are defined that deal with multiple rows from a single table, or that deal with one or more rows from multiple tables. Under this second violation, an incorrect insert, delete, or modify is more difficult to understand than if database processes are in third normal form. In addition to increasing ambiguity (undesired), the quantity of programs that have to be well defined, thoroughly debugged, and precisely documented dramatically increases.

Because both violation types produce undesired results, organizations often require—through standards—that a database change (add, delete, or modify) only affect one row in one table. Even though such a standard may ultimately require more computer resources than otherwise, the rationale is that excess resource expenditures in the name of data integrity is a small price to pay.

Most commercially available DBMSs cannot directly support all the different types of data integrity rules. Because of this, individual programmers have to be relied on for the correct interpretation and inclusion of all the appropriate data integrity rules. A review of the different data integrity rules specified in Section 5.5 in Chapter 5 shows all the different types.

Because of the critical importance of maintaining database integrity, and because of their potential complexity, all data integrity rules must be both specified nonredundantly and implemented nonredundantly.

Having database integrity is probably more important than having correct database design. Missing or badly organized data can be quickly recognized and projects can be readily mobilized to fix the database designs. However, database integrity is more subtle. If, for example, there is a personnel database with 10,000 employees, a slightly imperfect referential integrity could cause the unrecoverable disconnection of a number of advanced education rows, or a number of attained skill rows. No one would ever know, except for the individual staff members.

Significantly more serious data integrity errors can occur if data integrity rules are changed from one suite of database update programs to the next. Whenever there is a large quantity of derived data elements, the possibility for loss of data integrity is very high. Therefore, it is very critical that all programmed data integrity be formally specified and implemented in nonredundant fashion, that is, through database processes.

6.2 Database Process Model Meta-Entities

The meta-entities that comprise the database process model are:

- Column
- Column & data integrity rule
- Database view
- Database view element
- Data integrity rule
- Database process
- Subordinate database process

These meta-entities are illustrated in Figure 6.1 The column meta-entity identifies the database table columns that are involved as database view columns in the database view.

A database view column is the column that matches the database table's column. The database view column may have a name different from the database table column.

A database view is the specification of the interface between the view columns and the database table columns. Because of the types of relationships between database view column and database column, it is possible that the view maps to multiple data model tables. In such a case, the view select clause (a long text meta-attribute in the view meta-entity) must contain not only row select statements but also the necessary intertable relationship logic to generate one or more view instances. Figure 6.2 shows the data structure part of the view DEPT_EMP_DEP. This shows that three tables, EMPLOYEE, DEPARTMENT, and DEPENDENT, were employed in the development of the view. The complete ANSI/SQL language statement is provided in Figure 6.2. The reason for using the ANSI/SQL language is because it is unambiguous and very common across many DBMSs.

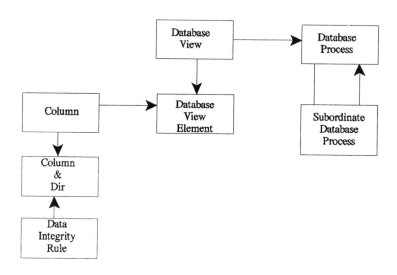

Figure 6.1. Process meta-entity cluster.

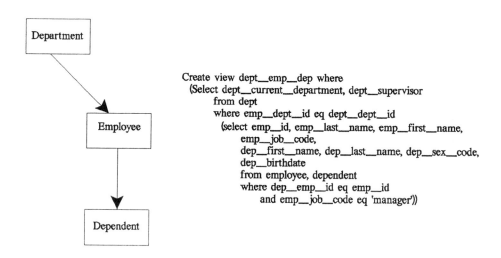

Figure 6.2. View definition for department, its employees, and their dependents.

Figure 6.3 illustrates the meta-entity types associated with view. *Clearly, from this diagram, it is easy to e view is the critical link among all the different models.*

While ANSI/SQL enables complex database accesses and relationship processing, such complexities are only absolutely safe during reporting. That is because no updating is occurring. During complex updates, multiple outside effects can take place on the triple-table row-set. The effects can range from various column editing clauses for values and NULL to the referential integrity clauses . If the update transaction fails, the DBMS is likely to merely return a transaction fails error code rather than an unambiguous statement of the exact reason(s). Consequently, the use of multiple-table views for updating is discouraged. Instead, there should be a view for each table that—during update—is acted upon by only one database process.

The database process meta-entity represents the pseudocode of the database process that will add, delete, or modify the view instance. The pseudocode for the database process module should be in third normal form. If subordinate database processes are necessary, they are represented through the subordinate database process meta-entity.

The data integrity rule meta-entities are a very critical component of the database process model. Before the pseudocode for a database process is considered either sufficient or satisfactory, the entire set of data integrity rules associated with the database column (and thus the database process) must be examined and determined to be either relevant or not.

A complete database process specification is thus one that:

- References all the appropriate data interfaces to the database

- Properly represents the required computer logic in unambiguous pseudocode for the database process and any necessary subordinate database processes

- Properly references and adequately includes all the appropriate data integrity rules

- Represents the necessary processes in a nonredundant manner

Responsibility for the correct definition and ongoing correctness of the process model must reside with database administration because the overall integrity of the database is the responsibility of database administration. In contrast, identification and specification of the business systems that use the database is the responsibility of the business organizations employing the database.

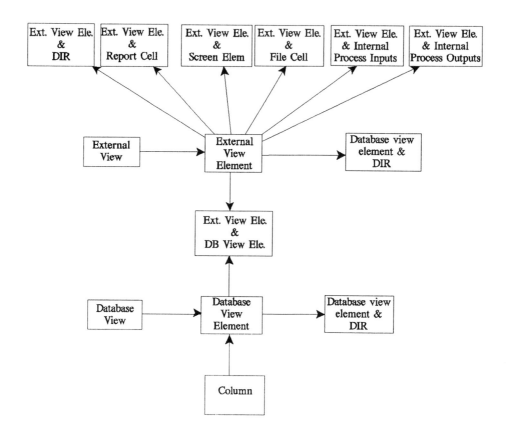

Figure 6.3. View meta-entity and all connectors.

Figure 6.4 presents a database process model schematic of a business transaction for adding a new customer. In this diagram, there are seven database processes:

- End transaction
- Insert contract
- Insert customer
- Insert order
- Insert order-item
- Rollback
- Start transaction

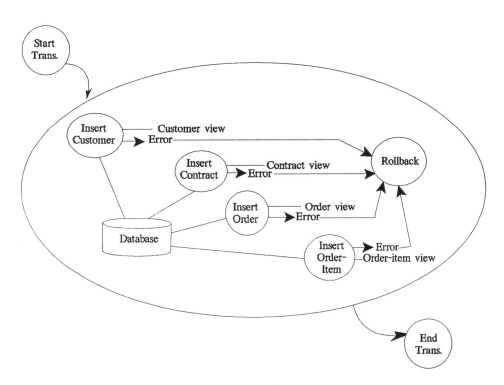

Figure 6.4. Process business transaction for ADD CUSTOMER.

While the behavior of each database process should be defined by database administration, the rationale and design of the overall business transaction, ADD CUSTOMER, is the responsibility of business analysts. Each node in Figure 6.4 shows an implicit sequence (upper left to lower right) with the specific required view (e.g., customer data), and then an error dataflow that leads to the rollback transaction. When the database process is successful, an update is posted to the database; otherwise a rollback occurs. Figure 6.5 presents an alternative view of the same business transactions. The execution sequence is presented in a linguistic fashion.

Figures 6.6 and 6.7 presents two versions of the INSERT_ORDER_ITEM database process: graphic and pseudocode. The database process presumes that the previous transactions, INSERT_CUSTOMER, INSERT_CONTRACT, and INSERT_ORDER, have successfully taken place. The INSERT_ORDER database process would thus be able to presume the existence of a valid contract, customer, and salesperson. The output from the INSERT_ORDER_ITEM database process would be the details for the specific items being ordered.

```
NAME:  ADD CUSTOMER

START TRANSACTION
¦ DO WHILE CUSTOMER EXISTS
¦ ¦ INSERT CUSTOMER, IF FAILURE THEN ROLLBACK
¦ ¦   DO WHILE CONTRACT EXISTS
¦ ¦   ¦ INSERT CONTRACT, IF FAILURE THEN ROLLBACK
¦ ¦   ¦   DO WHILE ORDER EXISTS
¦ ¦   ¦   ¦ INSERT ORDER, IF FAILURE THEN ROLLBACK
¦ ¦   ¦   ¦   DO WHILE ORDER-ITEM EXISTS
¦ ¦   ¦   ¦   ¦ INSERT ORDER-ITEM, IF FAILURE THEN ROLLBACK
¦ ¦   ¦   ¦   ¦ END ORDER-ITEM
¦ ¦   ¦   ¦   END ORDER
¦ ¦   ¦   END CONTRACT
¦ ¦ END CUSTOMER
¦ END CUSTOMER
END TRANSACTION
```

Figure 6.5.   Business process pseudocode.

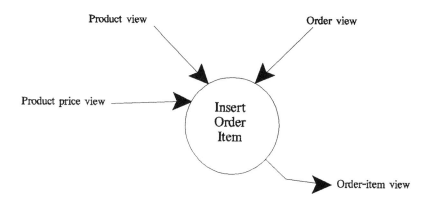

Figure 6.6.   INSERT_ORDER_ITEM process graphic.

NAME: INSERT ORDER ITEM

PROCESS LOGIC: ACQUIRE AND VALIDATE ORDER ITEM
        VALIDATE EXISTING CUSTOMER
        VALIDATE EXISTING CONTRACT
        VALIDATE EXISTING ORDER
        VALIDATE EXISTING SALESPERSON
        INSERT ORDER-ITEM

AFFECTED RECORD TYPE: ORDER-LINE-ITEM

Figure 6.7.   Primitive data transformation pseudocode.

The INSERT_ORDER_ITEM database process requires input data from two tables, and generates output data for the ORDER_ITEM table. The output view for ORDER_ITEM conforms to the restricted view approach. The role of the input views is to validate the correctness of the data contained in the ORDER_ITEM, that is, the proper product is being ordered, and the price contained in the order item transaction is correct.

6.3 Building Database Processes

Each database process, by definition, is to accomplish only one discrete action against the database's tables. Well-organized collections of these database processes serve to represent more and more recognizable business activities. The following example serves to illustrate how database processes can be defined and then collected to achieve these purposes.

There are three tables: EMPLOYEE, PERSONAL_EQUIPMENT, and EQUIPMENT_PASS. These tables serve the purpose of tracking the current locations and all in-and-out history for all employee personal equipment. The entity-relationship diagram for this example is provided in Figure 6.8. This figure shows that the EQUIPMENT_PASS table is related to other tables through optional, one-to-many relationships. For each EMPLOYEE there may be zero, one, or more EQUIPMENT_PASSes. And, for each item of PERSONAL_EQUIPMENT there may be zero, one, or more EQUIPMENT_PASSes that has tracked its placement into and removal from COMPANY_LOCATIONs. If an employee does not bring any equipment into a company location, it is not in the database.

Figure 6.9 enumerates the various columns contained in the EQUIPMENT_PASS table. In this table definition two columns are really from other tables: EMPLOYEE_ID and EQUIPMENT_SER_NBR. Figure 6.10 identifies

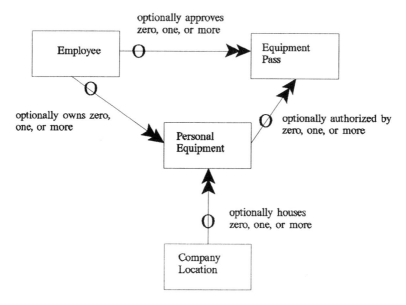

Figure 6.8. Entity relationship diagram for personal equipment and equipment passes.

the three different keys that are critical to the database. There is one primary key (EQUIPMENT_PASS_PKEY) and two foreign keys (EMPLOYEE_REF and EQUIPMENT_REF). The former is used to reference the EMPLOYEE table and the latter references the PERSONAL_EQUIPMENT table (see the relationship lines from Figure 6.8). Notice that the referential integrity rules also state the referential action to be taken when the referential integrity rule is violated.

Figure 6.11 presents a schematic for the meta-entities necessary for storing the data model metadata. In the keys box there is a relationship between the primary key of one table and a foreign key of another table. The Data Elements meta-entity type is necessary to contain the names and definitions of data elements that are used for columns. Figure 6.12 presents an example of all the metadata stored for this single table. The enterprise-wide data elements (Sequence Numbers, State, etc.) are shown along with their relationships to their column use in the Tables & Columns block. The EQUIP_PASS_PKEY metadata item in the Keys block shows the three columns that comprise the EQUIPMENT_PASS's primary key along with the sequence of the values from the columns that will make up primary key values.

The initial goal of the database process models is to define the primitive data transformations for all database tables. To this end, there are three classes of database processes for each table:

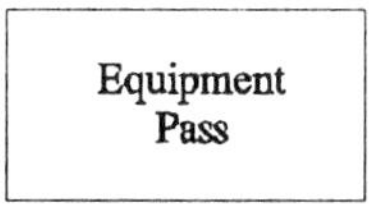

```
                    ┌─────────────────┐
                    │   Equipment     │
                    │     Pass        │
                    │                 │
                    └─────────────────┘
```

Table Equipment__Pass

    equipment__pass__seq__nbr number (9,0)
    date__of__entry date
    employee__id number (9,0)
    equipment__ser__nbr char (25)
    pass__state CHECK (pass__state in ('open', 'closed'))

Figure 6.9.   Table for equipment pass.

- Row existence
- Column validation
- Referential integrity

Figure 6.13 illustrates these three classes of database processes that are to execute against a specific row. Figure 6.14 also identifies the sequence of their execution. The first test class, row existence, is to determine if the operation should proceed or be aborted immediately. For example, if by some fluke a new equipment pass is to be stored so as to bring a piece of equipment into a location but the database shows that this piece of equipment is already present, an immediate error should occur because a piece of equipment cannot be brought into a location if it is already there.

Assuming the success of the row existence tests, the second set of tests is the column validation tests. There are two types: individual values, and combinations of values. In the first type, both the DATE_OF_ENTRY and the PASS_STATE are checked. In the former case, the 33rd of February would be rejected because it is an illegal date, and the state of KANSAS (see Figure 6.9) would also be rejected as illegal. The second type of column validation tests might require that all the columns be NOT_NULL and that they will have passed their individualized validation tests.

The third type of tests is the relationship tests. Figures 6.8, 6.10, and 6.12 identify that there are two different referential integrity tests. Each must be conducted and, if success is achieved, the referential integrity actions (see the ON DELETE phrases in Figure 6.10) do not execute.

```
                    ┌─────────────────┐
                    │ Equipment       │
                    │ Pass            │
                    │                 │
                    └─────────────────┘
```

Primary key: Equip__Pass__Pkey
   employee__id
   date__of__entry
   equipment__pass__seq__nbr

Foreign key: Employee__ref
   employee__id REFERENCES employee
   ON DELETE reject

Foreign key: Equipment__ref
   equipment__ser__nbr REFERENCES personal__equipment
   ON DELETE reject

Figure 6.10. Critical keys for the equipment pass table.

All three types of tests (instance, columns, and relationships) must be successful before a new row can be inserted. When a row is modified, the instance test would be to retrieve a row. If not present, then that is an error. The column tests would occur only when a column with restricted values changed. The referential integrity tests would be invoked only when a referencing column value is changed. *Note*: When a referencing column value is changed, the relationship between the rows of two different tables is also changed. These types of changes are thus nontrivial.

The three sets of actions are depicted in Figure 6.15. Note the control logic, that they all interact with an EQUIPMENT_PASS row through an SQL view, and that they all commonly either set a rollback flag or pass control on to the next database process. Figure 6.16 presents all three sets of tests and database processes inside one overall transaction. In this figure, there are nine distinct database processes: the overall, one each for the three test types, one for the first, two for the second, and two for the third. Now, Figure 6.17 then puts this set of nine nested database processes within an overall database transaction environment, which contains three additional database processes: begin transaction, the nine database processes, and the rollback or success message. The total quantity of processes is fourteen!

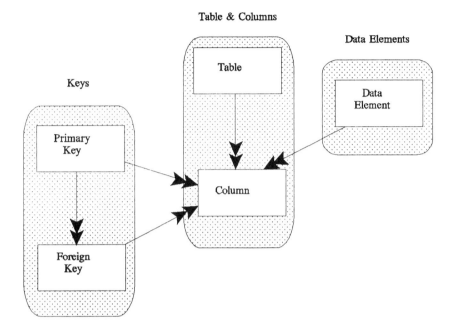

Figure 6.11. Table meta-entity cluster.

All is not finished yet. Figure 6.18 depicts a very critical relationship between EMPLOYEE and PERSONAL_EQUIPMENT. In the EMPLOYEE table there are two columns, NBR_PE (number of personal equipment items) and TOT_VAL (total value of personal equipment). Each of these is a form of derived data. That is, its value is derived from one or more rows from another table. There are a number of distinctly different rules, and collectively they are called Data Integrity Rules. In Figure 6.18, the data integrity rule is provided at the figure's bottom.

Figure 6.19 shows the database processes necessary to accomplish the data integrity rule database processing for an ADD or MODIFY transaction. These two sets of data integrity rules are each encased in a database process that contains two database processes. The left set of processes counts the quantity of personal equipment. The right set of processes computes the value of the equipment. Errors, if any, set the rollback flag, which passes to the outside of the overall transaction. If FAIL, then all updates (ADDs or MODIFYs) are reversed.

Figure 6.20 depicts the overall collection of both classes of database processes, all enclosed in one overall database process for an ADD or MODIFY action. The upper left process is the set of processes from Figure 6.16. The lower right set of processes are from Figure 6.19. Collectively they comprise one overall set.

Keys   Table & Columns   Data Elements

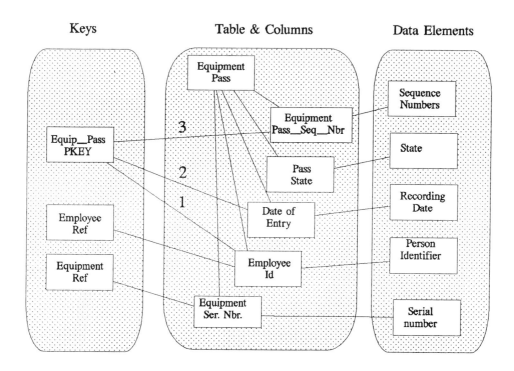

Figure 6.12. Property pass metadata example.

DELETE operations are different from ADDs and MODIFYs, as Figure 6.21 depicts. Comparing Figure 6.21 to Figure 6.20 (and its nested Figures 6.16 and 6.19) shows the logic to be different. On DELETE, the relevant database processes are two types: existence and referential integrity. If the row is present, the delete operation continues. The referential integrity rule is specified in the member/child row, but is perceived from the context of the owner/parent. For example, if an EMPLOYEE is deleted, the delete operation FAILS if there are any PERSONAL EQUIPMENT rows present. The referential integrity rule ON DELETE REJECT is specified in Figure 6.10. The other two types of referential actions are ON DELETE SET NULL or ON DELETE CASCADE. The first alternative allows the parent row to be deleted with the referencing column (foreign key value in member/child) having its value set to NULL. The second alternative, ON DELETE CASCADE, causes the member/child row to be deleted when the owner/parent row is deleted. Figure 6.21 depicts a simple child row delete operation with referential integrity checking.

None of the database processes deal directly with database tables. Rather, they interact with the database tables through views. Figure 6.22 illustrates the

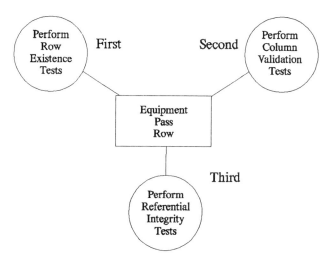

Figure 6.13. Three classes of primitive data transformations (PDTs) from among the many classes.

interaction. The database processes deal with the database control system (DBCS) through views. The DBCS in turn deals with the individual database tables. Figure 6.23 shows the two table definitions for EMPLOYEE and PERSONAL_EQUIPMENT along with the SQL language for the view EMPLOYEE_EQUIPMENT. The actual database process only deals with the individual instances of the view. Figure 6.24 shows the instances of data that are representative of the view. In Figure 6.24, the selection clause (WHERE . . .) and the ORDER BY clause reference a view column. There is no JOIN clause because it is specified in the WHERE clause of the view (Figure 6.23). What the view accomplishes is the complete insulation of the database process from the database's data model.

6.4 Developing Objects

An object, by commonly accepted definitions, consists of two parts: data structures and methods. The data model is specified in Chapter 5. The database process model is specified in this chapter. The set of meta-entities that fully specify objects are:

- Column
- Compound data element
- Database process

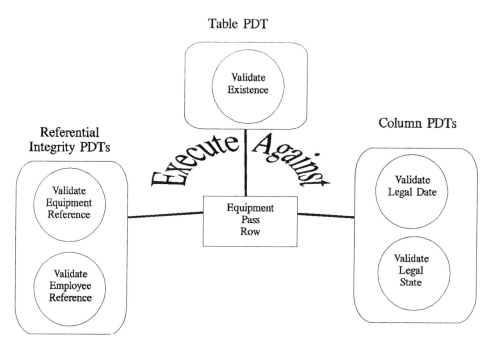

Figure 6.14. Sequence of execution for the complete PDT set for equipment pass.

- Data element
- Data element domain
- Data integrity rule
- Database view column
- Derived data element
- Foreign key
- Object
- Primary key
- Subordinate database process
- Subordinate compound data element
- Table

The meta-entities that interrelate all the other meta-entities are:

- Data element & compound data element
- Data element & data integrity rule
- Data element & derived data element

- Data element domain & data integrity rule
- Column & data integrity rule
- Derived data element & compound data element
- Foreign key & column

The purpose of the object meta-entity is to identify the name and description of the object itself. The complete specification of the object is the metadata rows stored in the remaining meta-entities and the relationship meta-entities. Figure 6.25 presents the meta-entities necessary for object specification. While the quantity of meta-entities may seem daunting, objects range from simple to complex. A simple object may consist of a single table, a reasonable set of columns, completely self-contained edit and validation clauses, and then just three database processes (add, delete, and modify). Most commonly, though, real-world objects

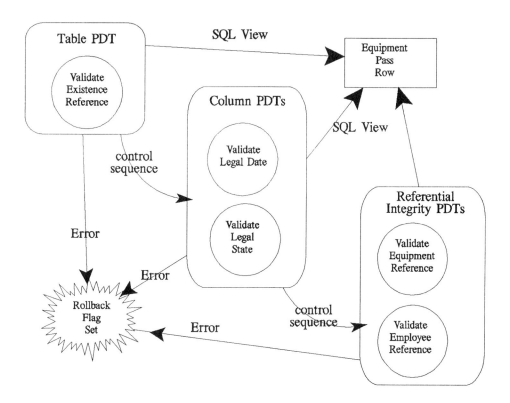

Figure 6.15. Process diagram of complete PDT set of equipment pass.

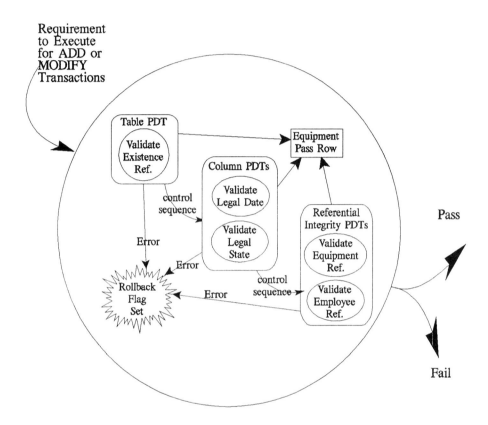

Figure 6.16. Process transaction environment.

sufficiently rich to accurately reflect object complexity.

One of the most critical aspects of objects is that they must be added to and deleted from the database in their entirety. For example, suppose that the complete set of employee data, as represented in Figure 6.8, consisted of EMPLOYEE, EQUIPMENT_PASSes, and PERSONAL_EQUIPMENT. Once an employee leaves the corporation, it probably serves little value to retain the EQUIPMENT_PASS and PERSONAL_EQUIPMENT rows. Thus, when the object EMPLOYEE is deleted, the EQUIPMENT_PASS and PERSONAL_EQUIPMENT rows should be deleted as well.

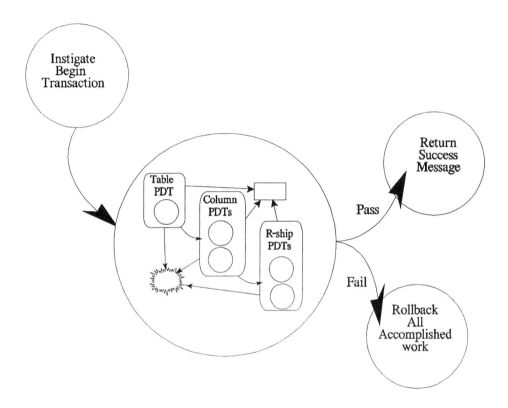

Figure 6.17. Database process transaction environment.

6.5 Database Process Model Summary

With the completion of the database process model, the technology-independent specification of the enterprise business model is complete. The remaining three models, systems, event, and organization, are all involved with the enterprise business model's deployment.

Finished is the definition of the mission of the business, and then the data and database processes necessary to carry out that mission.

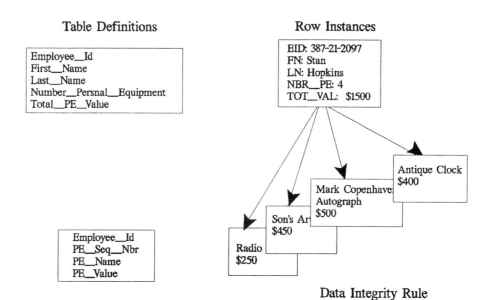

Table Definitions

Employee__Id
First__Name
Last__Name
Number__Persnal__Equipment
Total__PE__Value

Employee__Id
PE__Seq__Nbr
PE__Name
PE__Value

Row Instances

EID: 387-21-2097
FN: Stan
LN: Hopkins
NBR__PE: 4
TOT__VAL: $1500

Antique Clock
$400

Mark Copenhave
Autograph
$500

Son's Ar
$450

Radio
$250

Data Integrity Rule

For each employee, TOT__VAL = SUM (VALUE)
AND NBR__PE = COUNT (ROWS)

Figure 6.18. Employee and personal equipment.

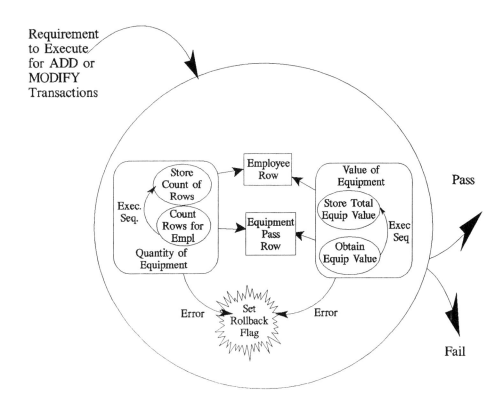

Figure 6.19. DIR database process transaction environment for ADD and
MODIFY.

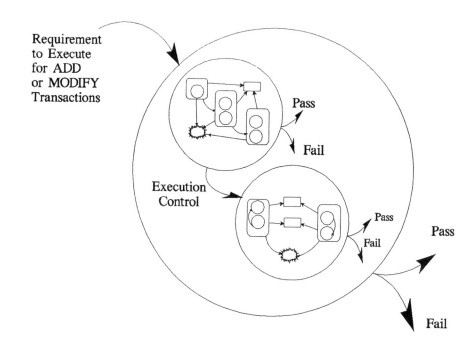

Figure 6.20. Database process transaction environment that includes DIR processing.

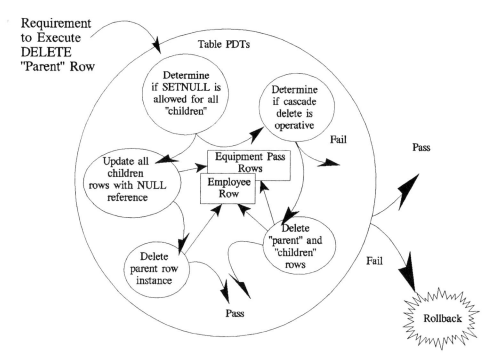

Figure 6.21. Database process transaction environment with DIR processing for DELETE operation.

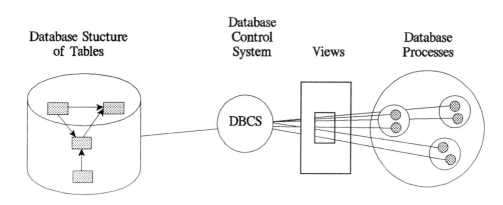

Database Stucture
of Tables

Database
Control
System

Views

Database
Processes

DBCS

Critical Issues

1. Complete Definitions for Tables
2. Proper Definitions for Views
3. Proper Nesting for Processes

Figure 6.22. Compete flow of activity from database to DBCS to views to database processes.

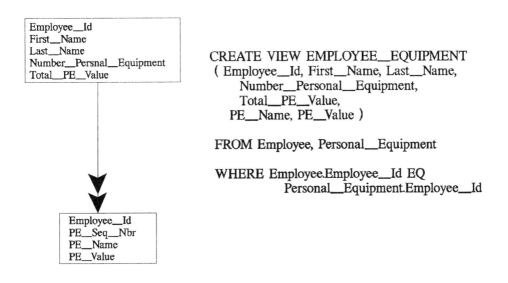

Employee__Id
First__Name
Last__Name
Number__Persnal__Equipment
Total__PE__Value

CREATE VIEW EMPLOYEE__EQUIPMENT
(Employee__Id, First__Name, Last__Name,
    Number__Personal__Equipment,
    Total__PE__Value,
    PE__Name, PE__Value)

FROM Employee, Personal__Equipment

WHERE Employee.Employee__Id EQ
        Personal__Equipment.Employee__Id

Employee__Id
PE__Seq__Nbr
PE__Name
PE__Value

Figure 6.23. View definition of combined employee and personal equipment.

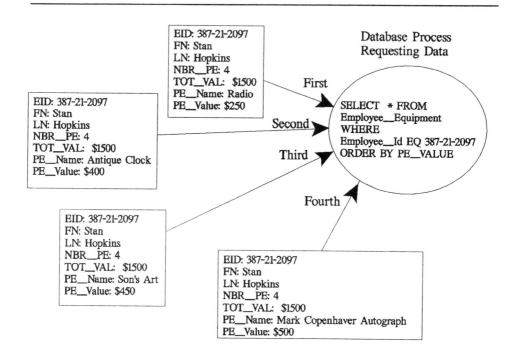

Figure 6.24. Instances of view rows for Employee_Equipment.

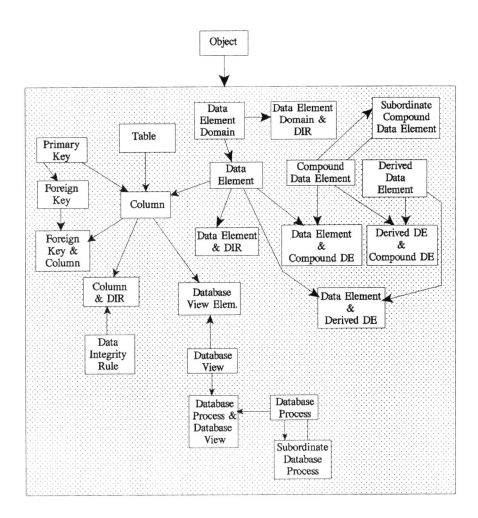

Figure 6.25.   Meta-entity cluster for object.

7

INFORMATION SYSTEMS MODEL

The information systems model actually consists of five subordinate models. These subordinate models are:

- Information system
- Report
- File
- Screen
- Internal process

These subordinate models do not interact directly with the database through views. Rather, they interact with database processes through the external views of information systems. Collectively, these five meta-entity models form an information systems architecture, as illustrated in Figure 7.1.

7.1 Information Systems Architecture

The meta-entity clusters defined by each of these models fall into groups. The first group of meta-entities provides structure to the overall information system. It essentially is a hierarchical structure chart of control logic. The next three groups, that is, report, file, and screen, define traditional data processing activities. That is, a report is produced, a file is read or written, and a screen's data is transformed into database data. It is important to note that these three sets of meta-entity clusters describe nonredundantly defined reports, files, and screens. If one or more information system units requires a particular screen, it only needs to reference the screen involved. The interface to the database is accomplished through one or more database processes. Database processes are described in Chapter 6. Because interface to the database is through database processes, all database interface is already known and should have already been completely debugged. The information system cannot impose any additional data integrity rules that apply to data that *should* have also been applied by another information system.

The fifth group, internal process, represents the specification of any process that is required by any report, file, or screen, or any aspect of a report, file or screen.

Each of these five meta-entity clusters is to be defined in a nonredundant fashion, that is, once. Each, however, may be employed as many times as may be appropriate. Each meta-entity cluster is a well-defined specification of an information system that interacts with the "outside" world and the database.

Examples of acceptable information systems under this nonredundant, multiple-use model are:

- One that only contains one report specification

- One that contains a high-level reports menu, and then a selection of a number of lower-level reports

- One that collects the data represented by a single business form

- One that offers a high-level menu data collection menu, and then a selection of a lower-level number of data collections through business forms

- One that represents the transformation of some set of internally stored business data to a database, or formatted into a report, or presented through a screen, or that is extracted from one database and is stored in another

The collection of all these business systems should thus represent the required set of all data entry, data validation, storage, and ad hoc and standard retrievals to support the total mission of the enterprise.

This collection of five meta-entity clusters provides an opportunity to develop a systems architecture that is:

- Nonredundant, because each meta-entity cluster is nonredundant

- Flexible, because each information system represents a *plug and play* use of one or more meta-entity clusters to support the other meta-entity clusters

- Robust, because each meta-entity cluster is well defined and is closed

This systems architecture supports:

- Traditional systems, where input, process, and output are well defined into a monolithic system that implements traditional well-defined functions

- Data collection systems, where all enterprise data is collected once through a common motif, edited once, and then stored in transaction format in the most appropriate physically distributed locations for later use in operational systems, and then in warehouse systems, and can be obtained for use in special studies

- Data reporting systems, where all enterprise data, from wherever it is stored, is made available through a set of standard reports, or through a standard report writing language

- A COTS environment under either a specialized, probably redundant data collection scenario, or that uses data that has been commonly collected and edited

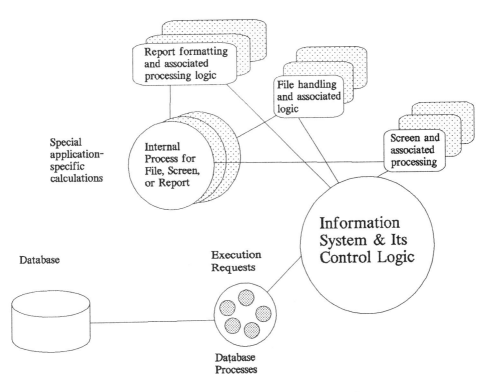

Selected combination of processing and I/O (report, file, screen) processes to handle the reporting, loading, updating, and deleting of database data.

Figure 7.1.   Information systems architecture.

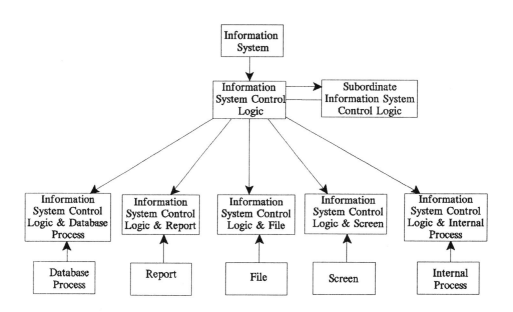

Figure 7.2. Information systems meta-entity cluster.

7.2 The Information System Meta-Entities

Figure 7.2 illustrates the set of meta-entities that comprise the information system. These meta-entities provide structure to the overall information system. The description of the information system is stored in the meta-entity information system. The logic represented by the information system is then stored in the information system control logic meta-entity. The sequence and the names of the subordinate control logic units is contained in the subordinate information system control logic meta-entity. Whenever an information system control logic meta-entity requires the "services" of one or more database processes, reports, files, screens, or internal processes, the reference to it is provided in the appropriate intersection meta-entity. The interface between any of these and the database is provided through the database process meta-entity.

7.3 The Report Meta-Entity Cluster

Figure 7.3 illustrates the report meta-entity cluster. The meta-entity cluster consists of a report meta-entity that describes the report, and then a set of meta-

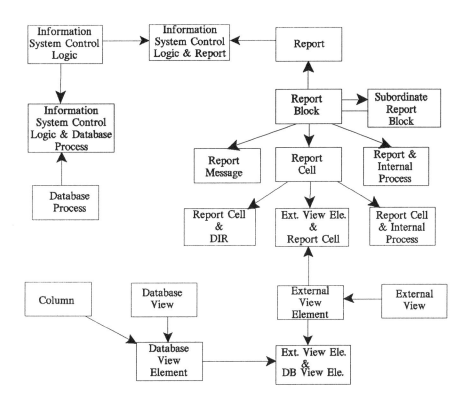

Figure 7.3. Reports meta-entity cluster.

entities that define the report blocks and the contents of these report blocks. Overall, the reports meta-entity cluster is to contain information sufficient to adequately describe a required report. The information is not supposed to be sufficient to feed a code generator, however. The top name and goal of the report is stored in the report meta-entity. If the report is hierarchical, that is, if there are subordinate report blocks, then those and their sequence are represented through the subordinate report meta-entity. For each report block that then contains report cells, the cell is mapped to an external view element through the many-to-many relationship, external view element, and report cell.

7.4 The File Meta-Entity Cluster

The file meta-entity cluster is depicted in Figure 7.4. The meta-entity cluster consists of a file meta-entity that describes the file, and then a set of meta-entities that define the file blocks and the contents of these file blocks. Overall, the file meta-entity cluster contains sufficient information to adequately describe a file. Like the reports cluster, it is related to the specific information system control logic meta-entity.

The file block meta-entity is further divided into a series of file cell meta-entities. If a file is divided into subordinate structures, as in the case of a COBOL record structure with multiple levels, the meta-entity subordinate file is provided. The purpose is to have all the file cells single-value.

If the file involves a particular process, that process is identified. The process referenced is the internal process meta-entity cluster. Actually, the records from the file are really involved in the process rather than the file itself. If any particular file cell is involved in a process, that reference is provided through the meta-entity file cell & internal process.

The file cell meta-entity is related to the external view meta-entity, and thus indirectly to the database view meta-entity. The relationship between database and external view is necessary to support any transformation between database columns and external view elements. For example, if the database contains three columns—first name, middle initial, and last name—and if the external view element only contained a single field, full-name, a process would have to rejoin them properly. In reverse, there would have to be some indicator of the end of the first and middle names within the overall full name string.

File cells are also related to data integrity rules. This is necessary to support both inward and outward data conversion and transformation. If for example, the file cell was a STATE_CODE that was two-letter abbreviations but the database column was two-digit integers, the transformation would have to be catalogued somewhere. If the transformation is only encoded in computer programs, there is no centralized location for the overall set of corporate semantics. Because of this, the information is defined into the repository, and then whenever the program's specifications are created that requires the transformation, all the DIRs associated with the file cell can be retrieved and acted upon.

7.5 The Screen Meta-Entity Cluster

The screen meta-entity cluster is depicted in Figure 7.5. The meta-entity cluster consists of a screen meta-entity that describes the screen, and then a set of meta-entities that define the screen blocks and the contents of these screen blocks. Overall, the screen meta-entity cluster contains sufficient information to adequately describe a screen. Like the reports cluster, it is related to the specific Information System Control Logic meta-entity.

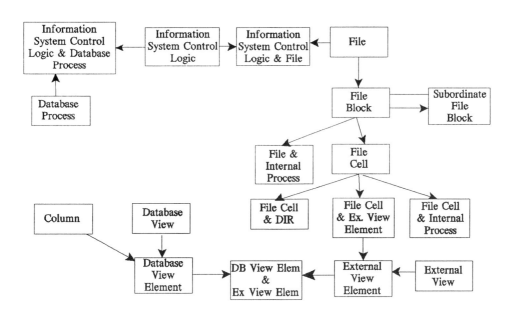

Figure 7.4.   File meta-entity cluster.

The screen block meta-entity is intended to represent one instance of a screen. Detailing the contents of the screen are function keys, messages, security requirements, and then a reference to one or more internal processes that are invoked either before the screen is displayed or after the screen is finished.

Screen elements comprise the screen. Within each screen element are references to data integrity rules that must be accomplished, screen element messages, security requirements, and if appropriate, references to any internal process that gets executed prior to or after the screen element is populated.

Ultimately, the screen element participates in an external view that, in turn, acts as an interconnection to the database.

7.6 The Internal Process Meta-Entity Cluster

The internal process meta-entity cluster is depicted in Figure 7.6. The meta-entity cluster consists of an internal process meta-entity that describes the internal process, and then a set of meta-entities that define the internal process blocks and the contents of these internal process blocks. Overall, the internal process meta-entity cluster contains information sufficient to adequately describe an internal process. Unlike the reports cluster, the internal process meta-entity is not

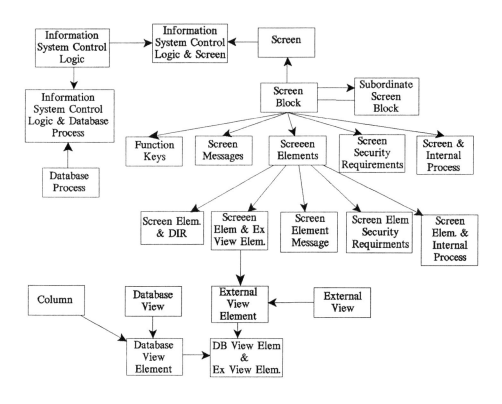

Figure 7.5.   Screen meta-entity cluster.

connected to a specific Information System Control Logic meta-entity. Rather, the internal process is connected to any of the components that invoke it, for example, file, file cell, screen, screen cell, report, and report cell. Through this technique, the processing logic employed by one of these *calling* meta-entities can be employed by any other "calling" meta-entity. It is essentially through this technique that data integrity rules are enforced.

The internal process meta-entity block contains metadata for messages, internal process inputs and outputs, and operator instructions. The inputs and outputs are both detailed in terms of the data integrity rules they enforce, the messages involved, and the external view interfaces.

7.7 Information Systems Summary

From the database point of view, the information system is a collection of database processes that as a collection makes business sense. Each collection of database processes that performs updates must be complete, that is, when the information system starts execution, the database is consistent, and when the information system's execution is finished, the database is again consistent.

An information system is analogous to a database process in that it must complete successfully before the entire business *activity* is considered complete. The scope of a business system might therefore be to *add a new employee to the payroll*. In such an information system, the activities involved might include:

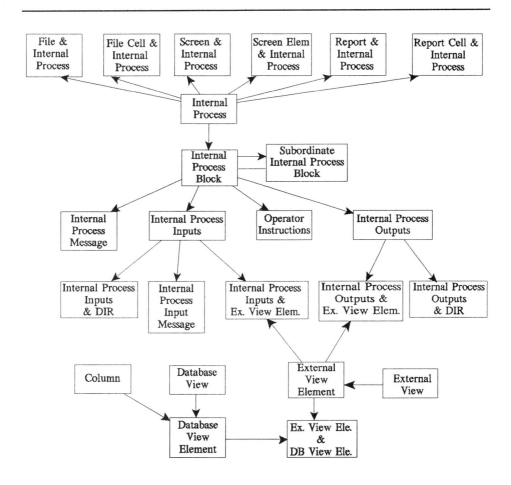

Figure 7.6.   Internal process meta-entity cluster.

- Getting an employee-number
- Obtaining all the tax information
- Benefits selection
- Department assignment
- Office assignment
- Filling out a computerized skills inventory
- Adding employee to e-mail and routing lists

Each of these data processing activities might additionally be information systems in their own right, but for another purpose. The keystone characteristic of this approach is that the information system consists of individually designed, nonredundantly specified components (information systems, database processes, screens, etc.) that are relatively easy to prove correct individually and in collections.

8

BUSINESS EVENT MODEL

The business event model defines the events that require information systems' services during the accomplishment of business functions. An example of a business event might be the monthly financial closing. Another business event might be to accomplish *project opening, project close-out,* or *client proposal development.*

A business event is not an activity of the enterprise. Activities of the enterprise are represented through the business function model. The business event model represents the automation interface between the business functions and the information systems. Because of this separation through the business event, the following occurs:

- There may be multiple styles of business functions that benefit from the information system.

- There may be information systems that are used by different business functions

- A business event hierarchy can employ different collections of information systems to serve the needs of different business functions.

Because business event is optionally hierarchical, with each node representing the invocation of an information system, there is the possibility of maximizing reuse while minimizing specification and design. This is essential to a *designed once used many times strategy.*

One business event, hiring plan development, could be in response to the Human Resources business function that call for the development of hiring plan projects every October for the next year, or on an emergency basis when an expected contract appears. The first need surfaces during the normal course of HR activities. The second occurs somewhat randomly. Regardless of the business function, the business event, hiring plan development must be performed.

The business event, hiring plan development, might include the execution of one or more information systems that take a snapshot of the current staff and creates several, multiple-year staff projections based on current trends in hiring, promotions, and attrition. Each node in the business event invokes one information system. Collectively, all the nodes produce all the information necessary for the development of the hiring plan.

This chapter contains a description of the meta-entities for incorporating the business event meta-model.

Figure 8.1 illustrates two interrelationships: one between business event and information system, and another between information system and business

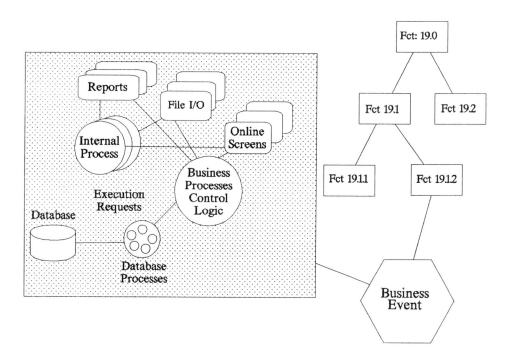

Figure 8.1. Intersection between functions, business events, and information systems.

function step. The information system is a reduced version of the illustration contained in Figure 7.1 in Chapter 7, which shows some process control logic, screen, file, and reports involvement, and also some internal processes to process screen, file, and report data. Finally, the information system involves access to the database through some set of database processes. This information systems activity is instigated by the business event. In short, because of the business event, the information system is independent of the business function that requires it. This strategy allows multiple business functions to be configured differently, while using the same information systems.

The business function-business event relationship shows which business function requires information system services. In Figure 8.1 the business function 19.0 is decomposed to at least three levels. Business function 19.1.2 requires information system services. This diagram illustrates that a business function is not required to need information systems services. Because of this, complete functional hierarchies are able to be shown.

In some cases, there are multiple information systems that are required by a single business event. Figure 8.2 illustrates such an arrangement. More

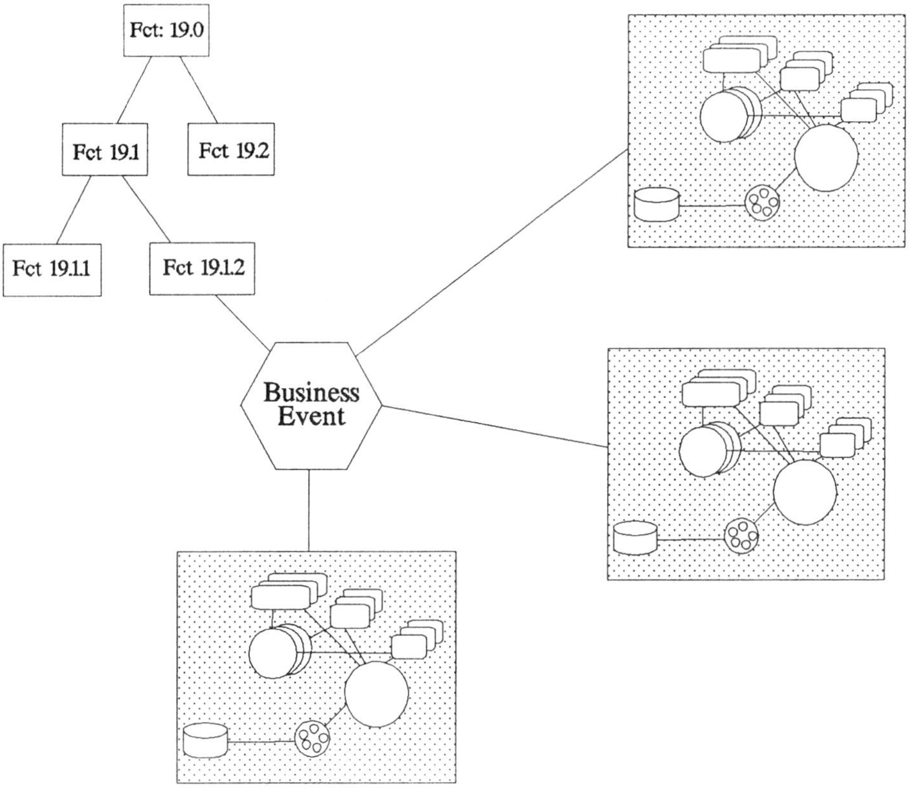

Figure 8.2. Multiple information systems servicing a business event.

commonly, a given information system is required by multiple business events. Figure 8.3 illustrates this arrangement. In the first arrangement, shown in Figure 8.2, the business event definitions are conserved. Since the information systems would have to be executed in a sequence, the business event meta-entity types have some sequencing data.

In the second arrangement, shown in Figure 8.3, the quantity of information systems is conserved. Two different functions are shown needing services from the same information system. This may be because the function hierarchies are really the same *functionally*, but differ in style. Or it may be that there are really two different sets of functions that require information from a commonly deployed information system. For example, if there are two different sets of finance functions, one for a company and another for a project, maybe the only difference

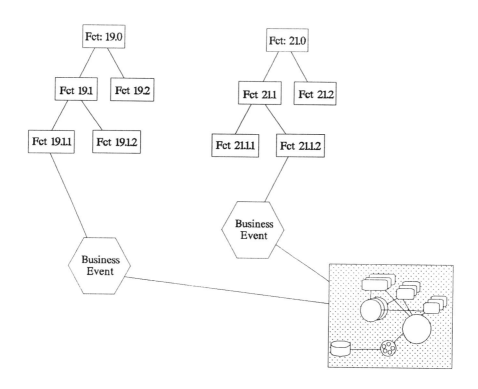

Figure 8.3. Information systems serving multiple business events.

needed for the information system to produce a balance sheet is the selection logic: one for company, and the other for project. Enterprise database strategies established along the lines of Figure 8.3 enable the nonredundant definition and implementation of information systems.

Figure 8.4 depicts the meta-entity types required for the business event model. Because the business event entity is simple, it serves mainly to intersect information system with business function. The business event meta-entity contains subordinate business events. This way, if there are multiple information systems tagged to a business event as in the case of Figure 8.2, the specific sequence for the execution of the information system can be stated.

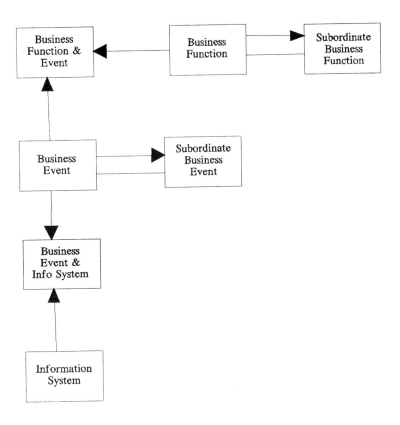

Figure 8.4.   Business event meta-entity model.

9

BUSINESS FUNCTION MODEL

The business function model identifies the set of activities that accomplish one or more aspects of a business's activities. In this book, a business function and its activities are manual. When ever a business function requires information systems's support, it is instigated through the business event.

Business functions discovered and designed through traditional structured systems analysis and design methods decompose into data processing systems, subsystems, programs and modules. This traditional approach has been discredited because it:

- Maximizes the quantity of defined systems
- Maximizes process redundancy
- Maximizes programming, test, and documentation
- Maximizes redundant maintenance

The approach defined in this book minimizes these important information system components by independently defining each and relating them through many-to-many relationships. While minimization of information systems components greatly benefits monolithic development, it is essential for client/server because the components have to be distributable across servers and clients. Chapters 5 through 10 accomplish the independent definition of the components and Chapters 11 and 12 defines the strategies by which they can be deployed in a client/server environment.

As an example, the business function, *validate invoice for payment*, as depicted in Figure 9.1, shows the three levels of activities (function rectangles) involved. The hexagons represent business event interfaces to information systems. The *invoices* rectangle represents the invoices that the business function *Receive and log invoice processes*.

Traditionally, these finance oriented business functions would have been hierarchically defined within the context of all other finance functions appropriate for centralized, function homogeneous enterprises, supported by monolithic systems. Modern enterprises, however, have more autonomous business units, each with their own business style. For some, invoice processing might be accomplished in a central department while for others, it might be accomplished in a client/server environment, with each department responsible for their own invoice processing. Due to this book's independent component definition, both strategies can be achieved. While each style results in a different contextual setting for these business functions, the actual business function, *validate invoice for payment*, would be the same. Identical too would be the supporting business event and information systems. The final result, stylized business functions with standardized, nonredundant information systems, achieves the critical minimums for information system components.

Another business function might be to accomplish human resources' candidate recruitment application processing, or the complete human resources function that would naturally include both candidate recruitment, and application processing.

A business function, once hierarchically defined, might require the use of various information systems in response to certain business events identified in the business function hierarchy. For example, in the human resources function of obtaining sufficient staff for a new contract, the business event, hiring plan development, has to be accomplished. The business event, in turn, causes the execution of the information system described above.

The business function model is accomplished through manual and automated systems. The automated component, information systems, was presented in Chapter 7. The manual component, business functions, actually consists of three models, which are:

- Business function
- Document
- Business form

These subordinate models do not interact directly with the automated information systems. Rather, they result in a requirement that a business event be satisfied, and that the satisfaction be accomplished through the execution of an information system. (The meta-entities representing these models are contained in Figures 9.2 through 9.4). Collectively, these three meta-entity clusters form a business functions architecture.

The complete set of meta-entity clusters from information systems, business event, and business function comprise what has been traditionally viewed as *process* or *function*. They are separated in this book so they can be defined nonredundantly and so that the man-machine interface can be clearly demarcated.

The document and business form meta-entity clusters represent the specification of a document or business form that is to be represented—traditionally—through a screen or a report. Clearly, then, if there is a large cache of business forms, each one's data and implied processing must be accommodated by the MIS.

In the traditional approach to an information system's specification, the business functions are identified, and then hierarchically decomposed until the processes are ready to be transformed into pseudocode. After pseudocode, actual coding, unit testing, system testing, and integration testing is accomplished.

The tradition approach is fatally flawed right from the start, because if the original hierarchical decomposition is done *incorrectly*, then the ultimate design and packaging of modules is also wrong. The paradigm defined in this book argues that there can be many different styles to the functional hierarchies. While clearly some can be flat wrong, there are many others that are just different, *not* wrong.

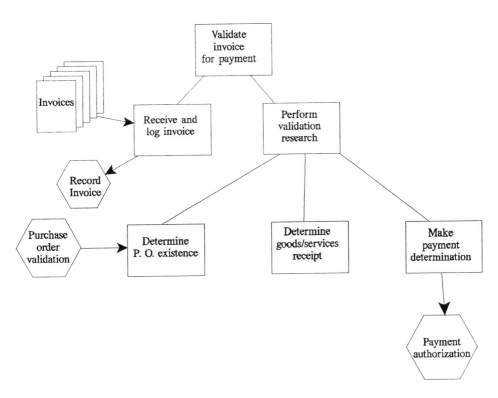

Figure 9.1. Invoice validation business function.

The paradigm in this book enables multiple sets of functional hierarchies that are effectively equivalent to coexist. From a systems point of view they are equivalent if the business functions decompose to a set of business events that reference the same information systems. A critical problem occurs if the referenced information systems are different. Whether one functional decomposition is better than another or more efficient can be a matter of personal assessment, and is outside the scope of this book.

There is more to a large-scale database application than just a series of databases and information systems. There are all the human systems of activities that collect data, perform manual calculations, do filing, and the like. If these manual activities are not optimized, the best of information systems will fail to deliver meaningful improvements. Two cases illustrate this point.

First, a service organization whose income was derived from memberships wanted to convert their manual membership system to an automated system. The organization hired a systems house that provided a package that would build a

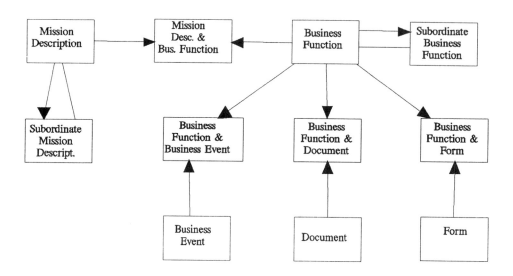

Figure 9.2. Business function meta-entity model.

database of membership information, issue receipts and invoices, and provide a variety of different reports on the current status of membership. The system was installed, the staff were trained, and everything seemed to be working fine. After a few months, the membership statistics were produced and the numbers were not good. While the quantity of new memberships kept up with expectations, the number of renewals was dropping. The statistics were reviewed a month later; the trends were the same. For the next several months, the trends stayed the same. An exhaustive audit of the information system was started and all the analysis showed that all notices went out on time, renewal notices were being mailed within the appropriate time of not hearing about membership renewals, and the like. Upon analysis of the members who failed to renew, it was noticed that they were all long-time members and were getting on in years. Then, someone remembered *Madeline*! It was her job to call those members who failed to renew after two notices. Was she doing her job? A quick check showed that the new system failed to generate the list of nonrenewals for Madeline to call. And, since she did not get the sheet, she did not call. A quick check of the nonrenewals showed that talking with Madeline was an annual social event, and they were merely awaiting her call before they renewed!

The second case involves a government agency's office of application processing. Overall, the process was to receive correspondence from an applicant,

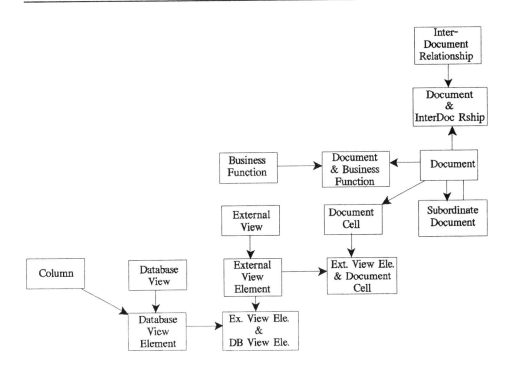

Figure 9.3.   Document meta-entity cluster.

perform some amount of analysis on the application in order to accept or reject the request, receive funds for all acceptable applications, and then go to the next major step. The office broke the application processing work down into such small steps that the overall effort was absurdly lengthened. For example, as the applications came in the door, one processing station divided the mail into batches of 25 letters. Each batch was assigned a number, and the log-in and log-out dates and times were noted on a batch processing slip. The entire batch was tied into a bundle for subsequent processing. The next step was to take the batch of 25 letters, untie the bundle, and slit open each envelope. The contents were removed, and a log sheet was created for each envelope. The materials were examined to ensure that all necessary components were present. The components were placed into a particular order, and then the whole package was clipped together. The analysis results were recorded on the log sheet. After the 25 envelopes were similarly processed, the batch of 25 was recreated and tied, noting the log-out time and date for the batch. Then the batch went to the next station. This station was to determine another very small aspect of the processing. And the following station performed another step, and so on. By the time the application processing was

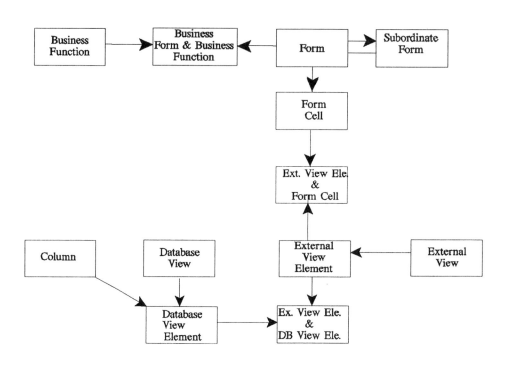

Figure 9.4. Business form meta-entity cluster.

completed, the overall processing time was almost four weeks, while the actual work for each application was less than twenty minutes. The organization had mistakenly presumed that if you break down work for machines and then get greater efficiency, you can do the same set of steps for humans.

The point to both case studies is that the human process must also be studied and optimized. In both case studies, critical mistakes were made. In the first, a critical human component was merely forgotten, resulting in important losses of the only asset the membership organization had, members. The business was not just a business; it also had a social dimension that could not be ignored.

In the second, the ability of a human component to perform a complete, multi-step job was ignored. The process designer totally ignored the amount of time to:

● Tie and untie batches

● Record batch logging

- Transport batches

- Relearn the information that each application presented in order to perform an almost inconsequential step

The functional analysis must be done with the knowledge worker in mind, not just the actual process. If the work is not tuned to the knowledge worker, mistakes will be made, critical steps will be forgotten, and valuable time will be lost. Only after a complete and proper analysis of the human process is done can optimizations be made.

The purpose of the business function model is thus to make the human dimension of a business system perform with the highest quality at the minimum cost. Since human factors engineering is outside the scope of this book, it is presumed that such analysis has taken place, and the role of the three meta-entity clusters is to record the results.

Figure 9.1 illustrates a function hierarchy that is appropriate and suitable for this type of analysis. Clearly, *Validate invoice for payment* is a subordinate business function to an overall accounting business function, and that to finance. In this example, there are three levels to the functions. At the second level, the business function *Receive and log invoice* is shown receiving documents (invoices) and generating information to the business event *Record invoice*. The actual details of the human activities are not detailed here. They may be in text attachments to a business function meta-entity.

The critical information required from the document is defined in the document meta-entity cluster (see Section 9.2).

This business event *Record invoice* represents the interaction with an information system that enters critical invoice information into a database.

At the third level the *Determine P. O. existence* function ascertains if there is a preexisting purchase order. Servicing this function is the *Purchase order validation* business event. The third function, *Make payment determination*, is serviced by the *Payment authorization* business event.

All the functions not serviced by a business event are entirely manual. There are, of course, manual activities in each function. These activities can be defined either as text addenda to the business event, or in separate policy and procedure books.

Whether the business functions illustrated in Figure 9.1 are performed by one person or many persons or in the sequence shown is not germane to the issue of what the documents, business events, and inferred information systems are. These are defined independently of the actual business functions. Because they are independent, they can be standardized independent of any local customs, traditions, and practices.

9.1 The Business Function Meta-Entity Cluster

Figure 9.2 contains the essential meta-entities for business function. The main meta-entity is Business Function. It can be subdivided into subordinate business functions through the recursive relationship to the meta-entity Subordinate Business Function. Business Function is connected through many-to-many relationships to:

- Business Event
- Document
- Form

The figure also shows a many-to-many relationship to Mission Description. This relationship is intended to merely be a shortcut relationship to answer the question: Which business functions address which missions? Actually, that question can be answered by following the inter-meta-entity relationships from business function through

- business event through
- information system through
- external view through
- database view through
- column through
- table through
- object through
- database domain, and finally,
- mission description.

Since such logic is likely to be tortuous, this shortcut relationship is offered. However, care must be taken to ensure that following the relationships in either direction produces exactly the same answer!

9.2 The Document Meta-Entity Cluster

Figure 9.3 presents the essential meta-entities for Document. A document is some set of materials that are considered important to an overall enterprise database effort. For example, if the enterprise database contains one or more warehouse databases, then some data is likely to come from external sources. Once such source could be the New York Stock Exchange market quotations. In this case, the day's overall list of quotations could be considered the document, and an individual stock's or bond's daily evaluation could be considered a subordinate document.

Another type of document could be a standard publication of the U. S. Census Bureau. This government organization produces standard sets of statistics about

Standard Metropolitan Statistical Areas (SMSAs). The entire dated publication could be the document, a particular SMSA a subdocument, and a particular type of statistic a subdocument underneath the SMSA.

Regardless of how the document and its subordinate documents are organized, the intention is to ultimately identify particular data facts that are to be captured by the enterprise database. These external facts are called *document cells*. Each document cell is then related to an external view element.

It is critical to remember that an external view element can be related to various data integrity rules. See, for example, Figure 5.11 in Chapter 5 and Figure 6.3 in Chapter 6. This enables inward data conversion. For example, an enterprise database data integrity rule might state that state codes are two-digit numbers (00 to 49), while the U. S. Bureau of the Census has them as two letters. The inward conversion would be to make the conversions.

The primary role of a document is to identify the source of data for an information system. The relationship is that the document's data would be loaded via an information system that would load data either through batch access of files, or online through screens. The relationship is between the document's cell and external view element. The external view element can be related to either a file cell or a screen cell, which are critical components of an information system. When finally put together, a business function would be accomplished that, in turn, would result in a business event that would be serviced by the information system that would operate either online through screens or through batch execution of programs loading files. While somewhat circuitous, it is nonetheless a method of performing the exact mapping.

9.3 The Business Form Meta-Entity Cluster

Figure 9.4 presents the meta-entity types for Form. A form is divided into subordinate parts, and ultimately into form cells. It is not uncommon for businesses today to have developed 500 to 1000 different forms. If an organization is going to have control over its data, the existing data entry forms have to be tackled. Each form must be examined. If it is deemed to be useful in the capture of permanent corporate data, it must then be carefully examined to ensure that it is in the best format.

Each form cell must be related to an external view element. Each external view element is traced to a permanent data element through

- external view, then through
- database view, then through
- column, and then through
- data element.

If the metadata for all these meta-entity types is carefully constructed, the directions for filling out a form can be clear and unambiguous. All corporate forms can be handled in this manner, and be properly filled out through the development of the appropriate business function.

9.4 Business Function Summary

In traditional information systems development, the creation of the business function was synonymous with information systems' design and development. That was unfortunate because it left uncontrolled and unaffected the existing morass of forms and documents, and left unanalyzed and unoptimized the existing sets of manual activities.

While great strides have been made in the automation of specific aspects of business processes, overall business processes are generally unaffected. Forms continue to grow, policies and procedures are developed in a conflicting manner, and the corporate data has critical semantic conflicts and different time synchronizations.

Control must be established. The first step of control is inventory. This is accomplished through the meta-entity cluster Business Form & Business Function. Once the inventory of all business forms has been entered, they can be related to the data and database process models.

For those forms and documents that are to remain, new business functions can be created to enter form and document data through specially created information systems that are also based on the semantics contained in the data and database process models.

Over time, business function efficiency can be judged and then optimized through different implementations. Because the detailed components of a business function are independent and nonredundant, the business functions can be optimized without fear of damaging overall business semantics and data integrity.

10

ORGANIZATION MODEL

This chapter describes the meta-entities required to store an enterprise's organization model. This is the last of the technology independent models. Figure 10.1 illustrates the set of meta-entity types required to represent the organization model. In Figure 10.1 the business organization meta-entity can contain subordinate business organizations. The relationship between business organization and business function allows multiple functions to be assigned to a business organization and the business function to be assigned to different business organizations. It seems simple, and it is. That is because of the presumed existence of the prior six models:

- Mission
- Data
- Database process
- Information systems
- Business event
- Business function

Organization is not last by accident. The mission model is done first because it defines the overall scope and domain of the entire enterprise database effort. The strategy by which mission is developed is apolitical. The mission descriptions are not to contain either *who* or *how*.

The data model is done second. It is the creation of the third normal form tables for the data requirements to serve the missions. Creation of this model is merely a technical activity and, since there are a number of self-correcting strategies, data models can be proven correct.

The database process model, accomplished next, causes the development of all the database processes necessary to uphold the integrity of the database. Since the database process model is a direct extension of the data model, it is done in a straightforward manner, without regard to business function details or corporate politics.

The information systems model can tend to be political. However, this book attempts to make the model as apolitical as possible by restricting an information system to be a set of business processes that result in a correct database transformation. If the transformation becomes broken or does not complete its processing, the entire transformation is rolled back.

The business event model serves as the interface between the information systems model and the business function model. It further enables an information system to be employed by multiple business functions, and a business function to employ multiple information systems.

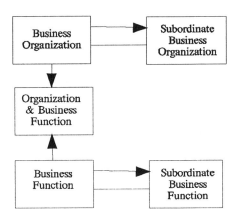

Figure 10.1. Organization meta-entity model.

The business function model is political. That is, it is a design calculated to achieve a particular scheme of data transformations and/or reporting. Because no two organizations would ever agree on the minute details of a business, it does no good to attempt to force a common set of business function definitions. Consequently, the paradigm of this book allows multiple, yet equivalent, business function hierarchies. The test of equivalence is simple: Are the results the same?

The organization model is truly political. Organizations are essentially styles of arranging people to accomplish particular business functions. Like a business function, this book allows for the creation of different organizations that achieve the same business functions. For example, if a large company has a local office in which all aspects of human resources, finance, and many support services are accomplished by a single office, does it matter that the organization is *one person doing all things*? Back at headquarters there may be separate offices for each of the business functions. Again, that should not matter. With the paradigm set out in this book, the information system is independent of the arrangement of the business function, and the orchestration of the business function is independent of the corporate organization.

The business function and organization models are purposely done last so that there already exist large bodies of agreement, accord, and compromise within the information systems, database processes, data models, and missions.

Figure 10.2 depicts the situation in which a corporation has a headquarters and an outreach office. The headquarters is organized into distinct functional units, one each for accounting, payroll, recruitment, and personnel records. The

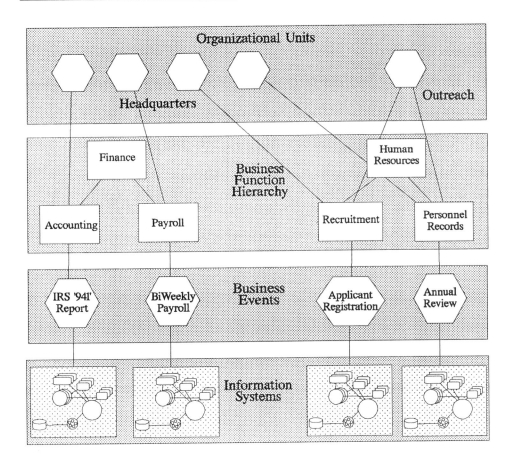

Figure 10.2. Interrelationship between business organizations, functions, events, and information systems.

outreach office has all four functions grouped into one organization. Regardless of organization, as these four functions are accomplished, they require services from information systems as illustrated through the business events. In this example, the business function hierarchy appears to be the same for both organizations. That may be true, or as in the case illustrated in Figure 8.3 in Chapter 8, there many be different configurations of business functions that result in a common business event that causes the execution of a common information system.

It is essential to have the organizational model as independent as possible from the business function model. If dependent, then as the organization changes so too must the business functions. This type of dependency is all too common with the consequence of too many, unnecessary enterprise database functional reorganizations just to reflect the organizational style changes.

Similarly, the information systems model must be independent from the business functions model. Independence prevents functional changes—commonly know as *management style*—from having an affect on information systems content and structure.

The mutual independence of the seven models (mission through organization) is crucial to the proper definition of enterprise database. These models must also be defined in a manner completely unconstrained by technology so that they do not bias any of the possible implementation alternatives.

If both these characteristics exist in the seven models, they can form the platform from which enterprise database can be efficiently and effectively deployed in any of the four different client/server environments. Heterogeneous organizations often require different and coexistent implementations of the same functionality. Different implementations are very difficult and/or impossible if the foundation models are defined in a technology dependent manner.

11

IMPLEMENTED DATA MODEL

11.1 Introduction

Over the years there has been a demarcation between the terms *logical* and *physical*. In this book the two terms generally imply unimplemented and implemented. In the information systems industry, logical and physical are seen as the two sides of the transformation of an item. The item (usually a database's design) is transformed to make its performance acceptable according to some established standards. For example, whenever a database's design is said to be in third normal form, it is said to reflect a *logical* design. But, if the initial performance is unacceptable, database design changes occur to make the performance acceptable.

These changes are not considered native or natural. Rather, they are necessary to accommodate certain physical constraints (e.g., space or speed). When this is done, the resultant changed state is termed *physical*. The database is now said to have a *physical design*.

The problem with these *logical* and *physical* terms, however, is not that they are opposing sides of a single transformation; it is that there are successive sets of these transformations. Each transformation starts with a *logical* form and ends with a *physical* form. That means that the physical product of one transformation is the logical input for the successor transformation.

To help end this confusion over states and transformation cycles, this book chooses not to use the terms logical and physical. Rather it uses the terms *specified* and *implemented*. A data model is thus in its specified design form up to the point of being submitted to the DBMS for schema compilation. The design of the database reflected in the actual language submitted for compilation is called the implemented data model. Once implemented, there may be additional transformations to make the database perform even better than when first submitted. Once all those transformations have been completed, the database's design is called the operational data model. In short, this book refers to three database design states: specified, implemented, and operational.

This chapter is about the implemented data model, which is necessary for two main reasons:

- Distribution of data to support client/server
- Performance

167

This book does not address changes resulting from performance[11]. Because of changes to a database's design due to performance, it is essential to maintain both the specified data model, all the implemented data models, and all the mappings among the specified and implemented models.

There are a number of different reasons for distributing data. Among the more important are:

- Placement of data closer to its responsible source

- Higher availability by placing multiple copies of critical data at different locations, thus eliminating a potential single point of failure

- More efficient data access, thus improving data management performance

- Application load balancing as it relates to data access

- Ease of application and user growth [12]

11.2 Types of Data

A critical issue affecting client/server is data distribution. There are two significant parts to a database: operational data and reference data. *Operational data* is the data that is entered, modified, or deleted in support of the day-to-day operations of the business. Examples are invoice line items, customer names and addresses, time charges from time cards, and personnel data. All this data exists or fails to exist depending on the existence or absence of the invoice, customer, time card, and employee.

Reference data, the second type of data, is the set of data used to validate operationally entered, modified, or deleted data. For example, an employee's city, state, and zip are all reference data, while birth date is not. Reference data is also commonly used for expanding codes into long values, for example, MD into Maryland. This data is therefore commonly used in joins between production data tables and the reference tables.

---

[11] A discussion of the various strategies to accommodate performance is presented in Section 6.10, Application Optimization of *Database Management Systems, Understanding and Applying Database Technology*, Wellesley, MA: QED Information Sciences, 1991.

[12] Berson, Alex. *Client/Server Architecture*, McGraw-Hill Series on Computer Communications. New York: McGraw-Hill, 1992, page 222.

In general, the four commonly employed data distribution types are:

- User extract
- DBMS-generated snapshots
- Replication
- Fragmentation[13]

Notwithstanding that user extracts are a form of data distribution, they are under user control and thus are not under any centralized, reliable control. This type of distribution is really a *buyer's beware* type of distribution and should be avoided whenever possible.

DBMS-generated snapshots are not the same as user extracts, even though the result may be the same, that is, a subset of the production data. Rather, a DBMS-generated snapshot is supposed to be properly defined, tested, and documented. Whenever a user executes a stored procedure that finds, collects, and then transports the snapshot to the distributed destination, the result conforms to policies and standards for such data distributions.

Replication is commonly used to accomplish the distribution of reference data. These replications must be centrally defined and are distributed in a controlled, scheduled manner.

Fragmentation is a very common approach to the distribution of production data. It comes in two forms: vertical and horizontal.

11.3 Vertical and Horizontal Operational Data Distribution

The two most common types of data distribution are:

- Vertical
- Horizontal

The terms, *vertical* and *horizontal* relate to a single table, which consists of columns and rows. If the distribution is *vertical*, then all the rows are partitioned. Some of the columns from all of the rows become part of one distributed table, while the remaining columns from all of the rows become part of another distributed table. A common column must exist in both tables to enable a rejoin. Further, the join values must be unique to ensure that the rows separated are those rejoined.

Horizontal distribution means that certain rows from one table (all columns) are stored in one distributed table, while the remaining rows (all columns) are stored in the other distributed table.

---

[13] Ibid., pages 226-230.

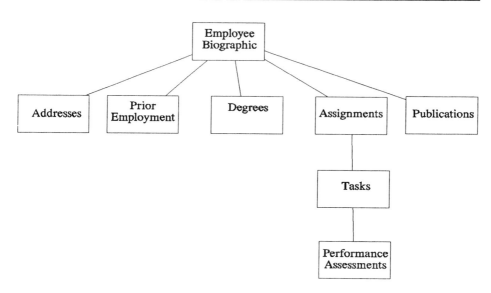

Figure 11.1. Third normal form data structures for employee object.

In addition to horizontal and vertical distribution, another important distribution consideration relates to granularity, that is, object or table. This book takes the position that either whole objects or tables are distributed, but not partial tables (i.e., subsets of columns).

An object represents an instance of a complete corporate policy. For example, all the data related to an employee represents a coherent statement about the employee. All the metadata about the employee object is the policy about employees. If the object is split into a series of tables, then each table is a policy subset about the object. For example, the dependents table represents the information deemed necessary for dependents of employees. It makes little sense to split tables. For example, with respect to the policy subset ADDRESS, what is the coherent subpolicy about Street Numbers and Zip Codes?

When the traditional distribution terms, vertical and horizontal, are applied to objects and tables, an object may be horizontally or vertically distributed, just as a table can be distributed. If an object is horizontally distributed then whole object instances are distributed, some to one server and others to other servers. In contrast, if an object is vertically distributed, then some of its tables are placed on one server while its remaining tables are located on other servers.

Figure 11.1 depicts the object EMPLOYEE, which consists of the following eight entities:

- Employee biographic
- Address

- Prior employment
- Degree
- Assignment
- Task
- Performance assessment
- Publication

When these entities are combined with the appropriate set of table, column, and other constraints, a complete object emerges. Figure 11.2 illustrates the various types of database integrity processes that must surround each entity to maintain its integrity. Chapter 6, covering database processes, provided a complete description of the various database processes required for database integrity.

Collectively, the eight entities and their sets of database processes comprise the object. Figure 11.3 depicts the complete EMPLOYEE object. In this figure, each of the eight entities is surrounded by the set of database processes required

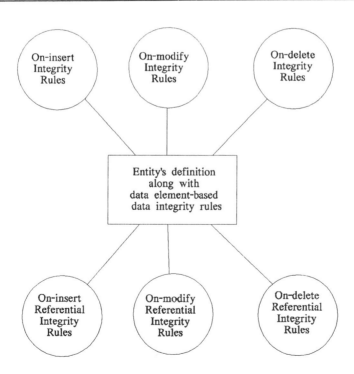

Figure 11.2. Complete policy definition for an entity.

to retain database integrity. These database processes must also be distributed if there is going to be any database integrity.

11.3.1 Vertical Object Distribution

Figure 11.4 depicts a vertical distribution for EMPLOYEE. On the first server, the HR server, all the data required for human resources is stored. The second server, mail, contains only the EMPLOYEE BIOGRAPHIC information, including the current location, telephone number, and e-mail address. The third server, project

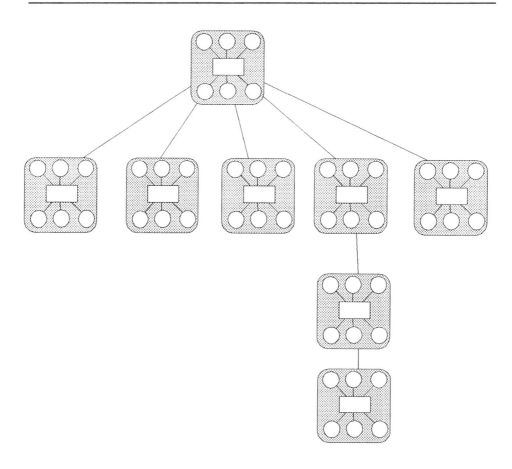

Figure 11.3. Complete employee *object* diagram showing both data structure and required processes.

management, contains the EMPLOYEE BIOGRAPHIC information and also the data required for project management. Under this distribution, individual project managers would use the project management server to plan and manage various projects. This should have security by project so that other project managers are unable to see the assessments of individuals not under their control. All employees would have access to the mail server for posting and retrieving e-mail messages.

A rationale for partitioning EMPLOYEE as depicted in Figure 11.4 would be to store all HR information about an EMPLOYEE on a server different from that controlling the project management information. Both servers would, however, contain basic employee information, for example, name, SSN, home address, department assigned, and job title. This information could be contained in an EMPLOYEE_BIOGRAPHIC table. In this case, the data is not to be distributed; rather it is to be duplicated.

Advantages to vertical object distribution include the ability to keep certain categories of data completely confidential or secret. Other advantages include the ability to perform reports against all instances of that type of data, for example, payroll tax forms at the end of a year.

Disadvantages to vertical object distribution relate mainly to the difficulty in getting all the information about an object in one place for the purposes of archiving, reporting, or elimination.

If vertical distribution is to occur, then the object's distribution should be along application lines. That is, all the tables related to payroll should be on one server while other tables that support human resources, for example, are on another server.

11.3.2 Horizontal Object Distribution

Figure 11.5 illustrates horizontal data distribution. In this figure, both servers, Boston and Seattle, contain some of the rows from all the tables from the EMPLOYEE object. This means that the complete work force is subsetted.

A rationale for partitioning employees in this fashion would be to store all EMPLOYEE information over different servers because the organization is completely decentralized, with respect to both data and processing. For example, if the employee objects are horizontally distributed, then so too must be the processing functions. If there are five employee object servers, payroll must reside and occur on each.

An advantage to horizontal object distribution is the level of autonomy that may be enjoyed by each distributed organization. Each processing system is allowed to contain and reflect certain customs and mores. If an organization is international, and if the employees are obtained from local populations, then each processing system may have to have messages and reports in the local language. Another advantage is that the local data may have to reflect local tax rules that might be difficult to gather and administer on a centralized basis.

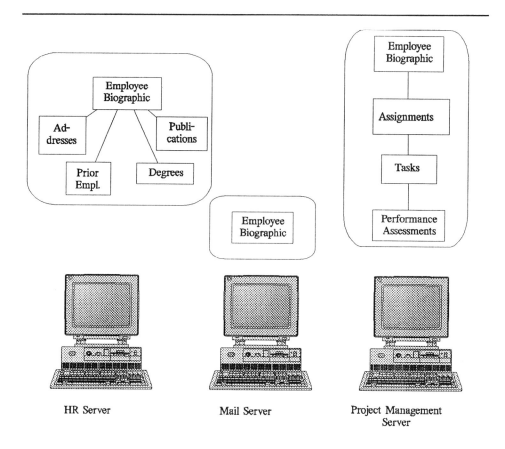

Figure 11.4. Vertically distributed employee object.

A disadvantage to horizontal object distribution is that certain economies of scale gained through centralization cannot be achieved. Every organization would have to be competent at every business function. Another disadvantage to horizontal object distribution relates mainly to the difficulty of getting critical information from all the objects in one place for the purposes of reporting. A final disadvantage relates to the simultaneous enforcement of semantics.

11.3.3 Mixed Vertical and Horizontal Object Distribution

The most likely type of data distribution will be one that is mixed. For those functions that are to be performed centrally, then for those objects, vertical distribution is preferred. This means that all employee data pertaining to payroll

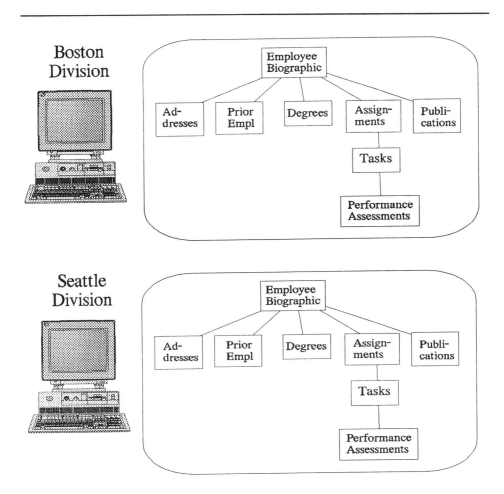

Figure 11.5. Horizontally distributed employee object.

would reside on a single server. For the remaining data, the activities against the data might better be served through horizontal distribution. Figure 11.6 presents a schematic for mixed data distribution. In this scheme, the Paris, France operations contain a complete set of EMPLOYEE information. The Kansas City and Seattle divisions contain only mail server data and project management information. Finally, all the HR information is stored on the Boston server, which is the corporate headquarters.

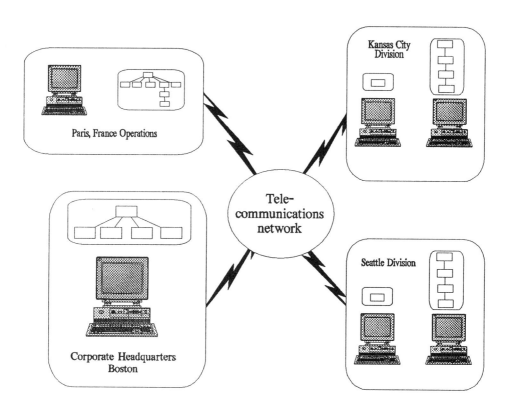

Figure 11.6. Mixed distribution of employee object.

11.4 Data Replication

A first-generation approach to data systems implementation was called stovepipes. This simply means that the data contained in a database all deals with the same narrow subject, but is stratified by operational, control, and then strategic. The first set of stovepipe data systems employed their own designed access methods. A second set of these systems employed commercially available DBMSs.

A second generation of data systems was an extreme reaction to the first generation. Formerly there was a database for every different reason; now there was to be one database for all reasons. This *one pervasive database* strategy was short-lived because its design was never able to be finished in any practical time frame and because the computing technology was not available to implement it.

A third generation of data systems combines the use of DBMS from the first generation, but narrows the scope from the second generation to embrace data from discrete subject areas. Examples are finance, contract/project accounting, and human resources. The subject area databases still exhibit stovepipe characteristics. That is, they contain operational, control, and strategic data. While these databases have broader subject areas, there are still two problems:

- No overall corporate viewpoint
- No common, corporate-wide set of semantics

The second problem can be solved through the development of an overall enterprise business model. The metadata for such a model is the subject of Chapters 4 through 10. The first problem is not so easily solved. The solution is not easy for three reasons. First, the granularity of the subject databases is likely to be different. Some data might be by trip (travel), by project, or by business event (tax report due).

The time synchronization of each database may also be different. For example, in a purchasing database, the time synchronization may be ad hoc, with reports monthly. The payroll records data time synchronization may be by pay period with reports dictated by various taxing authorities. To overcome these difficulties, an additional database concept has been developed: *warehouse*.

Warehouse databases are designed to regularize both granularity and time synchronization. This type of database then enables researchers and business planners to explore business data without having to constantly adjust granularity and time units. Quality warehouse database designs always maintain backward *pointers* into the production database from which almost all the warehouse data is derived. Some warehouse data is obtained from outside sources such as government agencies, business trends, and the like.

Because the warehouse database is largely redundant or duplicated data, these databases are not really a form of data distribution.

11.5 Reference Data Distribution

Regardless of how the production (invoices, employees, and time cards) data is distributed, a number of the database tables must be distributed with every subset, that is, the reference and validation data. If the employee object is distributed, say payroll information on one server, education data on another, and so forth, reference data such as state codes, sex codes, position codes and titles, salary ranges, and department numbers are common to all the distributed subsets. In this example, the reference data may have city, state, and zip codes, which would be used whenever a paycheck address is needed or a school's address is entered.

The columns from each distributed production data table must be examined to identify the reference data tables that must also be distributed. Whether all the rows from the reference data tables must be distributed depends on the rows from the production data table. If the production data table contains addresses for employees, there is a high probability that only the city-state-zip rows within a radius of 50 to 100 miles have to be present in the required reference data. If the base table is education, virtually all degree types and majors would have to be included.

When data is inserted, modified, or deleted in the production data table, the reference table must either have all the necessary values, or be able to be updated to contain a new valid value. In the latter case, there will then be different sets of rows within the various distributed reference data tables. Such differences have to be managed in a coordinated way.

11.6 Distributing Database Processes

Database processes are those processes that are required to maintain the quality and integrity of the database. The processes (bubbles) from Figure 11.2 identify the different types of database processes that can affect data distribution integrity or quality. Some of the database processes are encoded in the actual table definitions. See, for example, the CHECK clause in Figure 6.9 in Chapter 6. In ANSI/SQL, the referential integrity feature allows for the definition of the relationship between the *referencing table* containing actual EMPLOYEE addresses and the *referenced table* containing the valid sets of cities, states and zip codes. In addition to referential integrity clauses, the referential integrity violation rules are also specified. These rules state what action is to be taken when a referential integrity rule is violated. For example, if the rule is SET NULL, then when the storage of an invalid value is attempted, a NULL value is stored and a message is issued. NULL means *don't know*. In the case of an invalid value, the data entry person might not know what the valid value is, thus *don't know* is appropriate. The other referential integrity actions are REJECT and CASCADE DELETE. In the case of an addition or modification, REJECT would cause the transaction to be rejected. In the case of the deletion, if a referenced table row is deleted, so too are all the rows from the referencing table. This is a very powerful capability and must be used very carefully. For example, if a referenced table contains the set of valid zip codes and the referencing table is a table of employee addresses, then if a particular zip code is deleted in the referenced table, all the addresses containing that zip code are deleted!

Other database processes include the calculation of derived data, the validation that the next invoice number is one larger than the previous, and the like.

11.7 Metadata Distribution

It should go without saying that the appropriate set of metadata, commonly contained in the implemented database's schema, is also distributed. If only a subset of tables from a specific object is distributed, then only that set of metadata is also distributed. The extent of the distribution is determined by the set of DBMSs employed in the distributed data environment.

11.8 Data Distribution Guidelines

The following are a set of practical guidelines for determining what data to distribute and how to distribute it:

1. Build a data usage chart for all database tables.

2. Analyze data distribution against optimization, execution site, and network throughput criteria.

3. Test, test, test, and test.

4. Accommodate security requirements. [14]

The data usage chart should identify the data table and then categorize the frequency of use (daily, weekly, monthly, annually) for local updates, local queries, remote updates, remote queries, and finally, the quantity of rows in the table. An example of a data usage table is contained in Figure 11.7. The data tables are then:

● Data tables that hold production data

● Summary tables for decision support use

● Static reference data that changes no more often than monthly or annually

● Dynamic reference data that changes weekly or daily

In general, the most common approach is to:

● Localize production data
● Distribute static reference data
● Centralize shared production data subject to update

---

[14] Agrios, Nicholas G. and Potochnik, Michael P. *Oracle International Conference Proceedings, Paper 300*, 1992.

The second step is to build typical queries (updates and reports) that can be used to assess performance. Then assess how these queries actually perform in the distributed hardware environment. Three criteria should be employed:

- Maximum possible optimization
- Execution site
- Network

Every query should be examined to ensure that it represents the most efficient configuration for the DBMS that is going to process it. There may be several different forms for a particular query that produce the same result. Furthermore, different DBMSs will react differently to each of the different configurations. Finally, different volumes of data and different physical layouts of stored data will further affect performance results. All of these variables must be factored into the final determination of the particular queries. Each computer site must be examined to determine which form of a query it best executes.

A significant variable in overall query performance is whether the query is to be run partially or completely at local or remote sites. Tests will show the effect of the communications network on the remote queries. A high-speed remote computer may have its greater performance overshadowed by a low-speed network. The goal is to determine the most efficient node for distributed query processing.

Once a complete set of prototypical queries is created and a preliminary determination is made as to the location of each of the data and reference tables, a comprehensive test plan must be constructed and then executed. A significant part of the test plan is determining strategies to be taken if certain test results occur. The test results should merely be the confirmation or rejection of hypotheses of certain types of performance. It is important to develop and then keep performance curves for all the queries, reflecting five variables:

- Volume of queries
- The volume of data with each query
- The state of organization or disorganization of the database
- The specific DBMS
- The configuration of the specific DBMS

After all the curves are plotted, the optimum set of queries, platforms, data, and processing distribution can be determined. Ultimately, these choices will reflect a series of compromises.

A very important consideration may be security. If all the data is open, everybody can access, and with appropriate access, perform updates. If the data is not open, security schemes have to be put into place. Development of a sophisticated security environment is very costly and time-consuming. It requires the identification of all possible users, their roles, the inventory of all applications, the types of permissions allowed within each application, and then the creation of

Table	Table Type	Update Frequency	Query Frequency	Remote Updates	Remote Queries	Rows in Table
employee	data	daily	daily	none	weekly	5000
equipment pass	data	daily	daily	none	monthly	7500
personal equipment	data	daily	daily	none	monthly	2500
company location	data	yearly	daily	yearly	weekly	25
pass state-reference	static reference	yearly	daily	yearly	none	2
zip code-reference	dynamic reference	monthly	daily	monthly	none	3000
state code-reference	static reference	yearly	daily	yearly	none	50

Figure 11.7.   Data usage table for determining data distribution.

all the proper interrelationships. If all of this sounds like a database application in its own right, that's correct! Once the security database is developed, it must be administered and maintained. Beyond all that, the DBMS and distributed database environment must be able to accept and enforce all these security dictates.

11.9 Recording Data Distribution Metadata

Figure 11.8 depicts the meta-entities required to store the critical information about the distribution of the specified data model. The figure contains two types of meta-entities: those representing data tables, and those representing database processes.

The intersection between the specified data model and the implemented data model is represented through the intersection meta-entity DBMS COLUMN & [database] COLUMN. The columns belonging to specified tables are represented through the meta-entity COLUMN. The DBMS tables contain DBMS COLUMNs. Figures 11.4 through Figure 11.6 provide examples of a distribution of a specified data model into an implemented data model.

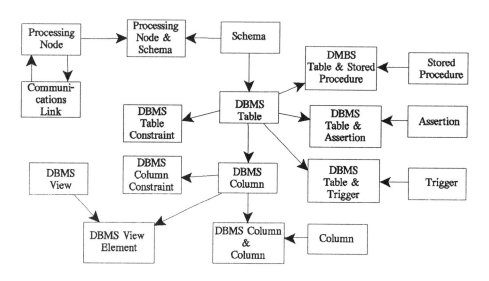

Figure 11.8. Implemented data meta-entity model.

The database processes are represented through the commonly found DBMS facilities:

- Table constraints
- Column constraints
- Domain constraints
- Assertions
- Triggers

A table constraint may be a unique constraint, a referential integrity constraint, or a table check constraint. Unique constraints apply to primary or candidate keys. Referential integrity constraints are an implementation of one of the data integrity rule classes.

A table check constraint or an assertion specifies a condition that must test true whenever a database action has occurred. If the test fails, the transaction is automatically rejected. A table constraint for an employee may test that the value from START DATE is less than or equal to the data contained in END DATE. The difference between a table check constraint and an assertion is that the former must be tied to a particular table while the latter is independently defined.

A column constraint specifies a condition that must test true before the row containing the column value is accepted; for example, that the SEX can only be M or F, or that START DATE must be greater than the incorporation date of the company.

A database trigger is the name for an action that occurs when a certain condition tests true. For example, in a student table there may be the GPA (grade point average) column. This column would be recomputed whenever a new grade is entered, one is deleted, or when a grade is changed. Once the procedure is executed, the derived data GPA would then match the actual data stored in the COURSES TAKEN table.

All the constraints except triggers are part of SQL/2 (1992). Triggers and expanded assertions are defined in SQL/3 (est. 1997).

12

IMPLEMENTED SYSTEMS MODEL

12.1 Client/Server Introduction

In the early days of online processing (back in the early 1960s), terminals were connected to the mainframe through cabling. Some of the terminals were local (directly connected), while others were remote (connected through a communication's concentrator). Independent of the connection type, all the terminals were *dumb*. That is, they were devoid of all processing capability. The first type of online terminal was really no more sophisticated than electric (no memory) typewriters. The computer sent one or more lines and they were typed out. The user responded by typing one or more lines and then sending a *return*.

The next generation contained a cathode ray tube (CRT). All data appearing on the screen was placed specifically and exactly by a computer program that was executing in the mainframe. Each mainframe program had to have intimate knowledge about each terminal type it was supporting.

With the advent of the personal computer (PC) in the early 1980s, the first hint of distributed processing appeared. Data was able to be entered and *scrubbed* by the local PC. The sole purpose of the PC was to prepare data for use by the mainframe. Telecommunication packages, such as CrossTalk™ were developed for the PC. These packages served three purposes:

- File uploading
- File downloading
- Interactive (but dumb terminal) interaction

While PCs were becoming more sophisticated and more powerful, mainframes were also becoming more powerful but smaller. Probably the biggest advance in the development of smaller but more powerful mainframes was the elimination of the need for special environments. Special environments typically have raised floors, air conditioning (or water cooling in many cases), special electrical sources, and endless special cabling. Today, computers just plug into normal or single-circuit outlets, normal room air conditioning is sufficient, and many offices today are wired with coaxial cabling just as they are wired for telephone.

As PCs became common on desk tops, they became interconnected through local and wide area networks (LANs and WANs). This permitted both data and process sharing. PCs today commonly have eight to twelve megabytes of random access memory (RAM) and have three hundred to five hundred megabytes of random access disk storage. It is now quite common for one PC containing a sophisticated package like a project management system to be accessed through the LAN by other office workers using their PCs. To classify the different roles the computers were playing, new terms were needed: *client* and *server*. Simply put, who/whatever is requesting the service is the *client*, and who/whatever is providing the service is the *server*.

Some servers are more comparable in size and processing capabilities to yesterday's very large and powerful mainframes. Servers today can have over 100 megabytes of main memory and billions of characters of random access storage. Because of their size, because of telecommunications, and because they do not need special environments, servers are able to be placed wherever needed. These servers are able to support any number of PCs acting as clients, and the servers are able to be interconnected with other servers. Through all these interconnections, multiple-site corporations are able to share data and processing as never before.

In a way similar to the shrinking of hardware, software has become more sophisticated. Fully functional DBMSs are available for PCs, servers, and mainframes. DBMSs that supported from ten to thirty users on a mainframe for a cost over $250,000 are now available to run on PC-based servers, (Intel 80486) running Unix supporting a similar quantity of users for less than $15,000.

Application system development has also become streamlined. Repositories and CASE (computer aided software engineering) tools are able to record the specification of simple systems and generate the application system in less than a week. Complex, more sophisticated application systems take longer to specify, but can be generated in a few days to several weeks.

A significant advance in application systems development has been the creation of specialized sets of software that are accessed through standard interfaces. An early development on IBM mainframes was CICS, an online transaction processing system. CICS is a large-scale software system that handles terminals, transaction processing queues, storage allocation, internal file accessing, recovery in the event of communications failure, and the like. Because of CICS, the mainframe application programmer could concentrate on the development of the application's processing logic without having to be concerned with the details of terminal and transaction processing.

Similarly, DBMSs allowed application programmers to stop having to define data structures, access methods, backup and recovery, concurrent operations, security and the like. With the advent of ANSI standard SQL in the mid-1980s, various programming languages such as PL/I, Ada, Pascal, C, COBOL, and FORTRAN could all read and write from the same database—unheard of just a few years before! Notwithstanding all these advances, there was still a monolithic concept of the application system. That is, the application system's execution domain was only one computer rather than a set of computers.

12.2 Client/Server Processing Alternatives

In the client/server environment, the concept of application is undergoing redefinition. The client-server application is no longer a monolithic, million-line system of programs. Rather, it consists of collections of well-defined software units that interface through standardized interfaces and that can execute on multiple computers at the same time in a coordinated, safe manner. This book deals with four types of client/server environments:

- Server and *dumb-like* operating client
- Server with computing systems running on the client to prepare data
- Server with data downloading and uploading
- Server and client in a fully cooperative environment

Figure 12.1 depicts these four client/server environments. The first environment is a mere variation of the traditional mainframe environment. The only real difference is that the client, possibly an Apple Macintosh™ or an IBM PC or PC clone, operates as a dumb terminal through some terminal emulation software. For Unix-based servers, the most common approach is to have the PC appear as an X-windows terminal. The PC software system performs all the screen formatting operations in response to data presented by the server.

In the second environment, the client may have fully functional application programs that interact with onboard storage devices for the collection and validation of data. A typical example is a time card system that has localized data and validation reference tables to preprocess a set of time cards. Once the time card data is acceptable, a final software module activates a server program that requests the data stored in the PC.

In the third environment, a computer program resident on the client activates a request for data from the server. An example is the acquisition of all project cost data (staff time and other direct costs). The client program is started. It then requests the project to be identified and the time frames delineated. Then the client program employs the user responses to finalize a set of interrogations for the server. The server's databases are accessed and the data is sent back down to the PC, whose program is awaiting it. The PC database is then accessed through a spreadsheet package or a PC/DBMS.

In the fourth environment, an application system is started on the client and whenever the client requires data from one or more servers, the query requests are automatically generated and dispatched to the appropriate servers. In other scenarios, the client might use the server as a source for data integrity validation, or might send the server summary data about a day's transactions. For example, if a client is performing point-of-sale processing, item prices for a day might be automatically downloaded to the client when the store is closed. But during the sales day, the client might upload hourly summaries of the number of different items that have been sold. The server might never care about each and every sales

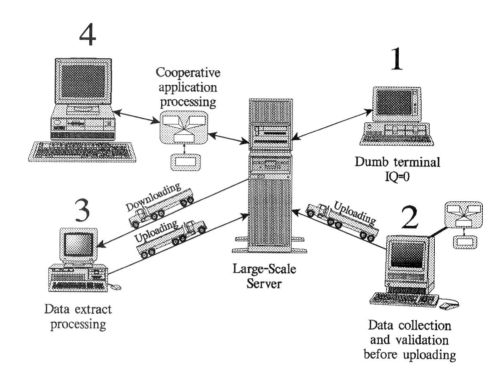

Figure 12.1. Four client/server architectures.

transaction. Rather, the design might only be the number of customers during the hour, the average sale amount, the sales tax collected, and the count by UPC (universal product code) number of the items sold.

All four scenarios illustrate that the traditional concept of systems and applications is changing. Application component parts are being factored into discrete components that are serviced by commercial, off-the-shelf packages (e.g., DBMSs and transaction monitors). Whole application suites are able to be created through the use of software generators that retrieve required metadata drivers from repositories. COTS (commercial off-the-shelf) application packages for traditional finance applications like general ledger, accounts payable and receivable, payroll, and inventory are now available in pregeneration (metadata) formats. Once the packages are customized and generated, production-class applications then exist for use by the enterprise.

12.3 Application Component Parts

From a functional viewpoint, an application system consists of four parts:

- Presentation logic (screen processes)
- Business data processing logic
- Data processing logic
- Database management system

The relationship among these four parts is shown in Figure 12.2. The first component is all the screen-handling capabilities. The second component is all the algorithms necessary to process a sale, update a general ledger account, generate report formats, and the like. The third component includes both traditional file reads and writes as well as access to commonly used databases.[15] As stated above, in the *old days* the application programmer was responsible for accomplishing all four activities. Today the application program utilizes a screen designer that generates all the actual screen painting and processing logic. Only the screen's name has to be referenced in the application program for it to be used. Similarly, database processing logic is accomplished by stating the DBMS commands for data selection, inserts, modifies, deletes, or for generating the report formats. What remains for the application programmer? The business processing logic, that's all.

An early client/server paradigm had these four application system components distributed in different combinations, from presentation logic only on the client, presentation logic and business logic on the client, to presentation logic and business logic and data processing logic on the client. This paradigm is too simple, however, especially in light of the sophisticated of PC-resident DBMSs and application development environments such as Clarion™.

12.4 Application Distribution Alternatives

Business processing logic can be distributed as follows:

- Entirely on the client
- Entirely on the server
- Fragmented between the client and the server

These three alternatives are illustrated in Figure 12.3.

---

[15] Berson, Alex. *Client/Server Architecture. McGraw-Hill Series on Computer Communications.* New York: McGraw-Hill, 1992, page 34.

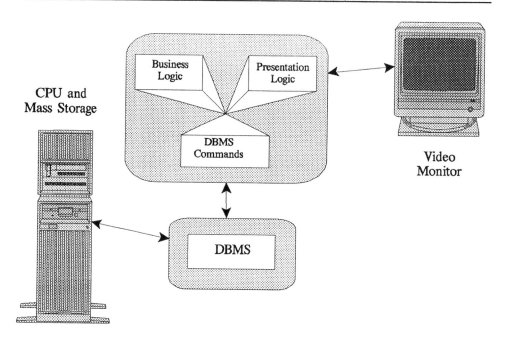

CPU and
Mass Storage

Figure 12.2. Application components.

12.4.1 Entirely on the Client

When the business logic is entirely on the client, the advantages center around the dedicated processing capability of a single processor versus the time-shared processing of a server. If the client is powerful enough, the ability to complete the process more than overcomes network transmission time required to bring necessary data from the server to the client.

A disadvantage is that the client is required to contain the exact same version of the application logic. If there are only a few clients and only a few applications, the effort would not be too difficult. If there are thousands of clients and hundreds of applications, the distribution coordination may present a logistics nightmare. Another disadvantage arises when the application is too large and too complicated for processing on the client. A final disadvantage exists when the processed data is shared data. Each client has to place update locks on the server-stored data, bring a current copy down to the client, update it, and transport the data back up to the server, replacing the locked but outdated data. In this case the network traffic times may outweigh the benefits of client processing.

A classic example of the need for a server is an e-mail system. The locations directory of various persons on the e-mail network is constantly being updated in

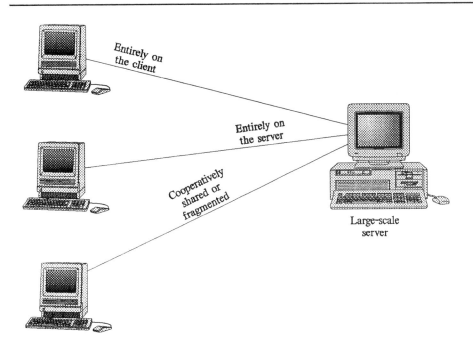

Figure 12.3. Business processing logic distribution alternatives.

a large company. This directory represents updated but shared data. Its only logical location is a server database. The e-mail messages are constructed on the client and then sent to the server for routing. When clients access the server looking for messages on either an ad hoc or a scheduled basis, the messages are downloaded to the client for recipient retrieval and disposition.

12.4.2 Entirely on the Server

When the business logic is entirely on the server, the advantages center around having only a few copies of the application software. If there are many different applications but their use is relatively nonintense, accessing a centralized server reduces the problems associated with software distribution and coordinated maintenance. Another advantage is that the only traffic on the network is the screen responses and other messages that appear on the clients. Finally, if the data that is being processed is shared data, the server's DBMS is the best choice for common, coordinated updates with minimum locking times.

Disadvantages center around using clients essentially as dumb terminals. Another disadvantage occurs when there are many hundreds of clients that perform significant processing and calculations against low volumes of stable, nonupdated sets of data. This exists with warehouse databases, which by design are updated only at regular intervals (usually weekly) so that data consistency is maintained for analysis and research reporting. In this case, subsets of the warehouse data are accessed, copied over to the clients, and then analyzed and researched at leisure.

12.4.3 Fragmented Between Client and Server

The third alternative is best when the advantages of the dedicated server can be combined with the advantages of client-based business logic processing. A good candidate application is one in which there is distributed data collection and validation to a centralized database that undergoes centralized processing after the data collection is completed. As cited above, point-of-sale processing is appropriate. Certain sets of data are distributed to the client. As the sales are made, sales summaries are created. On queue these summaries are retrieved by the server and used to update the server's understanding of the day's sales, including adjustments of all current inventories. As new inventories are entered into the store these new inventories are entered into the goods receipt client, and then, when all the inventory is received, the additions to the inventory are uploaded to the store's server.

Another good use of a cooperative processing approach is a student registration system. The course catalog can be replicated on each client. As students are registered, the class requests are entered into the client. When all the course requests are entered, the data is sent to the server, which attempts to enter the student into course-sections.

The algorithm might be such that the business logic looks for the course-section from all the course-sections of all the requested courses with the least openings and then places a temporary hold on a seat in that course-section. Then the business logic proceeds to the next course-section of the next course and so on. When all the course-sections are honored, another part of the business logic makes all the temporary class holds permanent and then produces a schedule for the student along with an invoice (of course!).

In this example, the clients accomplish the initial data gathering, and the server performs the process-intensive class scheduling effort. The client then receives the class schedule, creates the invoice, and prints it for the student.

While the fragmented approach offers the opportunity to minimize disadvantages, it clearly offers the significant disadvantage that the business logic is fragmented. Fragment interfaces must be carefully defined and the testing plan meticulously developed. At each step of the way, data must be preserved in the event a downstream processor fails.

12.5 DBMS Assists to Client/Server Processing

Database management systems are an essential component of client/server processing. The most commonly found DBMS is one that conforms to the ANSI/SQL language. SQL/86, the first version of ANSI standard SQL, was merely a fundamental core. It contained basic table definitions, some integrity constraints, and the basic data manipulation language commands. SQL/89 offered referential integrity and standards for embedding SQL commands in various third-generation languages. SQL/92 (commonly called SQL/2) offers the first facilities critical to cooperative processing. It contains enhanced constraints, independently defined assertions, and enhanced data manipulation language capabilities.

SQL/3, expected to be technically finished in 1995, contains the critical components for a fully functioning client/server environment. ANSI and ISO processing is expected to take another two years, for a release year of 1997. First of all, SQL/3 contains stored procedures, triggers, and the ability to define and manipulate objects. SQL vendors—Oracle Corporation, Ask Software (Ingress), Sybase, and others—are working on implementations of all these facilities. The vendor implementation schedules parallel the standards efforts.

DBMSs provide assists to the client/server environment as follows:

- Column check clauses
- Table check clauses
- Referential integrity clauses and actions
- Assertions
- Triggers (SQL/3)
- Stored procedures (SQL/3)
- Security (roles and grants)
- Savepoint
- Destroy savepoint
- Rollback
- Commit

Chapter 11 presents information on the first six of these items. Security facilities enable the database administrator to set up screens to prevent certain types of updates and other access to database users.

Transaction management in SQL is accomplished through the SAVEPOINT, DESTROY SAVEPOINT, ROLLBACK, or COMMIT commands. In ANSI/SQL/2 transactions are implicitly started. There is no BEGIN TRANSACTION statement.

A transaction is ended through either a ROLLBACK or a COMMIT. If ROLLBACK, all work since the implicit start transaction is undone.[16]

The SAVEPOINT facility is like a temporary, nested commit. An overall transaction may have a number of temporary commits (savepoints). As work is performed by the user's program through the DBMS the user, upon error, can invoke DESTROY SAVEPOINT, which restores to the last established SAVEPOINT. The transaction can then proceed, or determine that the work should COMMIT, or that the entire transaction should ROLLBACK.

12.6 Transaction Management

In traditional data processing, user programs completely control the concept of a transaction. Simply put, the program starts, WRITE locks are posted against files, records are updated, locks are RELEASEd, and the transaction is ended.

With the advent of online processing, two types of interaction are popular: timesharing and transaction processing. Time sharing provides the user program a discrete slice of time. For example, sixty users each get one-sixtieth of the available time. Some timesharing monitors are sophisticated enough to recognize a file access interrupt and transfer control to the next slice.

In general, transaction monitors control the acceptance of online transactions, their invocation of user-written programs that accomplish file reads, locks, writes, and releases, and the return to the user of any messages and data produced by the user-written online programs.

Transaction processor developers recognize that breaking up an MIS-type transaction into discrete time slices is not worth the effort. In contrast, transaction monitors swap control to the next transaction totally on the basis of I/O interrupts. Sophisticated transaction processors have multiple queues, and transfer control based on established priorities. For example, if there are six queues, and if transaction interrupts are even, then a 1-2-3-4-5-6, 1-2-3-4-5-6 sequence is even. However the sequence 1-2-1-3-1-4-1-5-1-6, 1-2-1-3-1-4-1-5-1-6 obviously biases the transaction processing to the number 1 queue.

When DBMS was introduced, it was naturally placed under control of the computer's existing online monitor (timesharing or transaction processing). Quickly, it became obvious that database activities are I/O-intensive rather than processing-intensive. Computer manufacturers who only had timesharing monitors

---

[16] It is important to note that as of July, 1993 a nested transaction capability is being pursued in the SQL/3 specification. That means that for SQL/2 all work is either committed or rolled back. Based on progress by some ANSI X3H2 members, SQL/3 will likely have a necessary set of transaction management facilities when it becomes an ANSI standard. A critical component of distributed, client/server transaction management is the protocols established by the RDA (remote database access) subcommittee of X3H2.

quickly developed transaction monitors if they wanted to remain competitive with those computer manufacturers already having transaction processors.

With the advent of DBMS, the interaction between transaction processor DBMSs became more complicated because sophisticated DBMSs perform their own transaction management. For example, a user-written program is accepted and processed by the transaction processor. The monitor then activates a special DBMS interface program that accepts DBMS commands. These commands are then assigned by the DBMS to one of its multiple queues for DBMS processing. As the DBMS encounters an I/O, control is transferred to the next appropriate DBMS transaction in the next appropriate queue. When processing is completed, data and messages are returned by the DBMS through the special interface program to the transaction monitor, which in turn provides responses back to the user. Tuning transaction processor environments is an art. Tuning DBMS environments is an art. Tuning them both together is an art of an entirely different kind!

Now enter client/server environments, with multiple processors to make the issue more complicated! Figure 12.4 presents a logical transaction diagram. It illustrates a human resources cooperative processing environment. In this transaction setting, three basic steps are required:

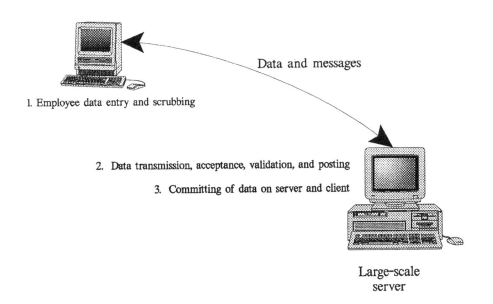

Data and messages

1. Employee data entry and scrubbing

2. Data transmission, acceptance, validation, and posting

3. Committing of data on server and client

Large-scale
server

Figure 12.4. Logical transaction for new employee.

1   Employee data (and possibly some new reference data) is accepted and scrubbed at the client.

2   The data is then transmitted to the server, validated, and if accepted, posted to the HR server database and possibly posted to the server reference database.

3   If all the information is acceptable, a commit is performed and all the data is made permanent at both the server and the client.

Because SQL does not support nested transactions, and because there are two different processors, the transaction environment has to be quite different. The necessary steps now are:

1. If the newly entered HR data requires the modification of client-based reference data, the reference transaction is accomplished and committed.

2. The client HR information is then validated, and if found acceptable, written to a client-transaction area and committed.

3. The data is transferred to the server.

4. If the newly server-entered HR data requires the modification of server-based reference data, the server-based reference transaction is accomplished and committed.

5. The server/client HR information is then validated and, if found acceptable, written to the server database and committed.

6. A message is returned to the client indicating that the server commit was accomplished or failed.

7. The acceptance message is interpreted to determine that either the server transaction was successful or failed. If it failed, the client program must provide an option to quit or to return to step 3. If successful, a delete transaction is created to remove the client-based version of the server transaction (step 2).

Two advances are becoming available to help client/server. The first is SAVEPOINT (SQL/3), and the second is the two-phase commit. With SAVEPOINT, the client and server can perform SAVEPOINTs at steps 1 and 4, respectively. COMMITs will still have to be performed at steps 2 and 5.

The two-phase commit will allow SAVEPOINTs at steps 1, 2, and 4, with only a *single client* and a *single server* commit occurring at step 5. Remember, however, there is no magic. The DBMS must perform all these steps. The only saving is in the area of user-written programming and subsequent checking.

12.7 Recording Information Systems Distribution Metadata

The meta-entities necessary for recording the distribution of information systems are presented in Figure 12.5. The meta-entity type, Processing Node, represents the identification of the client or the server on which an information system is to be located. Actually, what is allocated to the node is a *job*. The job may consist of job units, which may contain subordinate job units. Ultimately the meta-entity type Job Unit & Information System identifies the specific information system that is to execute on the node. In addition to job unit, roles are identified to have access to specific job units. The allocation between users and roles is presented in Chapter 13, Security.

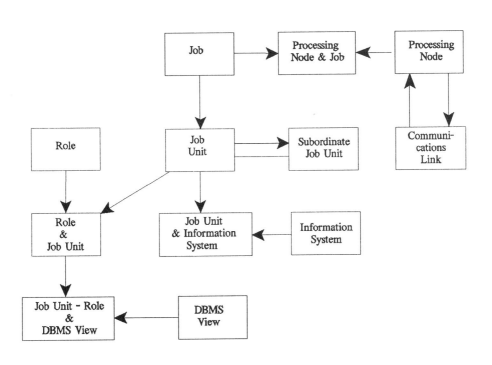

Figure 12.5. Implemented process meta-entity model.

13

SECURITY MODEL

Database necessitates sophisticated security and privacy. Databases centralize diverse data and important relationships, and allows access through easy-to-use languages. Security, therefore, must be available in different types, levels, and forms; its establishment and maintenance must be easy to learn and use.

Prior to the existence of database and DBMS, only the computer programs specially designed to access data files could make sense out of data. In essence, security existed because the data's semantics were fundamentally a part of the computer programs and not the data files. The data files and the programs were normally kept separated, providing additional security. The data files were on tape in a tape library, and the programs were kept in card trays at the programmer's work station. Since the separation of the data's definition from the data was a drawback to the generalized use of data by many different languages, technology came to the rescue and made the data's definition part of the data, giving rise to databases. Now, *that* solution *is* the problem, because anyone who has access to a generalized DBMS query language can access a database since the database contains both the data's definition and the data.

In short, database use necessitates sophisticated security and privacy, since well organized collections of enterprise data are readily available through easy-to-use, rapid-access, natural languages. To protect the database, security and privacy facilities must be provided.

There are more than just data record instances that need to be secured. In fact, the entire database environment, including the logical database, physical database, interrogation, and system control, needs protection. Client/server has greatly exacerbated the whole security issue. Formerly, a database resided on *one* computer and was accessed by *one* DBMS, and by *one* set of users. Today, with client/server, all these *one*s have become *many*.

This book does not address DBMS security, however. It is addressed elsewhere [17]. This book concentrates on recording what is to be held secure. Once the *what* is known, the DBMS's and operating system's security facilities can be employed to implement the enterprise database, client/server security.

---

[17] Michael M. Gorman, *Database Management Systems, Understanding and Applying DBMS Technology*, QED Information Sciences, Inc., Wellesley, MA, 1991, Section 6.8.

13.1 SQL, Almost to the Rescue

Properly installed security prevents user access to specific data. Access includes reading, writing, and selection. Specific data includes specific rows and specific columns. A quality security scheme thus controls:

- columns
- rows
- selection (reading)
- insert
- delete
- update

The view mechanism within DBMS addresses three of these components: column, row, and selection. The specification of the view explicitly identifies the columns from the specific tables that are allowed within the view. The specific rows are controlled by the use of selection criteria contained within the various where clauses of the view's specification. A more complete explanation of the purpose and value of a view can be found in *Database Management Systems, Understanding and Applying DBMS Technology* [18].

The read, write, and other action controls are also provided through ANSI/SQL facilities. READ and UPDATE are controls allowed to tables and also to views. Specifically, the critical actions that can be controlled in SQL/2 [19] are:

- SELECT—viewing or reading data
- DELETE—removing data from the database
- INSERT—placing new data into the database
- UPDATE—changing data from one value to another

By only GRANTing SELECT authority to a view, persons restricted to those views are thus restricted from all other types of access. The SQL VIEW facility is thus sufficient to control access to data.

When SQL was first standardized in 1986, the language contained two verbs for administering security: GRANT and REVOKE. The GRANT verb additionally contain the ability to GRANT with GRANT option. That meant that someone granted privileges with the GRANT option could in turn, pass some or all of those

---

[18] Ibid, Section 5.5.

[19] The database language standard SQL/2 became an ANSI standard in late 1992. Copies can be procured from the American National Standards Institute (ANSI) in New York City.

privileges on to someone else. SQL/2, completed in 1993, has not changed that model. Thus, there are still only the two main verbs.

A technical paper, commonly called ROLEs, was presented and accepted. However it is a component of SQL/3, which is not expected to be completed before 1997. A ROLE is a job with an associated set of privileges. For example, accounting clerk is the role, and the privileges are the actions required to successfully the job. Once roles are established, specific users are allocated to the role. By inference, all the privileges assigned to the accounting clerk are also assigned to the users performing the role of accounting clerk. The role concept is very useful because it provides a level of indirection to the establishment and maintenance of security.

13.2 Identifying What to Secure

While the establishment and maintenance mechanism is important, it is even more important to create a scheme for determining exactly which rows are to be held secure. One scheme is to create an artificial security code that is employed as a column in each table. If the WHERE clause always contains a selection based on the security code column, then the rows selected will only be those passing the security criteria. At first, such a scheme looks elegant. But, what the security code is really masking is the underlying data access policy that must be in place in order to establish the appropriate set of security code values. Suppose, for example that an organization consists of DIVISIONs that contain Departments that, in turn, contain SECTIONs. A two bit code can be created that identifies which rows are accessed. By definition, division users can select all rows. If the left bit contains a 1, then only DIVISION users can access the row; department and section users cannot access the row. If the right bit contains a 1 then only division and department users can access the row; sections cannot access the row. The only rows accessible by section users are those that contain 00 or 10.

While this scheme, or one similar, looks attractive, two problems are immediately apparent. First, the number of security levels is fixed by the mere construction of the code: three. Second, there is no horizontal segmentation (the Engineering Department only accesses Engineering's rows, not Marketing's rows). The first problem cannot be fixed except through traditional database reorganization, regardless of which technique is chosen.

To solve the second problem, there would have to be additional columns representing the identities of the individual departments, divisions, and sections. But, of course, if the department, division, and section names or their code surrogates are present, to facilitate security by organization name, then the security code is not needed. In general, the only security scheme that works is one that is based on the identifiable and *natural* columns (specific uses of business facts) present in the tables and their data values. If data is to be secure by ORGANIZATION, then one or more ORGANIZATION columns and their ORGANIZATION NAME values must appear. If SALARY data is to be segregated by TITLE and ORGANIZATION, then both those columns must appear in the employee information.

13.3 Client/Server Complications

Client/server introduces the additional problems of distribution of data and process. In regards to data distribution, Chapter 11 recommends for example that:

- Data should be fragmented such that local production data remains on the local server, given that there are multiple distributed servers. But if the system has only one server, then the local production data could remain on the client if updated by only one client, or remain on the server if updated by multiple clients.

- Static reference data should be distributed to the client if there is only one server, or to the server and then clients if there are multiple servers.

- Shared update production data should be centralized, making some servers acting as both a server to owned clients, and as clients to the shared update production data server.

- User extracts should be downloaded to the client from a single server or to the server from a multiple server.

From Chapter 12, there are four different techniques for distributing the process model:

- Server and *dumb-like* operating client, with few or no self-contained processing capabilities.

- Server with computing systems running on the client to prepare data

- Server with data down- and uploading

- Server and client in a fully cooperative environment, possibly with a fully functional DBMS on the client.

This greatly complicates security because if data is fragmented, there may be a single schema that is distributed. If the data is truly localized, there could be multiple schemas. If there is a single schema but horizontally fragmented data, the various WHERE clauses in the views would have to be different to correctly apply row-level security. Because of these complications, an effective security scheme must deal with:

- View (and by inference the rows and columns, as well as the view's owner schema with its physical database identity)

- Job (and by inference, the node on which it operates and the information system it is executing)

- User identity and password

- User's organization

- Activity role

In addition to managing the security related to these items, security must exist in two forms: specified and implemented. Specified security relates to the security necessary to protect the data inferred by the meta-models contained in Chapters 5 (data model) through 7 (information systems). Implemented security relates to the security necessary to protect the databases that reside on the clients, servers, or both (described in Chapter 11), and the information systems executing through jobs (Chapter 12). The reason that security must be represented in both specified and implemented manners is that a given specification may be implemented in different ways due to physical computer architectures. A given human resources application could be implemented simultaneously on both Sun™ servers with Apple/MacIntosh™ clients using an ANSI/SQL DBMS such as Oracle™, and also on an IBM mainframe with IBM 3270™ terminals using a CODASYL DBMS implementation of CA's IDMS™ [20].

Security requirements must therefore be comprehensively specified prior to their implementation. Once specified, the various implementations can be created such that they achieve the same protection.

13.4 Required Security Meta-Model

The meta-model for security is a mixture of meta-entities from the implemented data and implemented systems model as well as some linkages to the specified data model. Figure 13.1 identifies the meta-entities and illustrates their critical relationships upon which the security is built.

Starting at the top, there is the role meta-entity. It contains the name of the type of activity that is being performed, such as payroll clerk. Associated with the payroll clerk is the job and job unit. The job may be payroll time card entry. There may be multiple job units associated with payroll time card entry, such as entry, validation, and reporting. Each job is possibly identified as being accessible

---

[20] IDMS has an SQL view equivalent facility.

by that role. The security policy thus specified reads: *the payroll clerk is able to enter time cards.*

Associated with the particular job unit performed by a role is the DBMS view that is necessary for proper interface with the database. This view would essentially be the CREATE VIEW statement that would contain all the necessary SQL selection and navigation logic to operate against the database as if there were no organizational security. The policy expressed at this place in the meta-model is that *the payroll clerk is able to enter time cards using the time_card DBMS view to the HR database.*

The action type meta-entity identifies the types of actions that can take place with that view. Actions include:

- SELECT--viewing or reading data
- DELETE--removing data from the database
- INSERT--placing new data into the database
- UPDATE--change data from one value to another

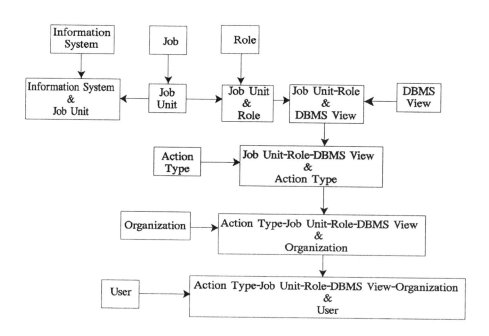

Figure 13.1. Security meta-entity model.

The security policy now reads: *the payroll clerk is able to enter time cards using the time_card DBMS view to the HR database in order to SELECT...*

Up to this point, the security model is both user and organizationally independent. The remaining two meta-entities add these levels of granularity. When fully specified, the security policy reads: *the payroll clerk, Joe Smith, within the Marketing Department, is able to enter time cards using the time_card DBMS view to the HR database to SELECT data.*

The collection of meta-data represented by the meta-entity types is actually the security definition database. As security is added, modified, or deleted, instances from these meta-entity types are changed. The revised specification then becomes the revised set of requirements for implementing in the client/server environment.

PART III

PRINCIPLES AND METHODOLOGY

Chapter 14, Project Management and Control, describes how effective project planning and management is critical to enterprise database achievement. Described as well is how the repository's design must be extended to contain all the critical meta-entities for quality project planning and management.

Chapter 15, Critical Staff Roles, provides descriptions of the various staff roles necessary to successfully accomplish enterprise database.

Chapter 16, Database Fundamentals, defines the fundamental principles that must be followed to achieve enterprise database success.

Chapter 17, The Make, Buy, or Generate Decision, presents the decision process surrounding the make, buy (COTS), or generate decision. In each information system's effort this critical decision is pivotal.

Chapter 18, Work Plan Development, describes a strategy for developing effective, high-quality database project work plans, and identifies prototypical work plans that have already been used to build various components of enterprise database. Included with each project plan are PERT charts as well as examples of the products produced.

Chapter 19, Typical Projects, presents the names and work breakdown structures (WBSs) appropriate for various types of enterprise model projects.

Chapter 20, Tool Selection and Evaluation, describes the critical nature of two of the most critical enterprise database tools, repository and DBMS, and then presents a strategy for their selection and evaluation.

14

PROJECT MANAGEMENT AND CONTROL

As a DP consultant, I've visited dozens of commercial shops, both good and bad, and I've observed scores of data processing managers, again, both good and bad. Too often, I've watched in horror as these managers futilely struggled through nightmarish projects, squirmed under impossible deadlines, or delivered systems that outraged their users and went on to devour huge chunks of maintenance time.[21]

There are three critical items in the description of this all too common situation. These are:

- Deadlines
- Outraged users
- Maintenance time

Projects with impossible deadlines must not be allowed to exist. If the project gets done within the deadline, the deadline was not impossible. If the project is not completed, the effort was a waste of time for two reasons:

- Valuable time has been lost and the objective was not achieved.

- The wreckage of the uncompleted project very likely cannot be used because too many shortcuts were taken that fatally affect quality.

If a project has outraged users, then where were the users during project proposal, during all the design and prototyping reviews, during system testing, and so on? Users must have equity (that translates to hard work) in the developed system. A project must not be allowed to start without estimated, scheduled, and contracted user commitments. Projects must not be allowed to go on beyond milestones without detailed user review that then translates to user equity.

Projects that *devour huge chunks of maintenance time* are those that suffer from either or both of the following:

- The design was not validated prior to implementation.

---

[21]   Page-Jones, Meiler. *Practical Project Management*. New York: Dorset House Publishing, 1985, page vii.

- The implemented system was not designed for maintenance from the outset.

When projects are estimated and scheduled, the typical project life span is calculated from the outset of the project through to first production implementation. This is quite flawed because it tends to reward project managers for cutting corners in the name of improvements of cost and schedule without determining the downstream negative impacts on maintenance costs and schedules.

It is imperative that the suite of projects comprising enterprise database not be characterized by Page-Jones' characterizations. To that end, this chapter defines the necessary components of methodologies that are sophisticated, repeatable, and reliable.

14.1 What Is a Project

At its very simplest, a project is a set of activities to accomplish a given objective, or to build a certain product. When the activities are formalized, they comprise a plan that, when certain techniques are used in preference to other activities, is said to follow a certain discipline or strategy. Formalized project plans with strategies have explicitly defined products.

Under the assumption that management wants to know both when products are to be delivered and how much they will cost, the project must be augmented by estimating techniques that can be produced to generate a schedule.

Given that the project is to be accomplished multiple times, for example, designing various databases, performance measures of activity by staff type and skill level should be taken so that future projects can be based on known accomplishment rates.

When all these project components are brought together, the project's methodology is sophisticated, repeatable, and reliable. Projects having these characteristics must embrace:

- Plan—steps for developing *what*
- Products—*what* is done
- Strategy—techniques for developing *what*
- Estimates—how much will *what* cost
- Schedule—*what* is done when
- Measurement—tracking performance against plan

Enterprise database cannot possibly be achieved in a single project because it would take hundreds of persons and five to ten years. During that time, requirements would significantly evolve, critical staff would change, and, if past is prologue, there would be at least two different generations of hardware. Because of these shifting critical elements, enterprise database is seen to be accomplished through a series of well-defined, 6 to 24 month projects with staff sizes of less than ten people. Common enterprise model projects are provided in Chapter 19.

A schedule for accomplishing a particular enterprise database project can only be developed through the use of a project management system such as Harvard Project Manager or Microsoft Project.

The final critical component, measurement, is accomplished through the capture of enterprise database project-based time cards that record critical statistics. This is defined in Section 14.3. The time card-based statistics are loaded into the project management database (PMDB) system.

When enterprise database is fully underway there will be a number of projects concurrently underway. Figure 14.1 illustrates this continuous-flow environment. It is critical that the enterprise database development methodology be configured to allow:

- Multiple, concurrent, but differently scheduled projects against the same operations database or warehouse database

- Single-database projects that affect multiple operations and warehouse databases

- Projects that develop completely new MIS capabilities, that can assess required changes to existing MIS capabilities, and that can accommodate a variety of systems generation alternatives (COTS, package, and custom programming)

Figure 14.1 presents a diagram containing the four major sets of activities for enterprise database's 6continuous flow environment. The user/client is represented at the top in the small rectangular box. Each of the ellipses represents an activity list to accomplish a specific need. The four basic needs are essentially:

- Need Identification
- Need Assessment
- Design
- Deployment

The box in the center is the repository. Specification and impact analysis are represented through the left two processes. Implementation design and accomplishment are represented by the right two processes.

In the first process, Create Application Model, the user provides requirements to an application's analyst, who interrogates the existing repository about the existing enterprise database. If the user's request can be handled by existing enterprise features, it is. Otherwise, the application's analyst formulates the requirement into an application request package (ARP). The ARP is represented as a need and includes a series of brief requirement statements in terms of additions to or modifications of an existing enterprise database.

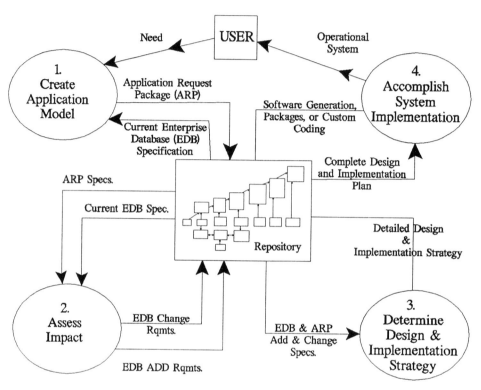

Figure 14.1. Continuous systems development method.

Because this is a continuous-flow model, an ARP may be handled by either existing enterprise database capability, or those now in implementation (process 4), or, in time, through process 3 (design) or process 2 (impact assessment).

At predetermined intervals, for example, monthly or quarterly, all the ARPs are bought into the second process, Assess Impact. During this process, all the ARPs are examined in unison against the then current enterprise database specifications. Because of the continuous-flow nature of this process, the enterprise database specification may have changed during the time when a set of ARPs is being batched. When the enterprise database add or change requirements are formulated, they will reflect the state of enterprise database at the time it is to be changed. The form of the enterprise database add and/or change requirements package is similar to that of the ARP. When the impact of a change is assessed, there may also be changes to existing facilities. These changes must be accomplished as well. Thus, when the final enterprise database add or change package is developed, it contains these additional change requirements.

The third process, Determine Design & Implementation Strategy, determines the actual detailed specifications of the computing systems environment changes. The detailed design of the change is in the form of specific changes to existing database schemas, views, computer programs, documentation, procedures, and the like.

In addition to the detailed design of the enterprise database changes, an implementation plan for a project has to be created, similar to one described in Chapter 19 (Implementation Strategy Project). Included would be the appropriate PERT chart, WBS, resource loadings, and then a Gantt schedule. Once this project proposal is received and approved, the complete set of changes becomes a new enterprise database version that moves on to the implementation process.

The final process, Accomplish System Implementation, performs all the normal implementation activities. At the end of test and integration, the new enterprise database release is accomplished.

Through this continuous-flow process, several unique features are present:

- All four processes are concurrently executing.

- Changes to enterprise database occur either quarterly or less often and in a very controlled manner.

- The enterprise database repository always contains all the enterprise database specifications, current or planned. Simply put, if some semantic is not in the enterprise database, it is not corporate information systems policy.

- All changes are planned, schedule, measured, and subject to accounting.

- All documentation of all types is generated from the enterprise database repository.

To keep all the work of several different projects coordinated, two tools are absolutely essential: the repository, and a project management database (PMDB) system. The repository is critical because it contains all the existing work products as well as all the work products under development. Multiple project leaders must be aware of each other's work. The second critical component is the PMDB system. Through this system and its attendant database, the specific work products that are being tackled can be discovered.

14.2 Project Management Database System

Correct project estimating is critical. In any estimate there are three components:

- What is done
- The quantity of what is done
- The work environment under which the work is done

The first component relates to the work breakdown structure. The critical question is whether the WBS is sufficient, and correct. If the WBS does not call for the correct steps or calls for an insufficient number of steps, then an estimate based on a defective WBS can only be correct accidently.

The second component of an estimate relates to knowing the quantity of work that has to be accomplished. If the work is well partitioned, then over time, certain statistical distributions can be developed. For example, for each subject area database there are—on average—40 tables. Each table contains on average 15 columns. And, on average, there is about .60 data elements per column. Thus, given the statistic of how many subject area databases, there are about 350-375 data elements. From this example, whole estimates can be developed from knowing only key component volume counts and the various *on-average* statistics. The amount of time is determined by multiplying the unit effort by the quantity of units. If it takes 4 hours for a data element's definition (including all research), then the time is about 1400 to 1500 hours.

The third component relates to the set of conditions under which work is being accomplished, for example, the availability of productive CASE tools, PCs, LANs, software generators, and the like. If the work environment is less than ideal, the unit effort must be multiplied by a factor greater than 1.0. If the final factor is 1.5, then the estimate of 1500 hours for data element definition must be raised to 2250 hours.

The objective of any estimating process is to create an estimate that is reproducible. If the estimate is reproducible, it is correctable. Errors in estimating will come from two sources: scope and familiarity. As more enterprise database projects are accomplished, the work will become better known. It is not uncommon for an organization to underestimate their own business's complexity. Policies and procedures will seem to slither out of every corner. But as time goes on, the estimating staff will better understand the nature of the company's business, and thus better estimate the scope of work. As the scope becomes better known, the statistical distributions will become refined. As time goes on, the metrics behind the estimates will become more accurate because users of the WBSs will understand the process better and the products will become more familiar.

The PMDB database consists of 16 tables, as shown in Figure 14.2. The fundamental strategy behind the PMDB database design is that each enterprise database has two different WBSs: local and standard. The local WBS is contained in the tables: project and work task. This allows the various organizations to design the WBS steps that they understand. For example, if there is a project to develop a prototype application for a particular mission of the business, the local eight-step WBS might be:

1. Plan and estimate security clearance project.
2. Identify and collect prior documentation of past efforts.
3. Determine requirements and review with proponent.
4. Develop logical database design for security clearances.
5. Present security clearance logical database and revise as necessary.
6. Build security clearance database prototype.
7. Revise security clearance prototype as necessary.
8. Create and finalize documentation of security clearance project.

The project's name is *Security Clearance Prototype*, which is stored in the *Project* table. The eight work tasks, identified above, are stored in the *Work Task* table along with a paragraph of description. Every task should be engineered to produce a deliverable, such as a plan from task 1 or the prototype in task 6. The deliverable is identified and recorded in the table *Delivered Product*.

To the proponent of the project, this WBS is probably detailed enough to understand the effort. But to the actual knowledge worker, the WBS is insufficiently detailed. A WBS is sufficiently detailed only when the same work products are produced at different times by different teams for essentially the same cost. Under this stricture the eight task names are not sufficiently detailed to achieve that result. For example, task 4 requires the building of a logical database. Since the task does not require that data-driven techniques be employed, one group of analysts may use process-driven techniques, which often produce very expensive, bad database designs.

If the WBS were sufficiently detailed, two unfortunate outcomes would result. First, the detailed WBS numbers and descriptions would all be tailored to embrace the needs of just the security clearances project. The next WBS might have 15 high-level tasks and sets of subordinate tasks. Thus many of the multiple local WBSs would all have different numbering systems. This would make project comparisons almost impossible.

Second, the descriptions of the WBS steps could be different when they were meant to mean the same work. This too would make work comparisons difficult.

Neither outcome is desirable, and furthermore, because of the lack of standard numbers, names, and descriptions, comparable work accomplishment statistics cannot be collected.

If, in order to collect work statistics, the WBSs all have to be the same, then either necessary steps must be omitted from some WBSs, or unnecessary extra work must be performed.

To solve these problems, the delineated strategy with PMDB is to have *customized* high-level WBSs with *standardized* low-level WBS extensions. Thus the eight tasks are created as noted, but are then extended to specify the critical subset of WBS steps from the complete WBS.

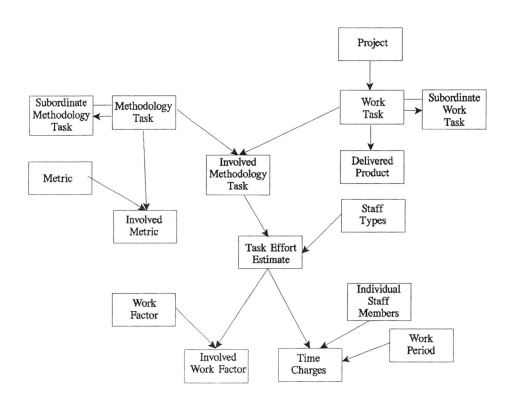

Figure 14.2. Project management database meta-entity model.

A review of the complete WBS shows that it is indeed detailed; some places are six levels deep. Experience has shown that if the WBS is inflicted at that level of detail, no one survives. Because of this overwhelming detail, the WBS should be considered only as suggested hints or strategies for work accomplishment at any level below the table of contents of the complete WBS. The level of detail contained within the table of contents was chosen for that specific reason. Because of this practical level of detail for the WBS, the only tasks from the WBS that should be stored in the *Methodology Task* and *Subordinate Methodology Task* are those that are contained in the table of contents tasks.

For each methodology task (stored in *Methodology Task*) there must be one and only one metric. This metric describes the product produced, and provides an estimate of the effort required to produce one of these product units by an average person, on an average day, with an average set of tools. These unit effort statistics have been derived from a number of different database projects since 1985. While they are correct on average, no one is average. The *Involved Metric* table enables a metric to be defined once but used many times over the WBS. For example, the metric *90 Name: Client review time of a deliverable* can be used in many different *methodology tasks*.

The table *Involved Methodology Task* is the intersection of a local WBS step (*Work Task*) and the standard WBS task (*Methodology Task*). A column that is computed in *Involved Methodology Task* is the amount of effort required to perform the work. The column *Involved_Methodology_Task_Total_Unfactored_Hours* is computed by multiplying the quantity of units by the *Involved_Metric* amount of time.

Work is accomplished by different staff types. The various staff types are contained in the *Staff Types* table. Each staff type consists of the staff title (systems analyst, programmer, database designer, etc.), and the billable rate in dollars per hour.

The gross amount of work is then distributed across all the different staff types according to the type of work. For example, if the task is: *2.02.04.01 Finalize database domain diagram*, the staff types might be functional experts, database administrators, and a repository tool specialist. The proportions might be 50 percent, 30 percent, and 20 percent. That would mean that if there is a staff size of ten on this task, five would be functional experts, three would be database administrators, and two repository specialists. Another issue that would have to be addressed is whether the work is actually split 50-30-20, or split by some other ratio. For example, if there is a 40-hour review, and the review team is five staff members, is it eight hours each, or is it a group meeting type of review where there are 400 staff hours consumed. The results of this analysis are stored in *Task Effort Estimate*.

Affecting the distributed task hours by staff type is the work environment. These assessments are made on behalf of each different staff type because their individual work environment may be different. The categories are:

- Experience of team
- Reviews conducted by the client
- PC equipment available for programmer/analyst
- Mainframe outages
- Extent of user contact

These factors were last updated in late 1992, so as technology advances, the third and fourth factors would have to be updated. When the work factor is identified, a new row in the table *Involved Work Factor* is created.

The work factors are designed to affect work in only a negative direction. The ideal environment causes all work factors to have no effect. As the work environment degrades, the work factors degrade the ability to work, making the quantity of hours rise. All the work factors are accumulative in their effect. For example, if the task is affected by the factors listed in Figure 14.3, the cumulative effect would be $1.20 * 1.20 * 1.07 * 1.16 * 1.30$, or for each 100 hours of staff time there would be an added amount of 112 hours. Thus if the original task was to be done by a single staff type, and if the original estimate was 100 staff hours, it would be increased to 232 hours. Additionally, this presumes an 8-hour day, 5 days per week, 52 weeks per year. If actual work experience shows that the staff is only available 90 percent of the time, then each work day can only be considered 7.2 hours. In this example, the number of work days would have to be 32.2.

This estimate is for the *work*. Added to it must be supervision overhead. While each company has its own strategy, a common one is to add 16 percent surcharge to the number of staff hours. In this case it would be about 37 hours. If all the hours are to be reported, a staff type of supervisor would have to be added and the hours calculated for inclusion.

The final calculated statistic is: *Involved_Methodology_Task_Total_Factored_ Hours*. All these hours by involved methodology task can then be exported and loaded into a project management package such as Harvard Project Manager or Microsoft Project. The package would have already had to have PERT charts built so that when the resources were loaded, the CPM and Gantt charts as well as costs can be computed. Once sufficient manipulation of the PERT is accomplished to achieve a satisfactory loading, the dates can be exported from the project management package for reloading into the PMDB database. A question naturally arises: Why have two packages, a PMDB and the project management package? One merely has to look at the types of data represented in the PMDB to see that

Factor Number	Name	Value	Description
13	Experience of team	1.20	Novice DP staff
23	Reviews conducted by the client	1.20	Reviews are generally not conducted
33	PC equipment available for analyst/programmer	1.07	IBM/PC AT or XT with only WordPerfect 5.1, telecommunications connection to a mainframe system for systems development and repository usage
42	Mainframe/server outages	1.16	For each hour below the average of six that the mainframe is unavailable
54	Extent of user contact	1.30	If users are available but only within ten business days of request

Figure 14.3. Unit effort work environment factors.

project management packages cannot fulfill the data storage, update, and reporting needs. And, PMDB cannot perform the project scheduling activities such as PERT, CPM, and Gantt. These two packages are simply two different tools that, while they have some functional overlap, are not functionally congruent.

14.3 Statistics Capture

The real value of PMDB is the capture of ongoing statistics, and the reporting of earned value. As projects are accomplished, time cards need to be created that record both the time spent on a WBS task and the quantity of worked units. For example, if the PMDB states that the amount of hours for a data element's definition is 2 hours and the environment factor is 1.75, and if through time card tracking the amount of time—on average—per data element is greater than 3.5 hours, then either the metrics or the environment factors need to be adjusted. Over time each organization will develop its own valid set of metrics and environment factors.

The tables involved in statistics capture in Figure 14.3 are *Individual Staff Members*, *Work Period*, and *Time Charges* (see Figure 14.2).

Figure 14.4 illustrates how actual delivered repository work and work accomplishment statistics can be related. Such a scheme presumes that both the work products (Chapters 4 through 13) and the project management data (Figure 14.1) are stored in the repository. Repositories that have modifiable meta-schemas and that are DBMS-based fill that requirement.

When the promises of proposals meet the work accomplishment of time cards, a statistic called earned value can be produced. Earned value simply is a measure of the amount of *funds* that have been earned based on work performed. It is common for projects to not really know what their earned values are because work performance is seldom tied to time expended. Figure 14.5 shows the intersection of these two repository components.

14.4 Summary

There are three key points about enterprise database estimating. First, virtually all initial projects will be estimated wrong. Time, if PMDB and the capture of performance-based statistics is installed, will cause continuous adjustments to the metrics and the work environment factors. Second, all early-on enterprise database projects should last less than one year and involve no more than about ten staff years. This will enable quick results for relatively small amounts of money. Third and finally, the repository is absolutely essential for enterprise database. It enables all project personnel to be aware of everybody else's progress and evolving corporate semantics.

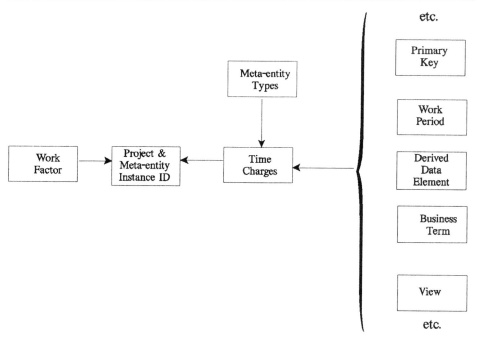

Figure 14.4. Intersection of project planning and project execution.

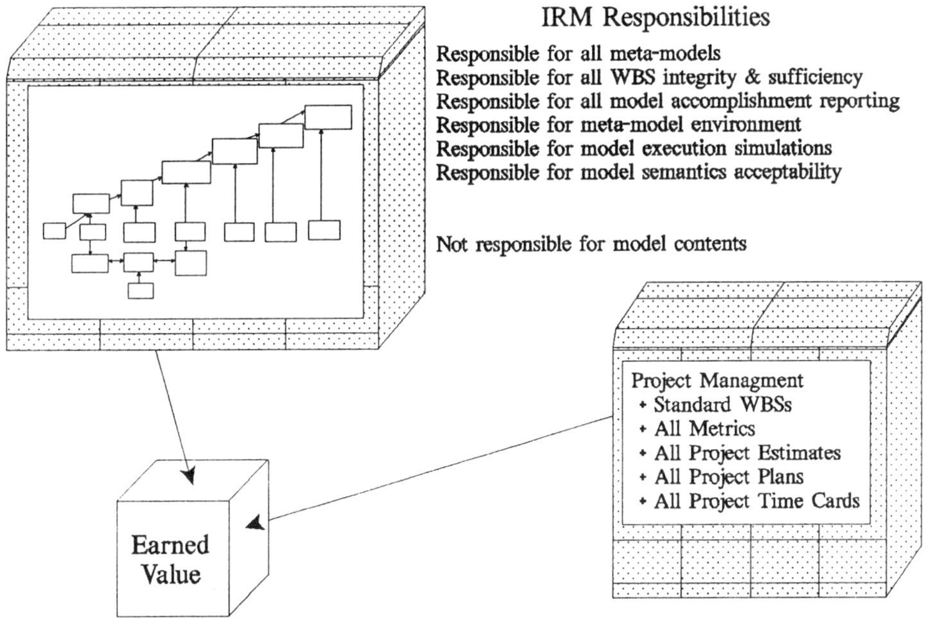

IRM Responsibilities

Responsible for all meta-models
Responsible for all WBS integrity & sufficiency
Responsible for all model accomplishment reporting
Responsible for meta-model environment
Responsible for model execution simulations
Responsible for model semantics acceptability

Not responsible for model contents

Project Managment
 ✦ Standard WBSs
 ✦ All Metrics
 ✦ All Project Estimates
 ✦ All Project Plans
 ✦ All Project Time Cards

Earned
Value

Figure 14.5. Connecting project work with project planning to generate earned value.

15

CRITICAL STAFF ROLES

Data administration, that is, the appropriate set of subject area administrators and application area administrators, is responsible for the *specification* of the overall enterprise business model data, while database administration is responsible for the *implementation* of the specified metadata. As a trivial example of the difference, data administration specifies the name, details, definition, and business rules associated with a travel order. Then database administration would first assist in determining how a travel order application system is deployed, and second, once decided, would create the DBMS-specific strategies for deployment. Included would be which DBMS, the DBMS schemas and application program views of data, the formulation of methods for business rule execution, and creation of appropriate procedures for backup, recovery, reorganization, security, and the like.

Figure 15.1 reflects a quick schematic of the kind of environment to be deployed.

15.1 Data Administration Role

Data administration is responsible for setting guidelines and standards for all databases. The policy set down would be followed by the individual subject area administrators. Additionally, the data administration is responsible for resolving any policy collisions among any subject areas.

15.1.1 Subject Area Administrator

The subject area administrator is responsible for the enterprise business model of that subject area. The enterprise business model consists of that mission model (the missions to be accomplished in that area), the data model (tables et al. required for permanent enterprise memory), and database process model (required changes in the value-states of tables). The subject area administrator is also responsible for cooperative interactions of data and database processes with other subject areas, and for the development of an overall enterprise glossary of business terms.

As can be seen, there is certainly more than one subject area administrator. In the enterprise database there are at least three, one for finance, another for human resources, and a third for support services. The subject area administrator is responsible for ensuring that all business rules, data, and processes are consistently specified within all the application areas of the subject area. A review of the mission description document will likely result in 10 to 15 subject area administrators.

The subject area administrator is responsible for the development of a common subject area data model across all application areas within the subject area. Each application area administrator proposes designs and requirements to the subject area administrator who then integrates them into an overall warehouse database design. Whenever there are policy intersections between subject areas, the committee of subject area administrators develops agreements. If the agreements affect contained processes, the application area administrators become involved.

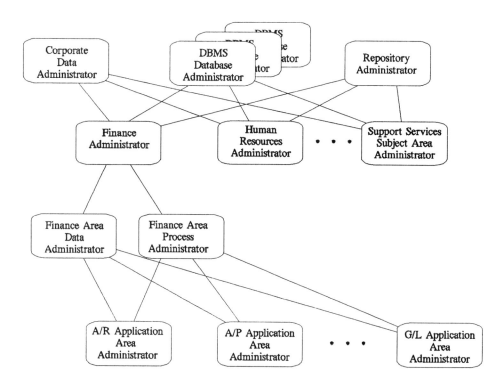

Figure 15.1. Interrelationships among persons supporting enterprise database.

15.1.2 Application Area Administrator

The application area administrator is responsible for the specific enterprise business model for the specific application, for example, accounts payable, accounts receivable, or general ledger, that may be deployed as an operational database or that may have its requirements included in a warehouse database. The subject matter experts are responsible for cooperating with their "peer" experts to ensure that all policy is common and consistent.

15.2 Database Administration Role

The DBMS database administrator is responsible for the installation and effective end user use of a DBMS. Within the enterprise, there should be at least be one database administrator for each DBMS. In general, a DBA:

- Assists in the creation of the DBMS's logical database design of the database

- Determines the requirements for the physical database

- Consults on the requirements of database interrogation languages

- Designs or reviews the system control facilities necessary to keep the database in optimum condition

- Designs, implements, and oversees the maintenance and reporting of the repository database application

- Helps create and participates in the formation of proper database environment support functions such as documentation, training, hotline support, and standards

15.2.1 DBMS's Logical Database

The DBA creates the DBMS's logical database design. For ANSI/SQL relational databases, this consists of the table and column definitions, initial access control (security), and ongoing development of views.

15.2.2 Physical Database

The DBA selects a storage structure for the efficient implementation of a logical database design. This structure must be compatible with interrogation languages and must utilize as little mass storage space as is practical. In conjunction with selection of the storage structure, he or she designs an access strategy to select, retrieve, and update data in an efficient manner.

The DBA helps evaluate data quality and helps design database loading from all the previously automated applications that are being utilized with this application.

Finally, the DBA selects the method and resources to support database backup during loading and ongoing database operation.

15.2.3 Interrogation

The DBA helps users of the database construct database applications. By examining the various interrogation languages, he or she determines the most appropriate language for application prototyping and then helps users select the most suitable interrogation language. The DBA assists in the development of interfaces to function between the database and canned applications such as word processing and financial modeling.

15.2.4 System Control

The DBA designs, creates, and maintains the appropriate audit trails, message-processing facilities, and backup and recovery procedures for database applications. These ensure that the database environment is protected against various types of loss, such as computer failures, DBMS failures, and data errors.

The DBA implements mechanisms to determine when physical database reorganization is necessary and then performs the reorganization. This involves coordinating the logical database change requests and making the changes during regularly scheduled times.

It is also the responsibility of this person to select, install, and maintain database security and privacy mechanisms that have been approved by management. The security violations log must be reviewed and the list of violations forwarded to management for action.

The DBA ensures that historical data that has been archived is retrievable under current versions of the DBMS.

Another task of the DBA is to determine which DBMS operations cannot execute concurrently and to eliminate as many of these conflicts as possible. He or she also determines which operations consume the most resources, and precludes such operations during prime time if possible.

Conducting reviews of database applications to provide recommendations for improving the operation of the application and the database is another very important task of the DBA.

The DBA supervises installation and maintenance of the DBMS and conducts tests to validate correct DBMS operation. As necessary, he or she constructs special DBMS versions to serve particular applications.

15.2.5 Repository Development

The DBA creates a repository implementation plan for the organization. Upon implementation, and subsequent to database loading, the administrator interrogates the repository to profile the ongoing database environment.

The DBA advises the data administrator on development databases, production databases, maintenance projects, and the characteristics of all databases within the organization.

15.2.6 Documentation, Training, Hotline, and Standards

The DBA receives, reviews, catalogs, and then distributes all documentation related to the DBMS. The DBA keeps a log of all persons having DBMS documentation so that updates can be distributed rapidly, especially if DBMS functions are found not to be working as described.

The DBA verifies that all documentation is added to the repository in a timely manner, distributes all database-related documentation, and produces a complete set of DBMS error reports so users can avoid the errors.

This person coordinates, designs if necessary, and attends all database training programs to ensure that students are receiving the most up-to-date material.

The DBA establishes, oversees, and reviews the operation of the DBMS hotline. All reported bugs are examined by the DBA to determine whether the user needs remedial training, or if the training needs to be changed, or if the DBMS has a bug. The DBA oversees and reviews the operation of the various database application hotlines to ensure that the best advice is given to the hotline's users.

The DBA follows up verified DBMS errors with the vendor and determines when a DBMS correction is to be available. The DBA oversees the creation of and adherence to standards relating especially to the design, implementation, and maintenance of databases and their applications.

The repository database, operating under Oracle RDBMS, for example, should contain all the metadata necessary for the development of production applications. *Note*: A production application need not operate under Oracle or any other DBMS. It is likely, though, that most applications will operate under some DBMS, whether it is on a microcomputer (PC), minicomputer, or mainframe.

15.3 Repository Administrator Role

The repository meta-model administrator is the person who is responsible for defining and enforcing standards and controls over the meta-products, their format and their interrelationships to other meta-products. For example, the repository meta-model administrator is responsible for stating that all database tables be properly named, defined, and in third normal form. If the content of a table (that is, its name, columns, and their descriptions) does not make business sense, then that is the responsibility of the subject area administrator (the "head" of business knowledge for that subject area), not the responsibility of the repository meta-model administrator. In short, the meta-model administrator is responsible for the existence, format, and interrelationships of meta-products but not for their content. There is likely more than one meta-model, but for a given architecture of information systems (e.g., commercial MISs) only one meta-model should be permitted.

16

ENTERPRISE DATABASE PRINCIPLES

A modern enterprise database development environment must embrace a systems development life cycle that:

- Is data-centered as opposed to process-centered

- Has the repository as the locus of all specification development, systems implementation, and ongoing maintenance

- Allows for the implementation of a continuous-flow, evolutionary systems development as well as discrete cradle-to-grave systems development

Critical to a successful database project environment is:

- The repository that contains the metadata representing the enterprise business model upon which all the database applications should be founded

- The discovery of the metadata for the mission, data, and process models by following critical enterprise database principles

- Choosing whether to implement a database application through a commercial off-the-shelf (COTS) package, through software generation, or through custom coding

16.1 Principles of Enterprise Database

Enterprise database must put into practice the lessons learned from the past. The main lesson is that data and processes must be specified only once, and if practical, be implemented only once. And, when maintenance is required, the single instance of the specification (data and processes) and the attendant implementation is the object of the modification and reimplementation. The first principle, then, is that

> *Data and processes are specified only once, and where practical are implemented only once.*

The second principle is that

> *The specification and, in turn, its implementation are modified together as a single unit.*

A corollary of the second principle is that

> *All maintenance activities begin with the modification of the enterprise database system's specification, not with the implemented programs or data.*

If these two principles are followed (initially or through maintenance), a significant reduction in redundant sets of processes will occur.

16.2 Comprehensive Model

For an enterprise database system to be successful, it must be based on a comprehensive model that consists of a completely specified, implemented, balanced set of data (Chapter 5) and processes (Chapters 6 through 9). The term comprehensive implies that all relevant data and processes, required for a complete set of business missions (Chapter 4), have been identified.

By balanced, it is meant that all data required by the complete set of necessary business missions has been correctly specified and implemented in the database, and that all the business processes necessary to represent the required set of business missions are also specified and implemented; furthermore, that the specified and implemented business processes deal with and/or produce persistent data (represented in the database).

A model of a balanced system consists of two components: data and processes. The data is represented as the data integrity model, and the processes are represented as the data transformation model. As stated above, these two models are functionally dependent on one another.

Prior to detailing the data integrity and the data transformation models, there must exist a single high-level statement that represents the overall scope and purpose of the business data and processes. The third principle, then, is that

> *The enterprise database system must be able to be represented through a high-level scope and purpose statement defining the functionality and boundaries of the included business data and processes.*

This statement is shorthandedly referred to as the corporation's mission description. The fourth and fifth principles flow from the third.

> *All data integrity model specifications must be based on the enterprise's mission description.*

All data transformation model specifications must be based on the enterprise's mission description.

16.3 The Data Integrity Model

The data integrity model is the representation of data that is both valid, and normalized. It further must contain all appropriate data dependency specifications (data integrity rules).

The data integrity model is valid if it contains all the data implied by the enterprise database system's mission description.

The data integrity model is normalized if all the data elements that are to be represented in the enterprise database are organized according to the rules of third normal form.

A data integrity rule is a statement that specifies an interaction between data elements (relational column) within one normalized structure (record type or table), between columns in different tables, between rows of the same table, or between a column in a collection of rows in one table and a single column of a row in another table.

The reason for having a data integrity model that is valid, normalized, and contains the complete set of data integrity rules is that the data integrity model only has to be defined once; the DBMS only has to store it once; the programs that add, delete, and modify the data only have to be designed, written, and debugged once; user training only has to be developed once; and finally, the data only has to be documented once. And with respect to maintenance, the specification is contained in only one place, requiring maintenance in only one place. Once the specification is modified, the attendant software and data needs to be modified once to carry out the specification change.

16.3.1 Valid Representation

The data represented by the data integrity model must embody all the data implied by the enterprise missions. To achieve this, the mission description undergoes further analysis to determine a database domain. This is then further divided into its major subdomains. Each is then defined and graphically represented through an entity relationship diagram. All the subdomain entity relationship diagrams are combined into a single diagram, which is then the graphical analog to the data required for the entire mission description. Each entity within the diagram is then robustly defined into objects. Those entities not surviving the definition process typically become data elements. The sixth principle, then, is that

The objects of the enterprise database system—in combination—represent all the data implied by the database domain.

The next step in the representation of a valid specification is the identification of data elements. These are found through analysis of existing reports, user interviews, screen layouts, and the like. These elements are examined with respect to the database domain and, if relevant, they become part of the enterprise database specification. The seventh and eighth principles, then, are that

> *Each data element represents a standalone business fact that is founded on policy analysis.*

> *All data elements of the database system—in combination—represent all the data implied by the mission description.*

16.3.2 Normalized Data

To achieve single-instance data specification, the objects and data elements must be joined and then represented as normalized tables in third normal form. An object may thus map into several third normal form tables. The ninth principle is that

> *To represent data only once, all data must be defined in third normal form.*

16.3.3 Data Integrity Rules

Data integrity typically consists of two types: acceptable data values and acceptable process results. Simply put, data integrity rules are the codification of business policy. Acceptable data values relate to valid and invalid values, ranges of values, and the like. Acceptable process results deal with calculations, selection logic, and so forth. In database, all such business policy rules must be "attached" to the database schema in such a way that these rules are automatically enforced regardless of the type of database access. If these business rules are encoded in programs and there are ten programs evoking these rules, then the rules must be specified identically ten times if the results are to be the same.

In addition to having single specification of business rules (a.k.a. data integrity rules), the enforcement of these rules by the database's schema allows for the utilization of nonprocedural languages encoded into database assertions and triggers. If the database's schema cannot automatically enforce these integrity rules, all updating programs must be written in a third-generation language since high-level nonprocedural languages do not allow for the definition of a large volume of business rules.

The tenth principle of the data integrity model is that

> *All data integrity rules that affect data interaction must be specified before an unambiguous specification can be achieved.*

A corollary is that

All data integrity rules must be specified before they are implemented in any programming language.

16.4   Data Transformation Model

The data transformation model is the representation of processes that are both valid and normalized. It further must contain all appropriate data dependency specifications (data integrity rules).

The data transformation model is valid if it contains all the processes implied by the database system's domain.

The data transformation model is normalized if all the processes that are to be represented in the database are organized according to process rules analogous to the data rules of third normal form.

While a good number of the data integrity rules are identified within the specification of the data integrity model, a number of them arise during the definition of the normalized processes.

The reason for having the data transformation model that is valid and normalized and contains the complete set of data integrity rules is that the data transformation model only has to be defined once, and the programmers only once have to design, code, and debug the programs that add, delete, and modify the data.

Furthermore, the user training for these processes only has to be developed once, and finally, the processes only have to be documented once. And with respect to maintenance, the specification is contained in only one place, requiring maintenance in only one place. Once the specification is modified, the attendant software and data needs to be modified once to carry out the specification change.

The eleventh principle, then, is that:

The processes of the database system—in combination—represent all the business missions implied by the database domain.

16.4.1 Normalized Processes

A process is in "third normal form" if it has:

- Only one purpose
- No nested subprograms
- No logic branching based on data values

If the data transformation model contains only third normal form processes, there is no process specification redundancy. These processes must also be implemented as nonredundantly as possible. The benefit of process normalization (nonredundancy) is that since enterprise policy (translated into computer programs) is specified and implemented in only one place, understanding, documentation, design, programming, debugging, and maintenance all become much simpler.

The twelfth principle is that

To represent processes only once, all processes must be defined in third normal form.

16.4.2 Process Integrity Rules

The data integrity rules that result from process analysis supplement those specified in the data integrity model above.

16.5 Repository

A repository, as described in Chapter 3, is essentially a database application in which the stored values represent the data about the database systems rather than data about personnel, loans, securities, and the like. Ideally, the data about data, or metadata, is able to be accessed by the DBMS so that it can more effectively manage the database system environment. The repository is the live specification of systems in development, systems in production, and systems during evolution and maintenance. The thirteenth principle is that

A database application cannot be achieved successfully without the aid of a repository.

By achieved successfully, it is meant that the database system must not only be specified according to the principles specified above, it must also be implemented and maintained according to these principles. If a system is only specified according to these rules, but not implemented and maintained according to these rules, then disintegration is the result. Figure 16.1 provides a graphic that depicts the overall database project methodology architecture. The time spans allowable for database projects are provided in Figure 16.2. Figure 16.3 provides the percentage distribution of effort by project phase. Figure 16.4 illustrates that a database project can be specified all at once, but be successfully implemented in waves.

Major Database Project Phase	Database Project Components			
	Logical Database	Physical Database	Interrogation	System Control
Business Model Specification	Significant effort	Little or no effort	Basic sketches only	Data gathering to make fundamental decisions
Business Model Implementation	Finalized designs & all details	Significant effort, R&D, testing, etc.	Traditional design, test, debug, and documentation	Significant effort for design, implementation, and test
Business Model Operation & Maintenance	Ongoing maintenance	Minor adjustments	Typical new applications & maintenance	Significant command and control effort and activities

Figure 16.1. Effort estimates for particular phases and components of enterprise database.

Major Phase	Detailed Phase	Length
Business Model Specification	Preliminary Analysis	1-6 months
	Conceptual Specification	3-7 months
Business Model Implementation	Binding	1-2 months
	Implementation	5-17 months
Business Model Maintenance	Conversion & Deployment	1-2 months
	Production and Administration	3 months to system life

Figure 16.2. Personnel involved and time spans for enterprise database phases.

Major Database Project Phase	Detailed Phase	Database Component			
		Logical	Physical	Interrogation	System Control
		Percent within phase			
Business Model Specification	Preliminary Analysis	100	N.A.	N.A.	N.A.
	Conceptual Specification	70	10	10	10
Business Model Implementation	Binding	5	30	5	60
	Implementation	10	35	20	35
Business Model Maintenance	Conversion & Deployment	N.A.	N.A.	N.A.	N.A.
	Production and Administration	10	15	50	25
	Overall Percentage	33	15	25	23

Figure 16.3. Percentage division of effort by project phase.

16.6 Why a Database Project Methodology?

A project's methodology is the set of steps required to develop the required set of products. For enterprise database, the various meta-models described in earlier chapters are the specifications of the required products. While all information systems methodology contains similar high-level steps, enterprise database, because it requires a special set of products, also contains a special set of steps.

An enterprise database methodology is needed because database is different from traditional data processing in seven significant ways. First, at the center of the database approach are databases, not reports. A database should never be designed to satisfy the needs of computer reports, but rather to enhance the orderly process of organizational decision making in some well-bounded area. The database thus becomes a computer-based model of that business area. Because it is a natural model, the fundamental design of the model lasts as long as the fundamental design of the business.

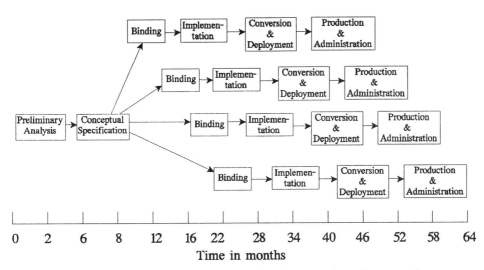

Figure 16.4. Enterprise database project implementation phases and iterations.

Second, the database is designed by users within the business. Since they know the organization best, they are uniquely qualified to design the database. The resultant design is a complete, user-defined, enterprise-policy-based specification of the organization for which it is being created. A database design is not a feat of technology but rather the practice of common sense.

Third, if the database project team has access to a relational-like DBMS, the database approach can greatly benefit from the building of a prototype of the entire database system during the first phase of the project. With a dynamic DBMS, this can be accomplished in a few weeks, with changes taking only a few days. When this prototype is demonstrated to and employed by the users, necessary design changes become obvious and a revised prototype can be demonstrated in a short time. This cycle of prototyping continues until the system design becomes stable. Then, and only then, is it time to proceed with the implementation of the operational specification.

Fourth, with the database approach, computer-generated reports (excluding interfaces to other automated systems) assume their lesser level of importance. This is because the goal of a database project is the design and implementation of the database. Only after the database has been designed and its physical database and system control components fully implemented is it time to begin work on the interrogation modules (reports). Because report modules are not part of the database project's critical path, they can be generated and altered without disturbing the design or operation of the database.

This fourth difference demonstrates an important dissimilarity between traditional systems and systems designed through the database approach. The traditional system design is today's use of data, whereas the database approach to system design is focused on the fundamental business policies that dictate data organization and structure. The former is like building a system on a foundation of shifting sands; the latter is like building on time-tested granite.

A fifth difference occurs because many DBMSs have multiple interrogation languages, and users are able to avail themselves of nontechnical query languages, semitechnical procedure-oriented languages, report writers, and very complex compiler languages such as COBOL and FORTRAN to greatly enhance the production of computer programs for data entry, reporting, calculations, and the like.

Sixth, the traditional approach requires the expenditure of about 85 percent of all the money and time allocated for system development before the design can be demonstrated. Changes required at that point are both expensive and time-consuming. Each change postpones the system delivery date.

The database approach, on the other hand, encourages the creation of design hypotheses and changes before system implementation. Only when the design becomes stable should implementation be considered. At that time, the system's delivery date can be predicted with confidence for these reasons:

- The design has already been shown to be correct.

- It is left to the user to write all or most of the ongoing interrogation subsystems using any of the DBMS language alternatives.

The seventh difference is in system maintenance. The database is designed on a foundation of organizational knowledge; thus changes to it should be minor. Major changes occur only when the database has not been correctly designed initially or when there is a fundamental change in the nature of the business. The first can be prevented; the second seldom occurs. Reports do change, but since they are not a critical part of the database system, the effect of such changes is not significant. And with the advent of sophisticated natural languages, old reports can be modified easily and new reports can be constructed in a few hours. In short, maintenance is part of the database approach to system design; because of this, changes become evolutions of systems, not revolutions.

Since a database project has as its goal the creation of a centralized, common database for all pertinent processes rather than a centralized set of processes that interact with data, it follows that a methodology designed to enhance the development of process based systems is not appropriate (except in a general way) to design a data-based system. With the emergence of high-quality, packaged information systems, the package decision is no longer just restricted to word processors, DBMSs, or spreadsheets. Entire sophisticated application packages in finance, human resources, and manufacturing are now available and should be seriously reviewed before proceeding with an information system's

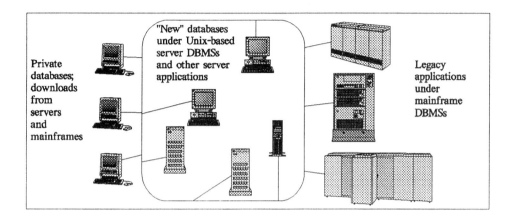

Figure 16.5. Common enterprise database architecture.

implementation. Regardless of which implementation alternative is chosen, a quality work plan must be developed.

16.7 Today's Systems Environment

Figure 16.5 illustrates a common information systems architecture that is found in businesses today. There is a mixture of mainframe legacy systems, a series of new client/server systems, and a large quantity of PC-based systems. It is not uncommon for these systems to have been developed over 20 to 30 years with varying types of technologies.

The characteristics of *old-time* systems are those characteristics that are presented in Section 16.6, giving rise to the development of a database project methodology. Old-time methods of the 1970s produced systems exhibiting these problem characteristics:

- No central, technology-independent design

- Each database has self-contained policy, allowing policy conflicts across databases

- No interdatabase data integrity

- Redundant data with different time synchronization

- No update synchronization for critical systems

- Ad hoc change requests; no central planning, management, and control

With the advent of sophisticated commercial-off-the-shelf application packages for bread-and-butter commercial applications like human resources, finance, and manufacturing, it is becoming common for organizations to acquire these packages as an alternative to a major upgrade from mainframe to client/server. Given that a common environment of mixed mainframe and client/server is presented in Figure 16.5, an all client/server environment can be depicted in Figure 16.6. What this figure presents that is different from Figure 16.5 is that the network has been expanded to include more servers, and the mainframes have disappeared. But what does this change in technology solve in and of itself? Nothing! In fact, it complicates the environment significantly. All the problem characteristics listed above still exist. Added to these are the following additional problems:

- Multiple databases containing distributed data of the same subject matter without update, backup, or reporting synchronization

- Ad hoc change requests that may move a consistent set of distributed database semantics and processing programs away from an initial central design to discordant semantics and design

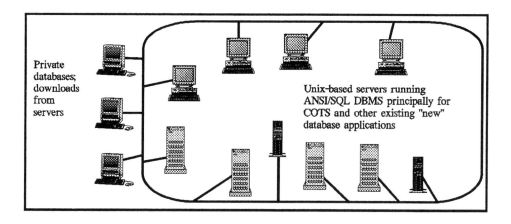

Figure 16.6. Effects of COTS seen as a silver bullet on enterprise database architecture.

Distributed processing has resurrected two problems that were previously thought to have been *killed*! They are:

- Centralized semantics
- Controlled redundancy

When commercial database first appeared in earnest in the early 1970s, one of the objectives of the DBMS proponents was to have centralized semantics and controlled redundancy. No longer would the meaning of data and the rules that controlled its values be stored in programs. No longer would there be multiple sets of files without centralized redundancy control. Semantics would be stored in THE database. Each enterprise would have its one centralized MIS and database. Well, it didn't work out that way, and the data processing situation of today dangerously parallels the situation of the late 1960s and early 1970s. The only difference is that we have replaced multiple, disjoint files with multiple disjoint databases.

DBMSs of the 1970s through the mid-1980s offered facilities that were significantly more advanced over the facilities available in programming languages in the 1960s and 1970s. During the mid-1980s through the early 1990s, however, DBMS took a significant step *backwards* through the adoption of the IBM-proposed relational model. While additional capabilities were gained in query flexibility, significant functionality losses were sustained in the areas of brute processing speed, data integrity, consistency, security, concurrent operations, and backup and recovery. Only recently have DBMSs started to regain those lost facilities. Referential integrity, standardized in DBMSs in the early 1970s and contained in the ANSI/NDL standard by 1980, did not become standard in ANSI/SQL until 1989. It is almost 1994, and referential integrity is only now becoming available in commercially popular relational DBMSs. That is 20 years after being commonly available in network and hierarchical data model DBMS [22]!

Now, with the advent of client/server architectures, the foundations just rebuilt are about to be lost again. DBMSs of the early 1990s are not fully capable of controlling distributed semantics or controlling consistency and redundancy as can DBMSs that control nondistributed data. While improvements are being made in DBMSs, it will not be until the turn of the century before high-quality, effective, efficient client/server distributed DBMS facilities will be in place.

Notwithstanding the above, a start must be made to achieve the highest control possible over distributed semantics. A necessary first step is to build the seven models described in Chapters 4 through 10. These models will then contain the technology-independent versions of these critical enterprise database building blocks. Figure 16.7 presents four levels of abstraction of a data model. The highest level, abstract, is too vague to be useful. The second level, high-level, is detailed

---

[22]   Michael M. Gorman, *Database Management Systems: Understanding and Applying Database Technology:* Wellesley, MA. QED Information Sciences, 1991, Chapter 3.

only down to the name of the entities, which may or may not be ready for third normal form attribution and quality checking. The third level, detailed, is in third normal form but is yet technically independent. To specify in third normal form is not the same as implementing in third normal form. The fourth level of detail, implemented, shows three different versions of technology mapping of the two detailed tables: P.O._Header and P.O._Line. Adabas, an independent logical file data model DBMS,[23] implements both tables as part of a single logical file. COBOL also allows a header-trailer file definition. ANSI/SQL requires that the tables be implemented separately.

The right level of data modeling is at the detailed level and not at the other levels for the reasons explained in the last column of Figure 16.7.

Figure 16.8 illustrates a strategy to control data semantics. All databases are implementations of the detailed form of data modeling. In the center of the distributed database environment illustrated in Figure 16.8 is the repository. Its control must be all-inclusive to the extent that:

- All data must be defined with its semantics centrally controlled.

- All captured data must first have its granularity and precise values (if they are to be controlled) being governed.

- All data combinations from disjoint sources must first be predefined through rules for engagement.

While these rules appear *and are* tyrannical, the facilities of DBMS necessary to make such manual rules automatic do not yet exist. When they exist, these rules will still have to be defined, but their enforcement will appear to be automatic.

The benefits of imposing such strong control is illustrated in Figure 16.9. This figure shows the three relevant levels of data models (high-level, detailed, and implemented). At the detailed level are iconic representations of both data and database process models for employee, purchase order, and contract. This detailed level along with the other models are then transformed into client/server applications. The employee becomes part of distributed human resources as well as part of corporate-wide project cost accounting. The purchase order is part of corporate-wide project cost accounting and a corporate-wide finance server. The contract is only represented in the corporate-wide finance server.

The value of this strategy is that the semantics are completely defined for all seven models (Chapters 4 through 10) down to the technology-independent detailed level. They are then transformed, as necessary, into implementation versions (the last three models, Chapters 11 through 13). And, as shown in Figure 16.8, they are all known and controlled through the single corporate repository.

---

[23] Ibid, Section 3, Data Models

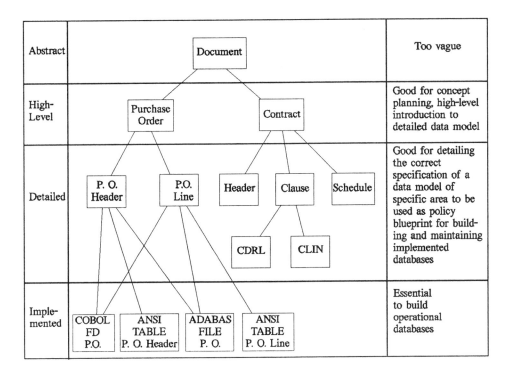

Figure 16.7. Necessity for multiple data architecture levels.

If this type of environment is installed, the problems listed at the beginning of this section can be addressed as follows:

- There will be centralized, abstract database designs, which are then detailed and implemented; they are consistent and top-down.

- COTS database differences can be known and bridged to eliminate and/or control conflicts.

- NonCOTS databases can have policy-consistent database designs.

- All databases can have data integrity through known implementation mappings.

- Redundant data can be controlled and updates time synchronized.

- Update synchronization for critical systems can be achieved through centralized planning and through an overall systems model.

- Outside vendor changes to COTS packages can be planned and controlled through DBMS component changes and through software generation of critical COTS components.

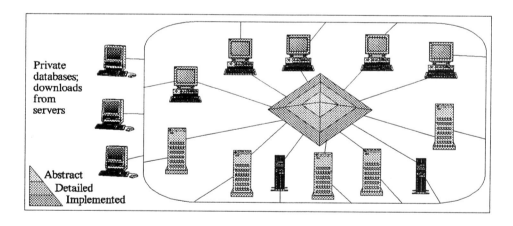

Figure 16.8. Repository based enterprise database architecture.

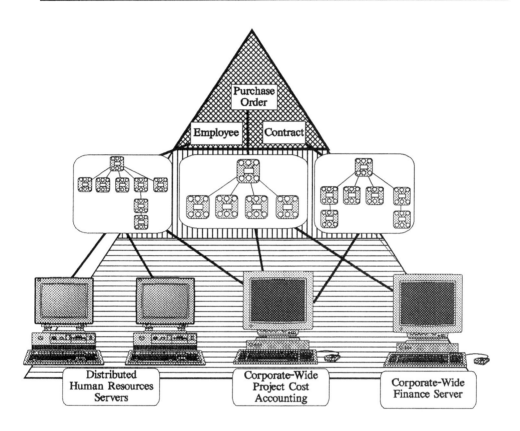

Figure 16.9. Distributed data architecture with consistent semantics.

17

THE MAKE, GENERATE OR BUY DECISION

Once the enterprise has completed the mission and a high level of the data model (entities only, without attribution), it is ready to start discrete projects for easily separable areas. An easily separable area is one that is either a significant originator of data or one for which the data is quite self-contained.

Implementing through pragmatic units versus the *big bang* approach allows for the benefits of database to be realized quickly while retaining a good measure of control and flexibility.

The necessary first step in each of these pragmatic projects is to complete the seven models. Completed then will be a mission-area-scoped, detailed data model, database process, information systems, business event, business function, and business organization. Once this is complete, a *make, generate, or buy* decision can be made concerning functionally acceptable application packages.

For the purposes of definition, *make* means the complete software development route, that is, detailed design, coding, and unit testing along with overall system testing and integration. *Generate* means that the metadata from the seven models and security can be readily fed into a sophisticated software package and that the complete software system is generated through vendor-provided software generation facilities. While individual tools may exist for screen design, report specification, and the like, *generation* here means the entire software application: screens, menus, calculations, reports, and so forth. Under this technique, knowledge workers develop, to a large extent, the first seven models, and the generator creates the remaining three models.

Buy means that the application system is ready to use once it is installed. The PC has made this market. Simply, the package represents all 10 of the models. PC based packages are available for almost every imaginable purpose: finance, human resources, word processing, spreadsheets, telecommunications, scheduling, project management, and so on. There are two big differences among all these packages:

- Single user versus multiple user
- The breadth, scope, and extent of tuning

The older and more complicated the business is, the greater are the requirements in these two areas. For the PC, single-user, simple accounting systems (G/L, A/P, A/R, Inventory, and Cash) can be purchased for $150. For the client/server environment, multiple-user, very sophisticated packages can cost well over $250,000.

Variations on the make, generate, or buy alternatives are becoming available. For example, rather than just being able to buy a generator, and then creating and feeding it with the organization's developed seven models, some software vendors are creating fully developed, functionally rich application packages with generators, and then marketing not the finished package but the generator and the installed metadata. In this form, the organization merely has to modify the generator-installed metadata and regenerate the application systems environment. This, for example, is the business strategy of Oracle Corporation with its human resources, financial, and manufacturing applications. For Oracle, the generators obtain all their metadata from Oracle/CASE.

If the make, buy, or generate decision is made too early, there will not be sufficient knowledge to correctly discriminate among the packages. As evidence, many organizations evaluate application packages solely based on the vendor's ability to meet their functional requirements (e.g., provide reports, promote end user access). Rarely, for example, are the package's data structures examined to determine if compatibility exists with the organization's way of doing business. Because of too-early picks, it is not uncommon to hear of a business buying a package and then spending from two to ten times the package's purchase price to have the package *fit the business*.

Once a package is picked, for example in the financial area, it can take up to 10,000 staff hours to finally install the package. Why so long as compared to a word processing package? After all, are not both commercial-off-the-shelf (COTS) packages? It is because of the quantity of different sets of reference tables (from 20 to 60), the number of specialized reports (100 to 200), the number of pair-wise validations (on a four-part validation it is can be thousands and thousands, which all have to be examined, determined, and set into place within the package).

It is important to understand the role of a COTS package. Simply put, if the business has no real position on how a business function is accomplished, then the COTS package becomes the defining strategy and implementation vehicle for the business function. This would be the case if a business was new, and if COTS packages were procured right from the beginning.

For most large businesses, however, procuring a COTS package is either an alternative to large-scale systems development or an alternative for a large-scale systems upgrade, for example, when migrating from mainframe to client/server. In this latter case, it is important to understand how few work steps are actually avoided. In terms of time and funds, a great deal is avoided. A COTS finance package could take as much as five years to develop with a team of 15 to 20. That would be a cost of well over $15 million. A COTS package changeover alternatively could be accomplished in two years or less with about 10 staff. That would be a cost of about $3 million. The savings is *potentially* substantive, and the time saving is 60 percent. However, if all the work steps are not accomplished, the whole effort could well be wasted. Appendix 2 contains a listing—at a very high level—of the critical tasks involved in a complete database project. Italicized are those steps that can be avoided by taking the COTS route. While the quantity of italicized steps seems few, they are time-consuming and costly indeed.

17.1 Definition: Functionally Acceptable

Because of this great amount of effort to tailor a package to fit an organization, a new definition of functional acceptability is needed. An application package is *functionally acceptable* if it meets the *majority* of both the data and business processing needs of the organization. These needs are defined in the six models: mission, data, database process, information system, business event, and business function. If a package is functionally acceptable, the organization should proceed to the next step of procurement.

If a package is only somewhat functionally acceptable, the organization must decide to either change the package to fit the rules of business or change the business to fit the rules of the package. In order to evaluate this decision, the following guidelines are offered:

- If the package is DBMS generator-based and, once tailored, can be made to regenerate the actual information systems, it is cost-effective to change the package.

- If the package is DBMS-based and is developed with natural (4GL) languages for data entry, processing, and reporting, it is cost-effective to change the package.

- If the package is not DBMS-based, nor generated, it may be cost-effective to change the rules of the business. Regardless, this package should be the only other alternative to *make* with a 3GL.

Less important is whether the package contains a full complement of reports since they can be obtained via report writers. *If, however, the basic data structures are not present to support the fundamental business needs, an overabundance of reports and the package's use of a DBMS has no value as a counterbalance.* This needs to be stated again:

> *If, however, the basic data structures are not present to support the fundamental business needs, an overabundance of reports and the package's use of a DBMS has no value as a counterbalance.*

17.2 Quality DBMS Packages

Unfortunately, it is not sufficient for application packages to be simply functionally acceptable and to utilize a DBMS. To be effective they must be based on a consistent set of semantics. If this is not the case, integration will not be achieved and the DBMS will revert to being used as an access method, thus negating its real value. In order to determine the possibility of integration, the following questions should be asked of package vendors:

- Do the data elements, tables, columns, relationship definitions, data integrity rules, and so forth, for all the applications under investigation have the same semantics?

- Do the semantics of the packages exist in a form that can be loaded into the DBMS's integrated repository system?

If application package vendors cannot affirmatively answer these two questions, then procuring these nonquality packages is merely a method of leapfrogging over application database development right into application database implementation.

Given these differences, if a package is available that both interfaces with a DBMS and satisfies the data and implied processing requirements of a project, it would be wise to procure that package.

As a final but very important difference, DBMS-based packages, if properly developed, enable the manufacturing of new information from existing data. That is because the semantics are data-based rather than program-based.

17.3 Package Conversion Versus Custom Software

If a quality DBMS-based package is not available, it is probably cheaper to create the custom software utilizing the site's DBMS than to convert a nonDBMS-based package for the following reasons:

- An analysis would have to be made of all the files handled by the package to determine the most efficient manner of converting the package's data model.

- Schemas and views would have to be constructed for all programs to utilize.

- All programs would have to be analyzed to discern the "real" program logic from the logic that serves as the access strategy, concurrent operations, and the like.

- The DBMS access logic would have to be installed in the programs.

- DBMS system control facilities would have to be installed, including privacy, audit trails, backup and recovery, row locking strategies, and the like.

In short, it is not difficult to see that the total cost of all analyzing, recasting, and code removal is likely to far exceed the cost of implementing the functionality of the package in a well-appointed DBMS.

17.4 True Costs of NonDBMS Packages

If a package is desired, and if an organization already has a nonDBMS version of the package, an analysis should be made of the true cost to keep the data outside the database versus the cost to acquire the DBMS version of the package. The costs of keeping a nonDBMS version of the package include:

- Not being able to integrate data with database data

- Not being able to access the data through natural languages (except through nonDBMS vendor report writers)

- Not possibly having the sophistication of:

    Concurrent operations
    Backup and recovery
    Transaction rollback
    Security and privacy

- Increased maintenance costs by the vendor because the vendor lacks the DBMS's ease of change capabilities

- Increased maintenance costs by the vendor due to the required inclusion of the following in many programs:

    Access strategy logic
    Physical storage management
    Transaction rollback
    Concurrent operations

A well-engineered DBMS version of the same application package has none of these extra costs. Additionally, many of the modules of a DBMS-based package may be written in natural languages, which both lowers acquisition cost and subsequent maintenance costs, and makes changes significantly easier.

17.5 Packages Procurement Strategy

Based on the foregoing, Figure 17.1 presents a tabular summary of the make, generate or buy factors. They are listed in decreasing order of preference. From this table, it should be crystal clear that it is never financially beneficial to purchase a functionally acceptable a COTS that is not DBMS-based application package. And, it should go without saying, to custom develop an application without DBMS assistance should never be an alternative.

Decreasing Order of Preference	ANSI DBMS-Based	Functionally Acceptable	Developer	Development Environment
1	Yes	Yes	COTS Vendor	Repository & Generator
2	Yes	Mainly	COTS Vendor	Repository & Generator
3	Yes	Somewhat	COTS Vendor	Repository & Generator
4	Yes	Yes	COTS Vendor	4GL
5	Yes	Mainly	COTS Vendor	4GL
6	Yes	Somewhat	COTS Vendor	4GL
7	Yes	Yes	COTS Vendor	3GL
8	Yes	Yes	Self	Repository & Generator
9	Yes	Yes	Self	4GL

Figure 17.1. A tabular summary of the make, generate or buy factors.

17.6 Packages Environment

An application software package must coexist in an overall information systems and database architecture framework. Figure 17.2 illustrates such a framework with just one functional area devoted to a COTS package. Shown is the outside ring for common user access, and then a series of COTS packages (geodesic dome) that commonly access one or more databases. Given the DBMS technology of 1994, interDBMS data sharing is problematic at best. Thus the only really viable strategy would be for all the COTS packages to use the same DBMS. Surrounding the ring that represents a common, end user interface for data entry, updating, and reporting are a series of user access devices. These, through open systems networking protocols, can range from PCs (MAC's, IBM/PCs, or PC clones) to dumb terminals connected to servers.

This data collection software ring is practical only if all the packages are from one COTS vendor, and if the vendor had formally decided to implement the COTS-to-user interface in that manner.

The goal is that a completely open environment be established and that, once security screens are satisfied:

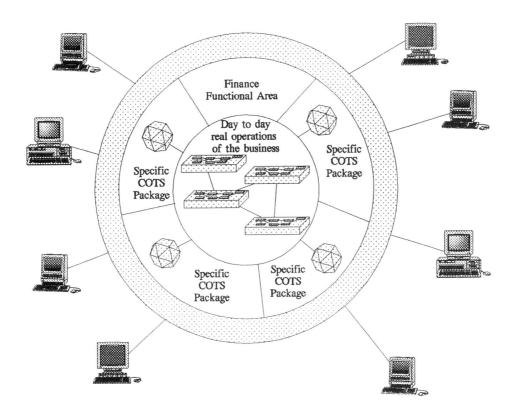

Figure 17.2. Functional area architecture employing COTS packages.

- Any terminal can access any form of commonly available computing resource. For example, any one can e-mail anyone else with document and diagram attachments.

- Anyone can access anyone else's PC-based terminal to run an application from that person's PC as if that person is a server and the accessing PC is a client.

- Anyone can access any server and access any data and any application package.

• Anyone can direct the output from any PC or server to any system printer.

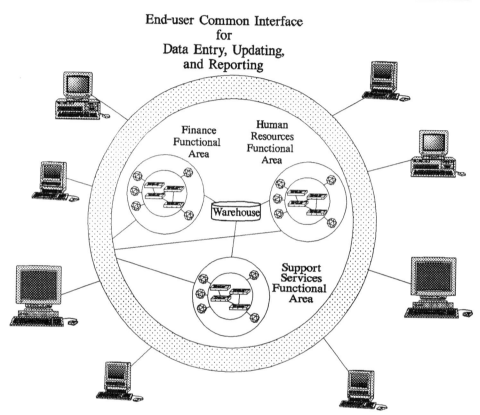

End-user Common Interface
for
Data Entry, Updating,
and Reporting

Finance Functional Area

Human Resources Functional Area

Warehouse

Support Services Functional Area

Figure 17.3. Three COTS-based functional area architectures with a common data entry interface and warehouse.

Figure 17.3 depicts two major functional areas, finance and human resources. The third area, support services, would support all forms of physical plant maintenance, computer supports, security, and the like. A common database called the warehouse is depicted as the location for all time-synchronized, longitudinal data.

It is essential, as stated above, that all the data from all the different COTS databases share the same semantics and also share a common granularity and time synchronization. If these databases do not share semantics, granularity, and time synchronization, then conversion programs, commonly called bridges, will have to be created. While COTS with bridges is better than a custom programming environment, it is not by much, because each bridge is an opportunity for delays, bugs, semantic mistranslations, ongoing maintenance, and so forth.

17.7 Packages Summary

If a business is starting, going with COTS is the only cost-effective route. Care must be taken, however, in the selection of the appropriate COTS package. The larger the business, the more complex the decision. Additionally, with the advent of client/server, issues of distributed processing, multiple DBMSs, and common user access must all be addressed.

Essential to a seamless COTS environment is the ability to maintain uniformity in data semantics, granularity, and time synchronization. Without integrity and overall consistency, rich functionality is completely useless.

18

WORK PLAN DEVELOPMENT

More software projects have gone awry for lack of calendar time than for all other causes combined. Why is this cause of disaster so common?

First, our techniques of estimating are poorly developed. More seriously, they reflect an unvoiced assumption which is quite untrue, i.e., that all will go well.

Second, our estimating techniques fallaciously confuse effort with progress, hiding the assumption that men and months are interchangeable.

Third, because we are uncertain of our estimates, software managers often lack the courteous stubbornness of Antoine's chef. [24]

Fourth, schedule progress is poorly monitored. Techniques proven and routine in other engineering disciplines are considered radical innovations in software engineering.

Fifth, when schedule slippage is recognized, the natural (and traditional) response is to add manpower. Like dousing a fire with gasoline, this makes matters worse, much worse. [25]

Enterprise database is developed through project plans that commonly employ work breakdown structures (WBS). A quality WBS involves six components. These are:

- W_vBS, that is, the activities to be performed
- W_nBS, that is, the products to be delivered
- PERT chart, a network chart showing precedence
- Unit effort estimates

---

[24] Written on the menu at Antoine's in New Orleans: "Good cooking takes time. If you are made to wait, it is to serve you better, and to please you." From Frederick P. Brooks, Jr., *The Mythical Man-Month*. Reading, MA: Addison-Wesley, 1975, page 13.

[25] Ibid, page 14.

- Factors affecting unit effort estimates
- Experience feedback cycles

18.1 Understanding WBSs

The term *work breakdown structure* is commonly employed in projects. Its first word, *work*, if not understood by all, can lead to significant confusion. Within the U. S. Department of Defense community, the word *work* is a noun. Thus, the term work breakdown structure implies a hierarchical decomposition of the actual product being delivered.

In data processing, the term work breakdown structure is also commonly employed in projects, but it is used as a verb! Thus, in DP, the term work breakdown structure implies a hierarchical breakdown of the activities.

The misunderstanding is not so bad, however, because in the continuous flow model in Figure 14.1 in Chapter 14, both types (verbs and nouns) are employed. The phrases that comprise the process bubbles are verbs, the set of W_vBS. In the repository, the storage location of the products of an MIS project, the breakdown is really a W_nBS. While the two are not the same, they are definitely related, for example, *Plan the Project* and *Project Plan*.

There is, therefore, a strong correlation between activity lists (W_vBS) and product lists (W_nBS). Not surprisingly, if one project's product list is different from another project's product list, the two activity lists are also likely to be different. This leads to the conclusion that since there are different and valid product lists (W_nBS), there must also be different and valid methodologies (W_vBS). The appropriate pairing of a W_nBS with an appropriate W_vBS is given this notation: $W_{n\&v}BS$.

> *For any particular project, then, if its product list is fundamentally different from that of another project, the methodologies must also be different.*

In addition to pairing appropriate sets of $W_{n\&v}BS$ for specific projects, multiple customers may require, for example, MISs in different subject areas. For example, one client had an MIS project for Government Grant and Loan Accounting. Another client had an MIS project for Program, Planning, and Budgeting (PPBS). While both projects are MISs, and both could have been developed through the same database project methodology, each client wanted to see *their own personalized* work plan. A $W_{n\&v}BS$ needed to be developed for each customer, that is, one for the Grants MIS and another for the PPBS customer. While the customers may be satisfied, a contractor performing the work will appear to have undertaken very different projects when, in fact, the structure and format of the real work products and the methodology employed are essentially the same. Lost from the contractor will be any internal attempt to measure work accomplishment or performance across MIS projects, and any benefits from common training, use of a multiple-project repository, and the like.

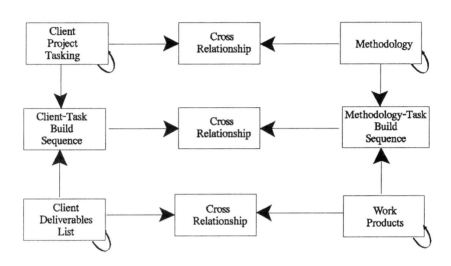

Figure 18.1. Interrelationship between standard and client work breakdown structures.

These losses can be avoided if the contractor first has its own $W_{n\&v}BS$ for MISs. From this internal MIS $W_{n\&v}BS$, the contractor can build relationships between its own $W_{n\&v}BS$ and that of the customer. Figure 18.1 presents a diagram that portrays such a set of relationships. Such an arrangement permits contractor methodologies to be evaluated, improved, and audited over many years and against many projects.

18.2 Homogeneous $W_{n\&v}BS$

In Figure 18.1, a project's methodology is represented by the methodology meta-entity and recursive relationship on the right. The product list of the methodology is represented by the repository schema meta-entity and recursive relationship also on the right. As steps of the methodology produce product, intersection meta-entities (called the *Build Sequence*) are created.

The *Build Sequence* intersection table is more than just an intersection table because it must have a sequencing all its own so that the methodology and products can be accomplished in a specific project-logical order. Figure 18.2 illustrates a set of $W_{n\&v}BS$. The W_nBS is on the left and shows the breakdown of the conceptual design. Conceptual design may be the name of the overall product

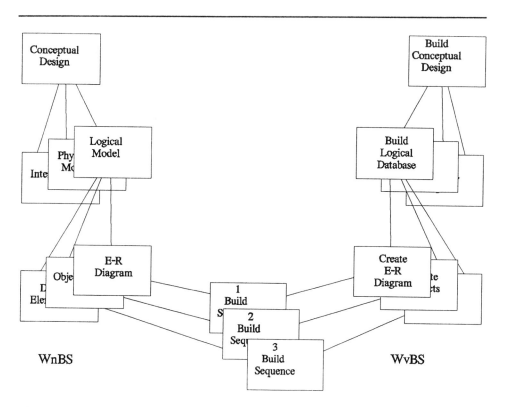

Figure 18.2. Interrelationships between W_nBS and W_vBS.

of the conceptual design phase. In a previous phase, Preliminary Analysis, there are other products such as mission model, high-level E-R diagrams, evaluation criteria, and so forth. In this hierarchy, three of the products, that is, logical model, physical model, and interrogation, are shown. Contained within the logical model are the E-R diagram, objects, and data elements.

On the right side of the figure is a W_vBS. It shows the verb sequence of *Build Conceptual Design* down through three of the steps within *Build Logical Database*. The intersection of the W_nBS and the W_vBS is shown at the bottom. Among the attributes contained in the Build Sequence table would be sequence, start date and time, and expected stop date and time. Other tables that could be attached to the build sequence table could be various time cards from staff members performing work. And, related to the various rows from the W_nBS table could be the actual work products themselves. For example, attached might be an entity-relationship diagram entity called Accounts Payable.

Analogous to the way the methodology and work products are organized and interrelated on the right side of Figure 18.1, the client's project tasking and deliverables list are represented on the left side. When requests for proposals

(RFPs) are issued, the buyer often issues what is on the left. *If the contractor is a quality contractor, the right side also already exists.* How to intersect the two? The intersection records, all labeled cross-relationships, provide the explanation.

Once the two $W_{n\&v}BS$ are created, a sophisticated contractor can quickly tell whether the RFP is one of quality. Assuming that the $W_{n\&v}BS$ of the contractor is valid, there will be a good match between the buyer's $W_{n\&v}BS$ and the seller's. If the match is not exact, four possibilities exist:

- The buyer is attempting to buy less than what is needed.
- The buyer is attempting to buy more than what is needed.
- The seller would build less than what is needed.
- The seller would build more that what is needed.

Regardless of which alternative exists, the discrepancies have to be examined and resolved before a quality proposal is generated and before a quality contract is consummated.

Contract performance disputes are almost always based on unknown mismatches between the client's and the contractor's $W_{n\&v}BS$.

Every project has a product list that is more or less unique. For projects with homogeneous product sets, for example, a human resources system and an operating system, the specific product list for the HR system is different from the product list for an operating system. Included in the differences would be the types of products, the types of tests, the interface products, and so forth. In this case, some of the products are likely to be the same in form but very different in content.

Additionally, there may be a difference in the significance of one product over another. For example, extremely detailed logic design is required before an operating system is coded, but only logic sketches are required for the HR system that is 4GL-based. Similarly, the database design section for the HR system requires significant effort, while the effort may be nonexistent for an operating system.

18.3 Heterogeneous $W_{n\&v}BS$

For heterogeneous projects, for example, a command and control system for the military, the product list includes software, hardware, training, documentation, quality measures, standards adherence, and so forth. Each of these products has a unique product list, that is, a unique W_nBS. Furthermore, a command and control system for the U. S. Air Force would be somewhat different than one for the Navy or the Army. A critical issue, then, is how to provide a unified $W_{n\&v}BS$ to the client for diverse product sets (W_nBS) and, by implication, diverse process sets (W_vBS).

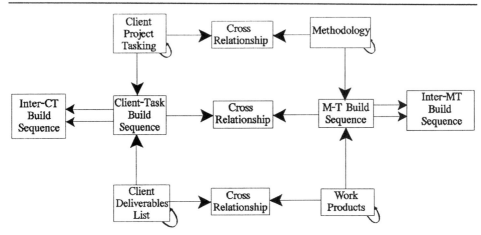

Figure 18.3. Interrelationships between multiple standard and client work breakdown structures.

Figure 18.3 shows the meta-structure of a repository to handle heterogeneous $W_{n\&v}BSs$. The center of the figure is the same as Figure 17.1 except that there are multiple hierarchies, one for each methodology. Similarly, there would be multiple subsets of the repository schema for each different product type. The additional meta-entities allow inter-W_nBS and inter-W_vBS relationships. Such relationships allow projects to identify, for example, the relationship between an HR data update subsystem, which is a product within an HR W_nBS, and a particular computing hardware subsystem from an appropriate hardware W_nBS. If the client's RFP is of quality, it too will have similar structures as depicted on the left side of Figure 18.3.

Figure 18.4 illustrates a heterogeneous set of $W_{n\&v}BS$. The project on the right side of the figure is a particular enterprise database project. From Figure 14.1 in Chapter 14, there could be a multiple of such projects underway. There would then be multiple sets of the right side of the diagram. Several might be for the concurrent development of detailed data models for particular aspects of an initial high-level E-R diagram effort. For example, there might have been the development of an overall E-R diagram that included the finance area, and then three to six smaller projects to develop detailed data models for accounts payable, procurement, receivables, general ledger, and cash flow management. Each of these projects would have their own W_vBS and would commonly contribute to different and to shared instances of the same W_nBS. There might also be, as depicted on the left side of the figure, a project underway to configure the overall set of hardware to accommodate an entirely new finance system. This, of course, cannot be done until the data and processing requirements of the various enterprise database projects are completed. Figure 18.4 thus shows how the $W_{n\&v}BS$ for each project type would be created, and then, as illustrated on the

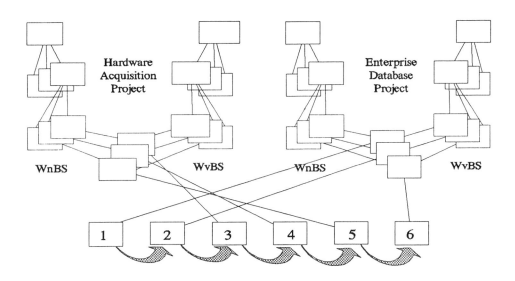

Figure 18.4. Interrelationships between heterogeneous $W_n BS$ and $W_v BS$.

bottom of Figure 18.4, the timing sequence of when all these project types should be finished.

Once all the various $W_{n\&v} BSs$ are developed, an overall schedule, satisfactory to both the client and the contractor, must be created. Figure 18.5 shows the meeting of the minds between the two parties. The two middle meta-entities at the ends show the client schedule and the contractor schedule. And, the meta-entity at the bottom shows the matching between the two schedules, or the detailed project schedule.

18.4 Work Plan Summary

The approach to database must be focused on only one objective: *the successful completion of a database project.*

A quality database project lifecycle provides a clearcut path, and a common-sense approach, to database projects. Using quality life cycles enables a project's costs and schedules to be accurately projected and managed. The controls imposed by a quality lifecycle enables the knowledge worker to identify what products are due, when they are due, and under what quality measures the products are judged. Because each product is well defined, project members can focus their

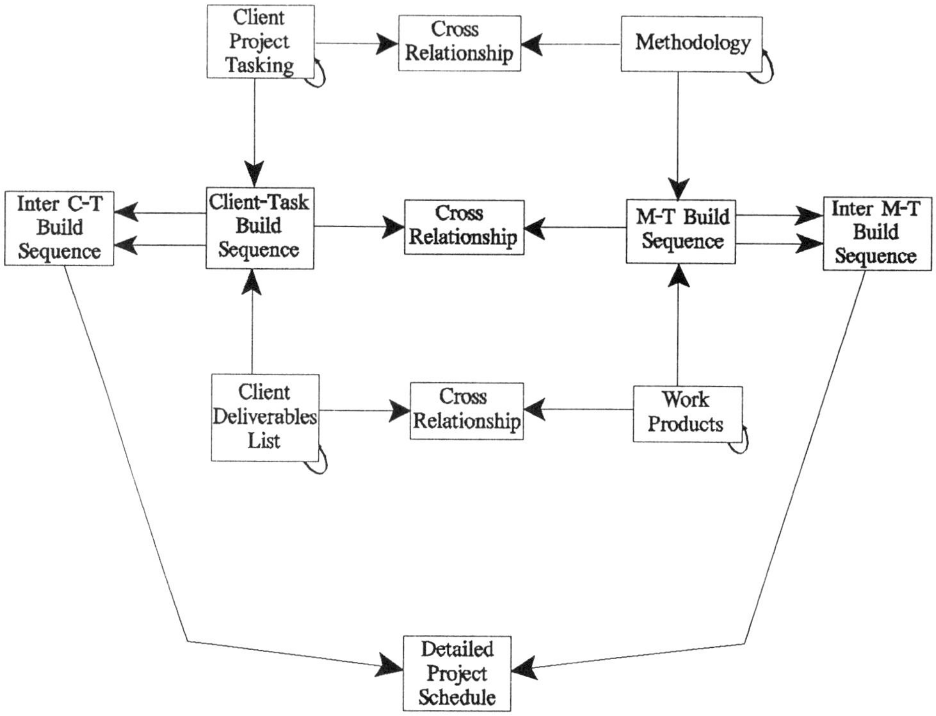

Figure 18.5. Interrelationships between $W_{n\&v}BS$, contractor and client schedules, and the overall resultant detailed project schedule.

work efforts. In short, knowledge work is accomplished more quickly and more accurately.

A quality lifecycle reduces project anxiety as each next step is already set down and is a logical consequence of the prior step. Again, sharply focused targets translate into quality work.

The methodology lifecycle, along with all the estimates, knowledge worker product specifications, actual products, and worker time cards indicating progress, must be stored in the repository. This ties project planning to product deliveries—in short, real project management and control. Because the repository is DBMS-based, cross-reference reports are easy to acquire.

A quality database environment, then, represents a complete solution to database needs. It represents the time-tested, rigorously defined products necessary for organizations to accomplish database projects successfully, the first time, and within budget.

The amount of work in creating a project plan and schedule, and then controlling and tracking a project through its entire lifecycle, should not be underestimated. Prudent project managers spend about 20-45 percent of the total project's cost on this task alone, depending on the overall size of the project. This means that on a ten *work* staff-year project, at least another two staff-years should be spent on its planning, scheduling, and ongoing control. Too little time causes:

- Bad initial estimates due to poor work assessments
- Inaccurate progress reporting during project execution
- Underdelivery of product, given required quality
- Underdelivery of quality, given required product

19

ENTERPRISE DATABASE PROJECTS

Most information systems are delivered late, over budget, and with less quality than promised. While there are a number of reasons, two can be immediately discarded:

- The staff is stupid
- Nobody works hard

While the quantity of remaining reasons are legion, two stand out: the work is underscoped, and the activities required to accomplish the work are both not well understood and are greatly underestimated. Hence the need for methodologies as a basis for estimating and for standard work practice.

19.1 Quality Methodology Characteristics

A quality methodology must exhibit the following five characteristics:

- It requires the correct set of products, no less and no more, and specifies the optimum build sequence.

- It has techniques for work accomplishment.

- It contains measures for judging work acceptability.

- It captures statistics about work performance.

- It interrelates project planning and progress reporting with actual products delivered.

Simply put, a methodology is a correctly sequenced set of hierarchically organized groups of work steps, each of which consists of a common-sense verb cluster that when followed results in a necessary and correct end product that exhibits maximum quality at the minimum cost.

Since the types of products required for a management information system are unique as compared to other types of systems, a methodology is acceptable if and only if it produces the correct product suite. If a methodology does not call for the creation of a necessary product, then the project team cannot help but be late, over-budget, and flat wrong.

While there any number of techniques for work accomplishment, the only ones acceptable are those that produce the correct products; for example, in the area of process modelling, since database projects use the product VIEW, the only correct interface between database process and entity is VIEW. Whether the process modelling technique uses square or round or rectangular process icons is unimportant; the fact that the process modelling techniques does not collect views and the associated ANSI/SQL syntax for materializing views is a critical flaw. The reason the flaw is critical is that database projects are not complete without views. And, the delivered product would have to be recast, thus making it underspecified, late, and of unacceptable quality.

When a product is delivered, there must be already existing measures to determine its acceptability. The more vague the measures, the longer is the evaluation, and the more unsure the evaluator, the more uneven is the evaluation of like products. If the measures are exact and published, the staff can work to the measures. This ensures that quality is built into the products right from the start.

Most projects are started with estimates that in hindsight are too ambitious. If the methodology contains sophisticated work-accomplishment mechanisms, as projects start to repeat themselves the estimates, based on collected statistics, will be more accurate.

Integration of promises with deliverables (or said another way, *the proof of the plan is in the delivery*) requires that the methodology be installed on the same platform as the repository. In this case, that means that the selected methodology must be installed as a series of extended meta-entity types in, for example, Oracle/CASE.

Such an installation, however, complicates the production of critical project management documents such as PERT, Gantt, and CPM. While that is true, most sophisticated project scheduling packages allow data importing and exporting. Thus, once a PERT is installed in Microsoft Project, for example, the WBS elements (PERT nodes) and associated resources (staff hours to perform a WBS element) can be exported to Microsoft Project from the repository through an SQL query such that Microsoft Project can then run the schedule (Gantt and CPM). Once the schedule is run, it can be exported from Microsoft Project and reimported into the repository. As work is accomplished, the work products can be tagged to the estimated quantities and percent accomplishment can easily be computed. Percent accomplishments are then exported from the repository to Microsoft Project as the necessary data for recomputing the project's schedule (new CPM and Gantt).

If the repository is enhanced to contain an appropriate methodology that supports the five characteristics cited above, accurate schedules and work cost estimates can be generated. These are critical to facilitate the software package make or buy decision. With estimation and scheduling licked, information systems can be delivered on time, at or under budget, and with the quantity and quality promised.

19.2 The Project's WBS

Each and every enterprise database project must employ a WBS that is localized and project-specific. The localized WBS identifies the specific products being built, staff interviewed, and named products produced. Chapter 18 provides an example of how to build a WBS that is both project-specific yet uses collections of standard work product development WBSs. The uniqueness of the individualized project WBSs provides three very important benefits:

- Project team ownership
- Independence from canned methodologies
- Individualized tailoring

Each project-unique WBS statement identifies, as lower levels, the standard set of tasks. Because of the standard tasks, work accomplishment statistics can be collected and compared to estimates and to other projects. Because of the standard work break-down structures:

- Projects are able to be accurately estimated because they use standard sets of activities.

- Products have standard formats and are related in already known ways.

- Training courses can be conducted that convey standard techniques.

- Work from different projects can be exchanged because they are accomplished through standard techniques and conform to standard quality reviews.

19.3 Typical Enterprise Database Projects

There are a number of discrete projects that accomplish enterprise database. Some projects are done only once, and others are done over and over. Some of the projects can only be done serially while others can be done in parallel. The following, alphabetically listed projects, are the typical set of enterprise database projects:

- Administrator Documentation
- Conceptual Specification
- Data Collection And Validation Systems
- Data Conversion
- Database Process Model
- DBMS Physical Database Specification And Implementation
- DBMS Schema And View Development

- DBMS Selection And Evaluation
- Detailed Data Model
- Emergency Maintenance
- Enterprise Model Audit
- Functional Area Implementation
- Functional Area Specification
- Functional COTS Implementation
- Functional COTS Selection
- Functional Prototype
- High-level Data Model
- Impact on Enterprise Model
- Implementation Strategy
- Interrogation Development
- Mission Model
- Repository
- Repository Evolution
- Standard Maintenance
- Standard Estimation
- System Control Implementation
- System Control Maintenance
- System Control Requirements
- System Documentation
- System Evolution
- User Documentation
- Warehouse

All projects, except the repository project presume the existence of a robust, online, and sophisticated repository environment that is available to all systems developers. Further, this enterprise database development environment requires that all system specifications be implemented, become operational, and/or are evolved only through standards, reviews, audits, and continuous evolution of enterprise metadata. The metadata that represents the enterprise's production databases and systems *is* correct. Any deviation, *is*, by definition, an error. If a mistake has been made in the specification, it must not be corrected exclusively by changing computer programs. The mistake must first be corrected in the specification before changing the computer programs. Simply put, changes to the specification must precede changes to the implementation.

As discrete application projects are started, two major assists must be provided. The first is to review the project's work plan to ensure that it produces the correct set of products for use in the evolution of the enterprise model. The second assist is to provide consulting assistance in the definition, formatting, and review of products that are necessary components of the enterprise model. In general, the seven steps are as follows:

1. Each application project creates a work plan that should be reviewed for sufficiency with respect to the enterprise model. Reviewed will be the correct inclusion of WBS steps, correct estimates for the generation of the WBS step products, and that there is sufficient time for review.

2. Each application development, acquisition or reengineering project creates a detailed/revised set of enterprise model components (data models, process models, etc.) to support its application. The model begins with the current subset of the enterprise model.

3. The project leader requests support at the beginning of the project. A staff member providing enterprise model component assistance is assigned to work with the project team to assist in the development of the enterprise model components and carry out the analysis required to detail, validate, and/or revise the model.

4. The detailed/validated/revised enterprise model component is peer-reviewed as part of the normal review process. Final review is the responsibility of the enterprise model function. Every effort is made to achieve consensus in the peer reviews before the final enterprise model review. The latter concentrates on ensuring that the model adheres to good practice, especially to standards. The final enterprise model review also resolves any open modeling issues from the peer-review process.

5. The reviewers of the detailed/validated/revised enterprise model components sign-off on the review, and (where practical) reviewers of previous versions of the model are asked to review the latest set of changes.

6. The detailed/validated/revised enterprise model components are installed into the then current development version of the repository.

7. As the application system enters the *test phase*, a review of the detailed/validated/revised enterprise model components is conducted to ensure that they conform to the components in the enterprise model repository. When the application system is migrated into production, the production repository of the enterprise model is updated to reflect the new production version of the enterprise model.

Each of these seven steps must be encoded as detailed WBS activities with unit effort estimates so that when volumes are determined, the required staffing can be easily created. Over time, as actual experience is recorded into the repository for these WBS activities, the estimates will become more accurate. Each project is briefly described.

19.3.1 Administrator Documentation

The administrator documentation project produces the critical information reports from all projects and all their developed work products from the repository. Given that all work products reside in the repository, the administrator's documentation consists of a hundred or so canned reports from the repository.

The only documentation outside the repository presentations to management. This should be minimal, and once the initial *selling* presentations are completed, most of the data for any management report should come directly from the repository.

19.3.2 Conceptual Specification

The conceptual specification project addresses the entire enterprise, which, depending on the organization's size and complexity, ranges from a few weeks to almost a year. The scope of the metadata for the conceptual specification project is that of the quantity of contained projects, which, listed in order of accomplishment are:

- Standard Project Estimation
- Repository
- Mission Model
- High-level Data Model
- Detailed Data Model
- Database Process Model
- Functional Area Specification
- System Control Requirements

19.3.3 Data Collection and Validation Systems

This project maps all enterprise forms to the repository and decomposes the forms to discover data elements. The project's main product is an enterprise-wide consistent set of semantics and a published set of directions for each corporate form to ensure high-quality data entry. This type of project is only practical if there is a generate or build decision for a significant majority of all the infrastructure systems. A single style of interface for all infrastructure systems is not possible if the decision is to buy, that is, to acquire commercial off the shelf software (COTS). That is because each COTS system is likely to have its own:

- Built-in data model

- Built-in, COTS-specific semantics that are either programmed or are drawn from internally stored reference data

- Multiple levels of data built into the internally maintained databases

- Internalized method of data capture that is interactive either on the screen level with multiple screens per transaction, or within the control of the screen

If the organization chooses the build or generate decision, then all existing enterprise data collection forms must be evaluated to ensure that they are still needed. For those that are, a PC-based data entry system that collects data and ensures consistent semantics for all entered data should be developed.

PC-based standard data collection systems that collect data from standard data collection forms are interconnected to be able to transmit data from site to site to expedite processing. The total collection of PC data collection application databases then becomes an enterprise-wide data collection system that obtains and places data into standard formatted data collection databases, which, in turn, are read by various legacy systems or developed systems.

This project is practical only if there is a large quantity of custom software development. For COTS packages, each is likely to come with its own set of data collection and validation software; thus this project type is unworkable.

19.3.4 Data Conversion

A data conversion project presumes the existence of production computer systems. There are two types of conversion projects:

- One-time
- Recurring

A one-time data conversion project presumes that data is being extracted from a set of computer files, and is taken through a number of steps that make it suitable for batch loading into a new production system.

Typical problems that must be overcome are conflicting semantics, for example, different quantities of codes for essentially the same data. One personnel system may have only two termination codes: voluntary and involuntary. Another personnel system may have a dozen or more. Each set must be determined, and a policy must be developed for each.

Another common problem is conflicting data. Employee addresses can be different. Which is more current? The basis for determining a definitive set may ultimately require accessing the payroll system, on the presumption that employees make sure that their yearly income tax records go to the correct address.

Another problem is missing data. Emergency names and phone numbers are missing. How is that to be collected? Does the new employee database process transaction prevent the entry of data if any is missing? If yes, then what about the bulk load from the old personnel system?

Data conversion projects can seldom be estimated correctly. Because of this, an experiment should be conducted that compares the total cost of understanding and repairing data versus recollecting the data. For the noncritical business data, it just might be faster and cheaper to recollect data rather than to discover errors and repair them.

Each automated file that is to remain permanent must be examined and an analysis made to correctly determine the bidirectional semantics. While it is simple to say that data conversion programs must be built to convert data from one set of semantics to another and then back again, it may be impossible to do so. For example, if data specificity is going from a more specific format to a less specific format, it becomes impossible to perform the backwards conversion.

19.3.5 Database Process Model

The database process model is the set of metadata that represents the necessary processes to keep a database in a consistent state, that is, without error.

The most critical component of the database process model is the transaction. It contains of one or more update (add, delete, or modify) processes that transforms the database from one consistent state to another. The transaction must be based on stated policy for correct values at the column level, and then at the table level, and then at the intertable level. Policies are expressed as data integrity rules.

The collection of data integrity rules are implemented differently from one DBMS to the next, and differently depending on the location of data.

19.3.6 DBMS Database Specification and Implementation

The DBMS physical database specification and implementation project consists of those activities that transform a completely specified database into a design that is suitable for a specific DBMS.

The data model of the DBMS is a critical characteristic that must be addressed. To ensure that the specified data model created through the Detailed Data Model Project work plan can be transformed into any DBMS' data model, it is in third normal form to ensure maximum specificity. If the data model is an independent logical file (e.g., Adabas, Focus, or Model 204) data model, then each *file* is able to contain vectors and repeating groups.

Hierarchical and network DBMSs, e.g., FOCUS, IMS, and IDMS are able to have many levels of nested structures. To guarantee discrimination among data instances within each structure, it is always preferable to create a relative primary key. A relative primary key is one that ensures that the instances within a structure (e.g., projects within a department, or addresses within an employee) are distinguishable.

In addition to physical database design development, all the data integrity rules would be examined to determine which can be implemented directly through schema clauses (referential integrity and action clauses), and which can be implemented through assertions, triggers, and stored procedures. While assertions, triggers, and stored procedures are all ANSI/SQL terms, these facilities are commonly available in nonANSI/SQL DBMSs.

19.3.7 DBMS Schema and View Development

The DBMS schema and view development project is one that produces the data definition languages necessary for the DBMS to then build the physical database. The activities include the actual transformation from specifications to the DBMS required language and sufficient testing to ensure that the desired physical database exists at the end of the effort. Included in this effort is the accomplishment of any operating system file allocation and formatting.

While DBMS schema is generally a one-time, low-maintenance activity, view generation is on-going. There are two extremes to view development: one view to serve all reasons, and a different view for every reason. Clearly, some happy medium must be accomplished. The goal of the view effort is to prevent the programmer from having to know about the implemented database's physical model. Such separation enables maximum data independence during the continuous evolutions that database designs undergo to serve the unfolding needs of the organization.

19.3.8 DBMS Selection and Evaluation

The DBMS selection and evaluation project enables the selection of the most appropriate DBMS for the current database application. Because of ANSI/SQL, there can finally be multiple DBMSs, each representing different performance characteristics that are able to be employed using standard languages.

Selection and evaluation of a DBMS should be on its internal characteristics, such as sophisticated index design, variety of physical database design tuning, and the like.

19.3.9 Detailed Data Model

The detailed data model project occurs after the high-level data model is complete. The detailed data model can be based on just a subset from the high-level enterprise data model. Even if the detailed data model is created for the entire enterprise, it is developed as a natural outgrowth of the entities contained in the high-level data model.

Each entity in the detailed data model is developed to third normal form. Hence these entities are as rigorously defined as third normal form relational tables. Because the detailed data model can be expressed as a table, it is not unacceptable to use the ANSI/SQL language as the linguistic mechanism. Simply because ANSI/SQL3 provides a rich set of facilities to express all the necessary components of a fully defined data model, it should be used. Another reason to use ANSI/SQL3 is because it is internationally known and unambiguous.

19.3.10 Emergency Maintenance

An emergency maintenance project is used to accomplish emergency maintenance to an existing database application. Once the emergency fix is developed, a standard maintenance project is automatically started. The standard maintenance project starts with the knowledge of the emergency maintenance fix, and then accomplishes the fix through the activities of a standard maintenance project. This ensures that the proper changes are made to the metadata contained in the repository.

19.3.11 Enterprise Model Audit

The complete set of metadata contained is the correct set of specifications, even if they are wrong! If the software is implemented correctly, but differs from the metadata contained in the repository, then by definition, the software is wrong!

Enterprise model audits consists of obtaining specifications for production software and comparing them to the output of the production software. If, for example, the specifications say that only valid state codes are allowed for addresses, then a transaction with an invalid state code would ensure that an invalid state code is not allowed. For existing data, an SQL query can produce the set of unique valid state codes that are being used. These can be compared to a list to ensure they are correct.

Each work product must be audited. Sometimes, the audit consists of a review by functional experts to make sure that the correct policy is in fact installed. For example, carefully contrived data may have to be run through a complex systems environment to ensure that correct answers are produced. The metadata contained in the repository should clearly indicate which procedures are to be executing. A set of data can be fed into a test version of the system that, when processed fully, indicates all the tests that were run and the results.

19.3.12 Functional Area Implementation

A functional area implementation project presumes that a functional area specification project has been completed and that the following set of metadata already exists:

- Mission
- Data
- Database process

The mission model should be complete for the entire enterprise. The data model should at least be at a high level, and if any of it is detailed, a good part of the database processes for the detailed data model components should be finished.

Further, upon analysis of the requirements for the functional area, all the necessary metadata already exists for the information systems model. That is, all the required screens, reports, and files metadata already exists. The information system implementation project thus consists of generating the actual information system components and assembling then into the appropriate sequences within the set of manual activities that address the functional area.

19.3.13 Functional Area Specification

A functional area is a particular set of activities that may stand alone or be part of a larger set. The total set of activities accomplishes a complete business purpose. For example, a functional area might embrace all the activities associated with accounts payable or accounts receivable. The domain of activities can be somewhat arbitrary.

Regardless of size and complexity, a functional area project causes a set of information systems to be developed to accomplish the functional area activities, or causes modifications to some information systems and the use of others. The only real question is whether the project is merely an implementation project or first a specification project.

A functional area implementation project presumes that the following models already exist:

- Mission
- Data
- Database process

When a functional area is identified for specification and/or implementation, both its required processes and data must be discovered. This is usually accomplished by performing a functional decomposition of the required activities. Functional decomposition is a well-known technique that is used to discover both data requirements and process logic. This expedition is usually accomplished outside-in. That is, the screens, reports, file operations, etc., appropriate for the function are identified and decomposed. Once these are entered into the repository in the appropriate subordinate models within the information systems model, their requirements are matched against the existing set of metadata that represents either production systems or systems that are in development. Three cases are possible, which, in increasing order of probability, are:

- Nothing exists

- All the data, database processes, and information system components already exist

- Some exist and some need to be developed

The first case, nothing exists, should be quite rare. What that really means is that the mission model completely missed a functional area of the enterprise. If the mission model is acceptably done, all the functional areas should be either directly addressed or certainly inferred. Under the assumption that the mission description missed the functional area, then not only must the functional area be developed, but so also must be the following models with respect to the functional area:

- Mission
- Data
- Database process
- Information system
- Business event

This means that the functional area project must include the WBSs and work for these project types associated with building those models as well.

In the second case, because all the metadata exists, the project is really a functional area implementation project.

The most likely case is the third. That is, most of the metadata already exists, but some new metadata must be created. In this situation, the project plan must clearly identify both what is missing and what needs to be changed. For example, if an educational system needs to report the percentage of handicapped students that participate in all activities, the student's handicapped status must be collected and stored in the basic student biographic information table. This will likely require a project WBS that embraces:

- Administrator Documentation

- Data Collection and Validation Systems
- Database Process Model
- DBMS Physical Database Specification and Implementation
- DBMS Schema and View Development
- Detailed Data Model
- Impact on Enterprise Model
- Interrogation Development
- Mission Model
- Standard Project Estimation
- System Control Implementation
- System Documentation
- User Documentation

19.3.14 Functional COTS Implementation

A functional COTS implementation project presumes that a functional COTS selection project has already been completed. It is critical to understand that a COTS's real purpose is to skip over the detailed design, coding, and unit testing. There still remain integration and system testing. Chapter 17, Make, Generate, or Buy, offers guidelines for the selection and evaluation of COTS packages. If these guidelines are not followed, success is at best accidental. Failure almost always results with a multi-million dollar price tag.

Once the COTS is installed, its design is almost always able to be tailored without compromising its package characteristics. Once its design is refined, the refinements must be installed into the corporate repository. Only after the design changes are incorporated into the repository is the first test-production version of the COTS generated. As Chapter 17 suggests, any COTS package that is not delivered in generator format is probably a very expensive poor choice.

A series of system tests will result in required changes. These changes are cycled through the repository and then fed to the generator to produce a new version of the production COTS. After a few cycles, the COTS will have been modified to produce production version 1.0.

19.3.15 Functional COTS Selection

A COTS (commercial-off-the-shelf) system, is a set of software that is preprogrammed to accomplish a complete functional area, for example, finance or human resources. The functionality of a COTS can range from complete to only marginally acceptable. Most COTS packages are able to be tuned to make a marginally acceptable package into an acceptable package. The critical issue is to determine the extent of changes required. Since the COTS package is being procured to accomplish a particular functional area, then the set of all requirements for that functional area should be the set of requirements that the package should satisfy.

This means that the following models have already been created and have served significantly as part of the COTS selection and evaluation:

- Mission model
- High-level and detailed data model for the functional area
- Database process model for the functional area
- Information systems model
- Business event model

These models should be complete to the point that a decision could be made to accomplish custom development, generate, or begin COTS customization. COTS selection should be based on conformance to the functional requirements evidenced in the above models. If a deviation from requirements is found, its fix must be determined to be:

- Inconsequential
- Minor but fixable within normal COTS tuning facilities
- Major but fixable within normal COTS tuning facilities
- Major but not within normal COTS tuning facilities

A normal tuning facility would be one that requires the setting of some constant. For example, the default number of CUSTOMERs for an accounting system might be 1000, but the parameter can be changed without effort. A minor but fixable would be that a new report format has to be developed and the changes do not affect subsequent distributions of the COTS software. A major but fixable problem would be one that requires the development of a new software system, but because the package is a generator-based package, only the metadata has to be developed for the new system to be changed. Major but not within normal COTS tuning facilities is the design and development of original 3GL or complicated 4GL systems that, when implemented, interfere with subsequent distributions of COTS software from the vendor.

Once all the packages are evaluated and a selection is made, a COTS functional implementation project starts.

19.3.16 Functional Prototype

A functional prototyping project shows the preliminary correctness of a design. If a code generator is available, the appropriate repository metadata can be used to automatically generate ANSI/SQL schemas. Facilities in the generator can be used to accomplish the necessary and sufficient process modelling. Once detailed, the process models are generated into real online programs and the design can be tested.

When the inevitable set of requirements changes arise, these can be accomplished from the top-down, and the application regenerated.

19.3.17 High-level Data Model

The high-level data model project addresses the development of a mission description document and a high-level data model. The mission description document defines the "turf" and the boundaries of all future activities. The high-level data model provides a standardized exposition of the standard types of data and the critical relationships that must exist among the data. For a large corporation, there are commonly about 50 to 60 application database diagrams. Typical application database contains about 15 to 20 entities. If defined redundantly, there would be from 750 to 1200 entities. Defined nonredundantly, there are about 400 to 500 entities.

The main benefit from nonredundant specification is standard definitions and potential shared data with common semantics.

19.3.18 Impact on Enterprise Model

The impact on enterprise model project determines the effects that a proposed new database application has on the already existing models stored in the repository. These changes are expressed in terms of both the direct changes that will have to be made in the corporate business model and also the changes that must be made to existing information systems that may be depending on a component that may be undergoing change.

19.3.19 Implementation Strategy

An implementation strategy project is one that determines the sequence for implementing specific information systems. The strategy should be based on delivering the most valuable business information at the earliest time possible in the most cost-effective manner.

The following models are presumed to have been built:

- Mission model
- High-level and detailed data model for the functional area
- Database process model for the functional area

- Information systems model
- Business event model

In addition, a complete inventory of the as-is systems, if not already stored in the repository, must be conducted. The level of analysis must be at the high-level data model, and an information systems model for each information system that is to be considered must be involved in the implementation strategy. The metadata from each of these as-is information systems needs to be interrelated to the metadata from the metadata of the models above. The mechanism of interrelationships are the nodes from the resource lifecycles of the business that should also be stored in the repository.[26] Since each node could be an information systems project, each node can be resource loaded with time, money, and staff, and then the entire network scheduled by a project management package like Microsoft Project or Harvard Project Manager. The resulting network, as seen in a Gantt chart thus provides the ideal implementation sequence.

The Gantt chart created through this technique is affected by two factors: precedence vectors and resource loading. Changing precedence vectors changes the order with which a project management system computes schedules.[27]

Changing the method by which an information systems project is implemented can also change the time to implement. For example, using a 4GL to create all the screens and reports versus using staff-intensive language constructs for picture-perfect screens or laser-perfect, multi-tone reports. Another significant resource manipulator is COTS. If there is more cash than time, and if a package can be found that causes faster implementations, then the duration of a node can be changed.

Once a sequence for implementing information systems is chosen, repository reports greatly facilitate generation of supporting materials necessary for accurate, high-quality estimates. As reality changes, the effects of the changes can be easily

---

[26] A resource life-cycle is the set of essential steps for manipulating a critical corporate resource. Examples of corporate resources are: employees, contracts, customers. Each resource life-cycle represents the minimum essential set of steps an instance of a resource goes through from creation to termination. Each resource life-cycle node is a convenient mechanism to attach the metadata from the models and as-is systems analysis for subsequent association and reporting. When the resource life-cycles are networked through functional precedence vectors, they can be perceived as a PERT chart. A detailed explanation of resource life cycles is contained in Ron Ross, *Resource Life Cycle Approach*, Wellesley, MA.: Database Research, 1993.

[27] A node from one resource life-cycle precedes another whenever it enables the succeeding node or provides significant benefit to the succeeding vector when accomplished.

remodelled through the project scheduling system. For example, a COTS package might be found that provides quick and efficient data conversions from old formats to new databases. This would cause a change in duration for all the data conversion projects that are a necessary part of any modernization.

19.3.20 Interrogation Development

The interrogation development WBS is used for the development of new interrogation (reporting) systems for existing database applications.

19.3.21 Mission Model

The mission model project is the very first project on the road to enterprise database. The form of the information is text and it is hierarchically composed. That means hierarchies should be natural, without any effects caused by the current organizational structure. The descriptions of the missions are goal- and objective-oriented. For many organizations, the mission description document is probably the first overall statement of their infrastructures.

19.3.22 Repository

The repository project is a critical first enterprise database effort. If there is to be any long-term success, the repository must exist and be of high quality. If a quality repository package cannot be procured, one must be built. Remember, the repository is really just another database application. Thus, it consists of schemas, load and update programs, and reports. Nothing more! Over the years, repositories similar to the ones illustrated via the meta-models in this book have been built in various DBMSs, such as IDMS, MANAGE, Supra, and PC/Focus. While you may start enterprise database without a repository, you will never finish enterprise database without one!

During the creation of the mission model, which should take several months, text materials can accumulate up while the repository is being built. The repository must, however, be built by the time the specified data model is started.

19.3.23 Repository Evolution

Most commercial repository meta-models have to be enhanced to fully represent the critical meta-models, leverage standard systems development, and significantly reduce systems maintenance.

There are many more aspects to an information system than just its data model. There are for example, organization, goals, objectives, business events, requirements specification and tracking, process modelling, progress tracking (via PERT, Gantt, CPM, activities, resources, etc.), evolution of sophisticated data conversion strategies, security and privacy access controls, business rules, and the like.

Each area needs to be identified and their benefits to information systems quantified. The benefits are really only one: money. But money has different forms. These include decreased decision making time due to increased data quality and interrelatability, decreased maintenance time because the domain of a maintenance activity can be accurately predicted, and so forth.

After the various benefits of the aspects are quantified and ranked, methods of their quantification and assessment, as well as the data required to observe their adherence and reporting can be developed. Once developed, a quality repository can be expanded by adding new meta-entity types along with their associated meta-attributes and meta-relationships. Once expanded, test data can be added to the repository and reports built that provide management the types of information necessary to track enterprise database progress.

For example, suppose that one of the goals is to minimize the number of different signature events required for various business forms. First, the business event OBTAIN_SIGNATURE is created and stored in the repository. Once it exists, it can then be related to whichever business form (another class of meta-entity type) requires signatures. Related to this business event is the organization required to provide the signature. Once these meta-entity types are defined (that is, Organization, Business Event, and Business Form), the instances can be installed as part of a business modelling effort and reports can be produced by the repository's report writer interface detailing the required set of signatures by Business Form and by Organization.

19.3.24 Standard Maintenance

A standard maintenance project WBS is used to accomplish standard maintenance to existing database applications that have been previously built through any of the above WBSs and that have had their appropriate set of metadata for the data and process models already stored in the repositories. System maintenance is an activity that repairs or improves malformed functionality.

19.3.25 Standard Project Estimation

Based on the standard WBSs, and on the identification of standard work products, unit work effort statistics must be developed that can reflect the various work environments in the development of information systems.

19.3.26 System Control Implementation

The system control implementation project can range from minor to major. If minor, then all the requirements for system control are readily available in the DBMS and merely need to be properly established in a production environment along with any developed user guides. If moderate, then some of the system control facilities have to be developed and implemented. Each must be estimated, staffed, scheduled and tested just as a regular project. If major, then significant resources have to be expended to accomplish the system control facility.

Regardless of whether the effort is minor, moderate, or major, any system control effort is always on the critical path.

19.3.27 System Control Maintenance

The system control maintenance project is one that causes changes to existing and installed system control facilities. Some system control facilities require shutting down the database environment while other changes are part of daily events. Changes in the first category are, for example, those to the physical characteristics of an implemented database, such as buffer allocations, file blocking sizes, and the content of audit trail logs. Changes of the second type include adding or deleting security and privacy profiles.

19.3.28 System Control Requirements

System control[28] embraces a number of DBMS facilities that control the system. System includes the DBMS, the database, and the application. The set of system control facilities are:

- Audit trails
- Backup and recovery
- Message processing
- Security and privacy
- Concurrent operations
- Multiple database processing
- Reorganization

---

[28] Chapter 6 of Michael M. Gorman's *Database Management Systems, Understanding and Applying Database Technology*, Wellesley, MA: QED Information System, 1991, contains a complete explanation of how these critical facilities can make or break any enterprise database environment.

- Application optimization
- Installation and maintenance

The system control project presumes that the following models are already built:

- Mission model
- High-level and detailed data model for the functional area
- Database process model for the functional area
- Information systems model
- Business event model

Each of these models is examined to determine its system control requirements in each of the nine areas. The system control WBS then identifies what has to occur to accommodate these requirements. The WBS also indicates how a candidate DBMS should be examined to determine its system control characteristics, and what must happen to remediate any deficiencies.

19.3.29 System Documentation

The system documentation project is either nonexistent or quite small. It is non-existent if there is no repository. That is because enterprise database cannot be successful without a repository, so given failure, there is nothing to document.

If there is a repository, then enterprise database documentation consists of a large collection of specially written reports. The reports of special interest to the system's documentation are those from the following models:

- Detailed data model
- Database process model
- Information systems model
- Business event model
- Implemented data model
- Implemented systems model

Across these models there could be several hundred possible reports. After a while, probably 25 or so will become the most popular.

19.3.30 System Evolution

A system evolution project WBS is used to accomplish evolutions and/or revisions to existing database applications that have been previously built through any of the above WBSs and that have had their appropriate set of metadata for the data and process models already stored in the repositories. A system evolution or revision is one that develops significantly new functionality.

19.3.31 User Documentation

In enterprise database, if the repository or some subset of it is active, that is, available to every application system, a great deal of user documentation is unnecessary. The business function model is of course very important as it provides the sequence for accomplishing various business activities. In the paradigm espoused by this book, there can be multiple and different business function models for essentially the same business function.

The user documentation that should be online and available through the information systems is that in support of the:

- Detailed data model
- Database process model
- Information systems model

As an end user enters data through an information systems screen, the help key should make available information related to a screen element (really a data element if traced all the way back) definition, editing and validation characteristics, and the like. If a transaction fails, the information contained in the database process model that enhances the detailed data model should provide a clear identification of the business rules (data integrity rules (DIRs)) that were unsuccessful.

Because all or almost all of this information is a critical part of the requirements definition, design, and implementation efforts, and since quality enterprise database projects always require repository updates before a task is deemed complete, generating any form of documentation (administrator, system, or user) is a small, trivial task.

19.3.32 Warehouse

The warehouse WBS presumes the existence of the high-level enterprise data model. The warehouse project calls for the development of a well-defined set of data tables that contain data appropriate for project management.

The WBS defines the steps required to create a set of database tables and the appropriate set of data loading and the update systems necessary to populate the warehouse database tables. The WBS additionally provides for ongoing evolution and maintenance of the database tables and data update and loading systems.

The data for the warehouse is expected to come from existing legacy systems and new database applications that may result from the enterprise data model.

20

TOOL SELECTION AND EVALUATION

20.1 Critical Client/Server Tools

There are three major tools that are a prerequisite for successful client/server database:

- A repository
- DBMS
- Configuration management

This books addresses only the first two. Configuration management is a book in its own right.

The right tool set for enterprise database is critical to its success. Since this book concentrates on software and projects rather than hardware and operating systems, the critical tools for enterprise database consist of the DBMS and the repository. Tool selection involves five distinct sets of activities:

- Application assessment
- Features assessment
- Features and performance benchmarks
- Comparative cost evaluation
- Final evaluation

These five activities are all oriented toward picking the client/server tools most suitable for a suite of applications.

The results of any client/server tools evaluation are of course directly related to the effort expended. In support of that, five points need to be made and understood.

- The average effort behind the implementation of a moderately sized database application costs about $2,000,000. Ten cost $20,000,000.

- The cost of the client/server tools compared to application implementation cost is of little significance.

- If the wrong client/server tools are chosen, about 50 percent of all application expenditures will have been wasted.

- The average client/server tools vendor will expend about $25,000 in support of a features evaluation of the product.

- The cost of an average benchmark to the vendor will likely exceed $100,000.

Therefore, to begin the evaluation of client/server tools without having first analyzed and statistically categorized the applications for which it is to be used, and without first having a well-trained and experienced DBMS evaluation staff, leads to a complete waste of both the vendor's and the evaluating organization's time and money. It would be better to award the evaluation on the basis of the flip of a coin, or the weight of the vendor's reference manuals.

The worst possible scenario would be for an organization to conduct a study, only to arrive at the *wrong* answer, that is, to have predetermined a winner, and then to undertake a study to support the conclusions. Two clients of this author did just that. When the study pointed to a vendor different from the one preselected by the clients, the study results were *reevaluated*, finally resulting in the selection of the *right* vendor. In the five years after those *studies*, one client was unable to complete his corporate missions (at a loss of about $100 million), and the other only got one database application running. The message is simple. If a study is attempted, it should be serious, budgeted, and valid. The results should then be believed, and acted upon.

20.2 Applications Assessment

Database applications assessment is a two part process. First is the identification and utilization of a methodology for the analysis of the applications and the capture of critical characteristics, and second is the utilization of a methodology to capture the metadata for all the critical applications.

Regardless of the methodology employed, a series of projects similar to those described in Chapter 19 will occur. Each project will create new or revised metadata, or cause the deletion of existing metadata. These metadata are fully described in Chapters 4 through 13. The metadata that resides in a passive repository is presented in Chapters 4 through 10. The metadata for the active repository is described in Chapters 11 and 12. Security, defined in Chapter 13, is employed in both the active and passive repositories.

20.3 Features Assessment

The evaluation instrument must be very carefully drawn so that at the end, the selection is not decided by flipping a coin. To that end, the features assessment instrument is first and foremost a test.

20.3.1 Goals

The features assessment instrument is really a test. Most people feel great distress getting below a 70 on a test. After all, that's a failure! But what is the sense in spending 70 percent of a test determining the gradation of failure, and only 30 percent determining gradations of success? Similarly, it should be assumed that each client/server DBMS can define, load, update, interrogate, and protect databases. That's passing! Now, the real goal is to distinguish the D systems from the C, the C systems from the B, and finally, the B systems from the A. How confident would you be in choosing a system if the scores for three contenders came out 85, 86, and 88, as opposed to 27, 48, and 86? Certainly a great deal more confident in the case of the latter set of scores than the former.

If the real goal of an evaluation is to separate systems as far as possible so that the selection can be decisive, a test must be made that evaluates as illustrated in Figure 20.1.

In order to achieve such a dramatic separation between systems, each and every question must possess three characteristics: validity, reliability, and discrimination.

20.3.2 Validity

A valid question is one that measures exactly what it is supposed to measure. It does not measure a characteristic that is not relevant to the fundamental goal of determining which is the best client/server tool for the application.

For example, suppose it is determined that a dynamic relationship DBMS is needed for the applications. Questions regarding relationship processing through

Numeric Score	Letter Grade
0-5	F
6-25	D
26-50	C
51-75	B
76-100	A

Figure 20.1. Proper spread of test scores to maximize discrimination.

pointers, linked lists, chains, and so forth are not valid because dynamic relationship DBMSs do not use these to accomplish relationship processing.

Even worse, scoring invalid questions and adding these scores to the overall rating would take away from the goal of selecting a dynamic relationship DBMS.

20.3.3 Reliability

A reliable question serves two ends. First, it is one that is unambiguous. It is not subject to misinterpretation. If two or more vendors understand a question to mean different things, the question serves no good end.

For example, someone asks the question: How many databases does your system support under a single run-time instance of the DBMS? At first blush that seems unambiguous enough. But suppose there had been no clear definition of database. One well-known DBMS would answer that question with the answer 255, and another would answer it with 9.

Obviously the first system is 28 times better than the other. But wait—a careful review of the definition of database would clearly require the 9 answer to remain 9, but the 255 answer to become 1. The difference is that one system clearly allows 9 separate databases to be attached to a run-time copy while the other only has 1 physical database, but allows 255 logical subdivisions within it, each also called a database—by the vendor!

20.3.4 Discrimination

The third characteristic that each question must exhibit is discrimination, that is, that each evaluated client/server tool is likely to produce an answer that is different in value from another proposed DBMS. For example, if one DBMS does not permit multiple database processing from within a single instance of a run-unit while another does, then one would score higher than the other in that category.

A nondiscriminating question would be: Does your DBMS support the character data type? It is assumed that all do, so to ask that question does not promote difference.

20.3.5 Assessment Alternatives

In general, there are three alternatives for assessing client/server tools:

- The fatal flaw analysis
- Features essay
- A yes/no questionnaire

20.3.5.1 Fatal Flaw Analysis

In the fatal flaw method, the client/server tool is evaluated until a fatal flaw—with respect to an application—is found, and the evaluation is terminated. An advantage of this method is that the evaluation period can be significantly shorter than a complete features analysis or a benchmark.

An example of a fatal flaw test would be as follows. Suppose that an organization is going to establish a number of databases within different departments encompassing a number of different applications, which are occasionally accessed together for corporate reports. The characteristic subjected to the fatal flaw test would then be that the DBMS must support multiple databases within a single central version.

The fatal flaw analysis requires, however, that all the features that are to be researched be first ranked in importance, from most important to least. In that way, in case all proposed systems have a fatal flaw, at least the one with the least important fatal flaw can be discovered.

20.3.5.2 Features Essay

A second approach is features essay. This method of evaluation is popular, although it is not thought to be an essay contest. In the typical features essay questionnaire there is often from 5 to 25 pages, containing from 50 to 100 questions, provoking a response of from 300 to 600 typed pages.

The problem with a features essay is that it is very sensitive to the writing skills of the respondent. To illustrate the truth of that statement, this author has answered a number of DBMS feature analysis questionnaires for a commercial timesharing service. Other time sharing services also answered the same questionnaire about the very same DBMS they were also bidding on.

Because of this author's writing skills (a touch of the Irish), the time sharing service consistently received higher evaluations in the DBMS section of the questionnaire. How is that valid, especially when all the vendors were bidding the same DBMS? Some of the vendors' answers about that DBMS were even judged as unsatisfactory when other vendors, bidding on that same DBMS, provided satisfactory answers!

In a features essay, what is actually graded is not the features of the DBMS but a specific intonation placed on those features of the DBMS that the vendor feels are the most important to your organization, given the application set described and the time available to provide the responses. No two vendors are ever going to agree on just what that intonation should be, notwithstanding the fact that all the vendors start with the same solicitation document.

20.3.5.3 The Yes/No Questionnaire

The yes/no questionnaire is also features-oriented, but instead of a feature essay questionnaire from 5 to 25 pages, containing from 50 to 100 questions, provoking a response of from 300 to 600 typed pages, the yes/no questionnaire is several hundred pages long, containing thousands of questions, each provoking only a *yes/no* response. While obviously longer than the features essay, it takes much less time to answer! This questionnaire offers the following advantages:

- Each category of questions is well-bounded, and deals either with a particular feature or with a well-bounded aspect of a feature.

- Each question within a category is very specific and deals only with a precise aspect of a particular feature.

- The answer to each question requires no writing skills, only technical skills.

- Each category is able to be weighted differently against all other categories within the same level.

- Once the correct answer is determined, there cannot ever be an argument about the vendor's response to the question. Either the vendor provides an all-right answer or an all-wrong answer. It is impossible to have partial credit!

An example of a set of questions related to the definition of the column is contained in Figure 20.2.

The only drawback to this questionnaire is that its construction requires a very high client/server tool technology skill level. While that skill level requirement may not appear to be required to develop the features essay questionnaire, the features essay questionnaire requires an even greater technical skill level to be able to discern the real facts within all the marketing hyperbole.

This form of questionnaire forces the evaluating organization to really know client/server technology and how that technology has been configured into the various commercially available DBMSs. Appendix 3 provides an enumeration of the categories of questions that have been asked in a DBMS *yes/no* questionnaire. Appendix 4 provides an enumeration of the repository question categories. These outlines have over 500 categories of questions. If each category has an average of 10 questions, then the complete questionnaire has over 5000 questions. Questionnaires along the lines of Appendices 3 and 4 have been used very successfully by the author. The results have always been very valid, very reliable, and very discriminating.

Category Number	Category Name
1.3	Columns
1.3.1	Column descriptions
1.3.2	Column data types
1.3.3	Column editing & validation
1.3.4	Column use types
1.3.4.1	Primary keys
1.3.4.2	Candidate keys
1.3.4.3	Secondary keys
1.3.4.4	Foreign keys
1.3.4.5	Multiple-use designators

Figure 20.2. Categories of questions for evaluating DBMS features related to columns.

20.3.5.4 Evaluation Methods Summary

Of the three evaluation methods, the *yes/no* questionnaire provides the most information. It also is a single, well-organized document for subsequent DBMS understanding for those who need a deep technical understanding without attending courses.

20.3.6 Validating the Questionnaire

After the questionnaire is constructed, and after the applications requirements analysis is completed, the questionnaire can be validated in three ways.

First, the questionnaire is issued to vendors for their comments. The responses will point up any missing areas and any client/server tool feature areas that are not commonly available.

Second, other organizations that have applications essentially similar to those being attempted are visited. These applications should have been running for several years. Key persons at those sites should review the questionnaire and indicate those areas of the questionnaire that are adequately addressed and those areas of the questionnaire not developed well enough to suit the needs of the applications.

Third, if possible, documentation from several client/server tool vendors is obtained and a brief effort to answer the questionnaire in house is undertaken. The client/server tools chosen for the preliminary evaluation should be from two types: one that is expected to be close to the organization's needs, and one that is expected to be far away. If the quick evaluation finds that the questionnaire does not provide very discriminating differences, the questionnaire must be faulty in one or more areas. If the differences are significant, the questionnaire has passed another validation test.

20.3.7 Finalizing the Solicitation Document

Once the solicitation document has been validated, it should contain whatever other components might be required for a legal contract and also:

- The time schedule for response and evaluation
- A sample response format
- The rating scheme

20.3.7.1 Time Schedule

A *yes/no* questionnaire takes the better part of a month for a vendor to answer. The vendor's decision to answer a questionnaire is multifaceted. Some of the factors that a vendor typically includes in the decision are:

- The amount of new business the vendor can handle

- The existing workload of the vendor's technical marketing staff for answering questionnaires

- The expected short-term profitability of the business

- The expected long-term profitability of the business

- The vendor's evaluation of the technical compctcncc of the client to understand the responses to the questionnaire

Because of these factors, the only thing a short response time will accomplish will be no responses from those who do not already have the questionnaire.

The time required to evaluate the responses varies, but should be inside three months. The total time, therefore, should be about four to six months from the issuance of the questionnaire to the onset of a benchmark.

20.3.7.2 Response Format

If the questionnaire is in the form of a feature essay, then *telephone book* size essays are the format of the returned answers. If the questionnaire is of the *yes/no* variety, the answers can be computerized and easily scored. It should be very clear to vendors that if they do not conform to the response format they will be immediately disqualified from evaluation. Appendix 5 contains an illustration of the directions for a response format to a *yes/no* questionnaire.

The goal of the evaluation needs to be clearly stated before a rating scheme can be developed. Certainly a good one is: to obtain the most responsive client/server tools for the applications that are to use it.

Once the overall goal is firmly articulated and agreed on, the subordinate goals can be set. These might include:

- Application development with minimum human involvement
- Attainment of maximum database integrity
- Minimization of conflict with ANSI database standards

Each section of the questionnaire should be assigned an overall percentage of total worth; for example, for DBMS selection, the logical database section is 30 percent, physical database is 15 percent, interrogation is 25 percent, and system control is 30 percent. Such a comparative assignment of values clearly indicates that the ability to specify the logical database and the protection of the resultant database are of equal importance, but both are more important than interrogation, and interrogation is more important than the physical database. An example of a detailed weighting scheme provided for DBMS is presented in Figure 20.3. It is divided into three parts, two for DBMS features and one for DBMS supports. Together they add up to 100 percent. In a similar fashion, an example of a detailed weighting scheme for repository is presented in Figure 20.4.

Then within each section a similar division is made until there is a percentage assignment for each and every question. At each level, the lower categories of questions are divided across a 100 percent. At the level of just questions, equal weights at the outset should be assigned. After several reviews, the individual questions might take on different weights. In this manner, a fully weighted evaluation scheme can be achieved. The weighting scheme can be easily computerized and a vendor's overall score can be easily computed by giving a pass value (1) for each correct answer or a fail value (0) for each incorrect answer.

20.3.8 Evaluation of Response

The formal evaluation of the responses should take a relatively short time. This is because during the time before the responses arrive, the team has been assembled and trained.

The first type of training is in the technology of database. No member of the team should be a neophyte in database technology.

The second type of training is in the questionnaire. All team members should be completely trained in the implications of the question. If discussion arises as to the meaning of a question, the author of the question should be asked to provide the thought behind the item. If agreement is still not achieved, a ruling must be made by the person in charge of the evaluation as to how the question is to be interpreted. No deviations in understanding of questions should be allowed. If they are allowed, the question becomes an unreliable source of discrimination among the respondents.

All responses should be reviewed to ensure that all questions are answered. If questions are not answered, the vendor should be offered an opportunity to provide the answer.

After one round of evaluation of all proposals by all evaluators, the evaluators should be brought together to determine the level of agreement or disagreement on responses of a particular vendor. On those questions of disagreement, further research need to be accomplished to resolve the differences. If further research does not resolve the difference, a ruling should be made by the head of the evaluation team.

The points assigned each question for each vendor should be entered into the scoring system. Each vendor should be shown their scores for possible correction or rebuttal. Of course, they should not be shown the other vendors' scores.

The final rating of the respondents is merely the summation of the scores on each question. Of course, the points awarded each question have been normalized to 100 percent for each section and then adjusted for the relative weighting among sections, and so on.

Weight		Section		Category
15		2.		THE LOGICAL DATABASE
	5		2.1	Requirements
	10		2.2	Database Schema
	30		2.3	Tables
	10		2.4	Columns
	30		2.5	Schema Relationships
	10		2.6	Logical Schema Definition Language
	5		2.7	Schema Maintenance
10		3.		THE PHYSICAL DATABASE
	5		3.1	Physical Database Requirements
	25		3.2	Storage Structure
	5		3.3	Physical Schema Definition Language
	25		3.4	Access Strategy
	10		3.5	Data Loading
	25		3.6	Data Update
	5		3.7	Database Maintenance

Figure 20.3. Very high-level weighting scheme for DBMS.

Weight		Section		Category
10		4.		INTERROGATION
	5		4.1	Requirements
	15		4.2	View Development
	10		4.3	Screen Development
	15		4.4	Host Language Interface
	15		4.5	Procedure-Oriented Language (POL) (or 4GL)
	15		4.6	Report Writer
	15		4.7	Query-Update Language
	10		4.8	Application Packages
10		5.		SYSTEM CONTROL
	5		5.1	Requirements
	15		5.2	Audit Trails
	5		5.3	Message Processing
	15		5.4	Backup and Recovery
	10		5.5	Reorganization
	15		5.6	Concurrent Operations
	15		5.7	Multiple Database Processing
	5		5.8	Security and Privacy
	5		5.9	DBMS Installation and Maintenance
	10		5.10	Application Optimization

Figure 20.3 (cont.).   Very high-level weighting scheme for DBMS.

Weight		Section		Category
10		6.		DOCUMENTATION
	40		6.1	IRDS
	40		6.2	DBMS
	20		6.3	Application Packages
10		7.		TRAINING
	40		7.1	IRDS
	40		7.2	DBMS
	20		7.3	Application Packages
5		8.		EASE OF USE
	40		8.1	IRDS
	40		8.2	DBMS
	20		8.3	Application Packages
15		9.		OPERATING ENVIRONMENTS
	30		9.1	IRDS
	30		9.2	DBMS
	20		9.3	Optional DBMS Components
	20		9.4	Application Packages
5		10.		COSTS
	30		10.1	IRDS
	30		10.2	DBMS
	20		10.3	Optional DBMS Components
	20		10.4	Application Packages
10	100	11.		WARRANTIES, REPRESENTATIONS, CERTIFICATIONS, AND CONTRACTS

Figure 20.3 (cont.).   Very high-level weighting scheme for DBMS.

Weight	Section	Category
2	1	Repository Naming and Control
3	2	Mission Description Components
14	3	Data Modelling Components
14	4	Process Modelling Components
13	5	Systems Model
2	6	Project Management
3	7	Repository Data Maintenance
2	8	Repository Database Maintenance
13	9	Repository Reporting
2	10	Repository-DBMS Interface
13	11	Repository System Control
2	12	Repository Installation and Maintenance
3	13	Repository Operating Environment
3	14	Measuring Repository Ease of Use
3	15	Repository Documentation
3	16	Repository Training
3	17	Repository Costs

Figure 20.4. High-level weighting scheme for repository.

20.4 Benchmarks

The second major component in the evaluation of a client/server tool is the benchmark. A benchmark occurs only after the features evaluation is completed, and only if necessary to distinguish between several client/server tools that are close in features.

In general, benchmarks offer the least return for the funds and time expended. This is simply because the development of a valid benchmark is beyond the scope of any client/server tools evaluation project. A valid benchmark will require several months batch and online use of the benchmarked application by client/server tool users for each different client/server tool. Such a requirement is prohibitively expensive for both the user and the vendor.

Using the benchmark approach as the primary method of client/server tool evaluation should be avoided. The vendor in a benchmark has only one goal: win! Many neat tricks are performed during such tests, and the evaluators of such tests cannot hope to either see or know of them all. Often, the system with the most tricks wins, rather than the one with the most useful features or functions.

The three kinds of benchmarks are:

- Standard industry benchmarks
- Running the organization's workload
- Application requirements performance tests

20.4.1 Standard Industry Benchmarks

A standard industry benchmark assumes that the organization is a standard industry, and that the work performed by this benchmark matches the work done by the organization. A popular benchmark is one that simulates the activity of a bank teller. A number of articles in recent literature seem to indicate that this benchmark may not even be valid for banks. If it is invalid for banks, it would be even more invalid for insurance companies, manufacturing plants, personnel departments, and government agencies. Additionally, client/server tool vendors are likely to tune their client/server tools to perform well on this benchmark, possibly at the cost of other types of client/server database applications.

20.4.2 Organization's Workload

The second type of benchmark, running the organization's workload, is the opposite of running a standard benchmark, which can be seen as someone else's workload. If an organization has a static relationship DBMS and wants to move to a dynamic relationship DBMS, there will be a monumental amount of work to be done before the organization's workload can be run on a relational DBMS, for example. The following are the steps required to convert a database application from one DBMS to another, regardless of whether the DBMS vendor or the evaluating organization accomplishes the work:

- Identify all the source data update file formats.

- Obtain copies of the source data for updates.

- Obtain copies of the data definition language.

- Obtain copies of all HLI programs.

- Create a source database data dump program to obtain a copy of all database data into source format, table by table, and in third normal form.

- Obtain a copy of all rules and regulations by which members are stored via owners, and reduce those rules to columns and values.

- Obtain a copy of all natural language programs.

- Obtain a complete description of all system control procedures.

- Diagrammatically create a model of the new database.

- Create new data definition language.

- Identify mapping rules for the initial data load.

- Create the conversion strategy for the initial data loader program.

- Create the conversion strategy for the various data update programs.

- Create the new database backup procedures.

- Create the conversion strategy for the HLI programs.

- Create the conversion strategy for the natural language programs.

- Create the conversion programs and execute these against the HLI and natural language programs.

- Create the test data for the source database.

- Load the source database with test data.

- Unload source test data with the database dump program.

- Load the target database with the test data through the converted loader program.

- Dump both the source and target test databases and compare the data content and organization.

- Construct the tests to compare the HLI and natural language programs to both the source and target databases.

- Create the new system control procedures.

- Create a parallel testing environment for both the source and target DBMS environments.

- Run parallel testing and adjust as necessary until the converted system performs appropriately.

If this seems like a lot of work, it is! Once all this work is done the enterprise's workload can be *benchmarked* through a month or two of parallel operations. Once this is accomplished for one DBMS, the next DBMS can be brought in, and the steps started all over again. Figure 20.5 illustrates the complexity of the problem of conversion between:

- DBMSs conforming to the same ANSI standard

- DBMSs of the same nonANSI standard data model from different vendors

- DBMSs that are from different data models

In this figure, the key is:

Low:	Conversion requires both significant redesign and recoding.
Medium:	Conversion requires recoding, but low or no redesign.
High:	Either no syntax conversion or light touches with an editor.

It should be clear that hoping to accomplish a benchmark by running the organization's workload will only lead to one or more of these seven possible results:

- Only vendors desperate for business will bid.

- Vendors with anything else to do will not bid.

- The incumbent DBMS vendor will win.

- Only the wealthiest vendors will participate.

- Only vendors conforming to the existing data model will even consider benchmarking.

- Vendors will participate only if there is a 20:1 return on the cost of the benchmark.

As to the last item, that would mean that a $1 million benchmark cost would have to be a $20 million DBMS sale to be worth the risk.

20.4.3 Application Requirements Performance Tests

The third type of benchmark, application requirements performance tests, involves the creation of a discrete set of tests that match the characteristics of the organization's applications.

These tests are not the applications. Rather, they represent critical characteristics of the applications that, if run with appropriate volumes and frequencies, will validly model the applications. These tests can be derived through an analysis of the database application statistics identified as necessary earlier in this chapter. The tests can be organized by the various DBMS functions, that is:

- Logical database
- Physical database
- Interrogation
- System control

The logical database tests consist of creating and compiling the data definition language for one or more databases that contain the same number of tables, columns, and relationships that mirror the needed databases. Timings could be taken of the compilation process.

The physical database tests consist of the storage structure allocation and test data generation and loading of the databases determined to be of the size and construction proportions required. Timings are performed on these specially created data loading efforts to assess their one-time or recurring costs.

The access strategy of the DBMS is evaluated by constructing queries that involve different types of select clauses and navigation logic. The repository contains the complete specification of the select clauses for all the different types of programs (data loading, update, and reports) and the various frequencies of execution if the applications assessment activity is performed. These select clauses can be executed against the test databases to obtain performance measures.

Tests can be done on the performance effects of immediate index updates, deferred index updates, and the like. Data update programs and streams can be constructed to simulate the actual data updates necessary for the various applications. These programs could easily contain the realistic select clause and relationship navigation logic. Finally, database backups can be taken of the different databases with different data volumes to determine the resource consumption estimates.

Interrogation tests can be conducted in the various languages such as HLI and natural. These programs can be operated against the test databases using realistic report formats, navigation logic, and select clauses. The frequency and periodicity of these reports can be obtained from the meta-base.

System control facilities can be performed on the test databases either as the transactions operate or in standalone mode. For example, the costs of the audit trails can be determined through timings of transactions with the audit trail facility, and can be deactivated.

Special update transactions can be created that affect only specific storage structure components so that measurements can be made of the performance degradation. Then the costs of reorganizations can be contrasted with the improved performances. Susceptible to degradations are indexes and the placement of rows across the disks.

The benefits of this type of benchmark are:

- The tests match real application requirements.

- The tests are much cheaper for the vendor to run than the workload conversions and tests.

- An inventory of performance measurements tests is built for future DBMS testing and for future applications.

- The workload costs can be predicted over time long after the benchmark is completed.

- The vendor can run the tests on its own computer prior to reaffirmation on the organization's computer.

- The tests can be used to test new versions of the product and to test new features.

The disadvantages of this approach are that it:

- Requires that the organization know its own applications

- Requires more staff time to develop the test specifications, data streams, and report specifications

- The organization's applications will not be converted for free

Of the three benchmark alternatives, none are free and all have some drawbacks. The third method, however, offers the most benefits to the organization. As to the

DBMS Component			Same Data Model		Different Data Models
			ANSI/SQL	Variation Within Type	
Logical			High	Medium	Low
Physical Database		Storage Structure	Low	Low	Low
		Access Strategy	Low	Low	Low
		Data Loading	High	Low	Low
		Data Update	High	Low	Low
		Database Maintenance	Low	Low	Low
Interrogation	Host Language Interface	Calls	High	Low	Low
		Data Manipulation Language	High	Low	Low
		Self-contained Languages	Medium	Low	Low
	Natural Language		Medium	Low	Low
System Control	Audit Trails		Medium	Low	Low
	Backup & Recovery		High	Low	Low
	Message Processing		High	Low	Low
	Reorganization		Low	Low	Low
	Concurrent Operations		Medium	Low	Low
	Multiple Database Processing		Low	Low	Low
	Application Optimization		Low	Low	Low
	Security & Privacy		High	Low	Low
	Installation & Maintenance		Low	Low	Low

Figure 20.5. Conversion probabilities by DBMS component and data model.

third alternative's drawbacks, the organization must know its own applications. To not know them is to admit a lack of control. There should be a centralized staff that knows how to design and implement applications. That staff can be employed for training and consulting after the DBMS is procured. Finally, the applications can only be correctly converted by the organization's staff. To think that a vendor is going to convert them for free is not realistic.

If these drawbacks are real inhibitors then the organization is destined to be a database failure site, regardless of the client/server tool chosen. *Most client/server tool vendors shy away from prospective sites that are database failures because while the failures are seldom the responsibility of the DBMS vendor, they are always laid at the vendor's feet.*

20.5 Cost Evaluation

The final component of a client/server tool evaluation is cost comparison. The categories and subcategories include:

- Staff

- The DBA staff, that is, lost staff time for training, user group costs for meetings, dues, conferences, and so forth, including the lost time for staff members

- Hardware, that is, permanent and temporary disk space for the database proper, scratch and work files, and for DBMS programs; and central processor costs that must be dedicated to DBMS work, or that is attributed to DBMS usage

- Client/server tool software, that is, software/hardware purchase or lease costs and the annual maintenance costs

- Training, that is, the *training* costs for in-house or vendor site training

- Documentation, that is, manuals and documentation costs for initial acquisition and for updates

- Applications development, that is, the application development costs for particular types of languages, different applications with specific language types, and finally the costs of database design

- Applications operation costs

- System control costs for backup and recovery and reorganization

The cost categories and subcategories have to be quantified and extended over the life of the DBMS, which is likely to be about 10 to 15 years. The recurring costs, for example, software and hardware maintenance, training, and travel have to be programmed to increase by a certain amount every year, for example, by 7 percent.

Of all these costs, the cost of application development is likely to be the largest. The cost savings attributable to a DBMS have to be verified and then compared to the different DBMSs. The DBMS that offers the most robust natural language is likely to have the lowest application development cost. For example, if an HLI program costs $60,000 to develop in COBOL, it is likely to cost only $15,000 to develop in a 4GL or report writer. None of these programs is, however, portable to any DBMS other than the one that created it.

With the recent advances in code generators that produce COBOL and that interface to DBMSs, the real advantage (productivity) of a 4GL (fourth-generation language) is diminishing. If the cost of generating a COBOL program rivals the cost of developing through a 4GL, then the generator approach should always be chosen as the COBOL program is portable between DBMSs.

The development of a comprehensive cost model is very important because the DBMS cheapest in purchase price may be the most expensive in the long run—all factors considered.

The features survey is required so that the right facilities can be chosen for use in the determination of application development and maintenance costs. The benchmark is needed to determine the actual cost of database application operation. In general, while an application is developed only once and maintained occasionally, it is often run daily. Thus the computer operation costs are valid to consider in the determination of the overall DBMS costs.

20.6 Final Evaluation of the Vendors

Critical to the final selection of the most appropriate vendor is an examination of the support services. These include the vendor's financial stability, the number and kind of user groups, the type and quality of the field forces, training, and the organization of the home office.

The vendor's financial stability is very important. For example, is the vendor geared to make continuing money from each sale? In other words, is the purchase or lease price sort of an initiation fee, but the vendor's real money is made from maintenance contracts? If this is the case, the vendor is going to really care for its old customers. If this is not the case, then maybe old customers are a source of financial loss, and the company can only survive on new customers. In such a company, the attention is paid to getting new customers rather than servicing the old ones.

User groups are important. They are a source of solutions to application problems that seem to be best known to old-time customers.

The availability of field forces is also important. The account representative should be technically knowledgeable in most installation and usage problems. Furthermore, the account representative should be able to contact the key technical personnel at the home office for tough questions.

Training is very important. Are there both basic and advanced classes in all facets of the client/server tools? Furthermore, there should be seminars in which advanced topics are discussed so that better solutions can be achieved.

Finally, the home office should be organized to handle both the resolution of a client/server tool software bug in an appropriate manner and also any technical questions through a toll-free number.

20.7 Client/Server Tool Evaluation Summary

Once the vendor sharpie has left, what then? is the title of an article that appeared in a popular publication. If the evaluation has been well constructed, the answer should be: *That's OK, we'll make it just fine!*

Part of *making it just fine* is that the procured client/server tools fit the applications to be served quite well. That can be due to a sheer accident or to a set of well-analyzed applications that, in turn, produced a highly accurate questionnaire, benchmark, and cost evaluation.

Another part of *making it just fine* relates to the availability of support services. The vendor should provide good training, quick turn around on bugs and technical questions, and readily available technical personnel.

A final part of *making it just fine* relates to the stable financial condition of the vendor. In short, the long-haul vendor is in business to make a good reasonable profit. If the vendor does, its continued existence is ensured and so also is client/server support, evolution of facilities, bug resolution, training, and so forth. If the vendor does not have a good financial model for continued existence, then shortly after it goes out of business, so also will the majority of your applications due to unresolvable bugs, antiquated technology, no training, no field support, and so forth.

PART IV

SUMMARY

Chapter 21 presents a summary of the entire enterprise database effort, stressing why it is critical to be successful in each of these areas to achieve enterprise database.

To be successful in database is to be organized. And, with an organized enterprise, the past can be researched, the present can be mastered, and plans for the future can be set into place.

21

SUMMARY

In the 1970s, productivity advances mainly occurred when chaotic system design and implementation techniques were replaced with structured methodologies. Most methodologies then were process-driven (Yourdon-DeMarco, Spectrum, SDM-70, IDEF-0, etc.). However, these methodologies were shown to be ineffective when dealing with data-intensive projects. New data-driven methodologies arose from Bachman, Chen, Finkelstein, and Martin.

These methodologies too proved less than perfect, as projects are usually a mixture of both process-driven and data-driven activities. Balanced methodologies arose that employed appropriate mixtures of data and process techniques as well as the other critical missing aspects of a complete database project.

Advances in productivity have also occurred because of DBMSs (database management systems), 4GLs (fourth-generation languages), and software generators (e.g., MAGEC and CLARION).

CASE tools have arisen and are generally classified as upper CASE (planning, analysis, and design) and lower CASE (generation and maintenance). CASE tools have also suffered because they typically were built around fixed meta-schemas that were tilted toward data or process. Thus, 50 percent or more of all projects had to be shoe-horned (or worse, toes were cut off) to make them work.

In the late 1980s, ANSI/IRDS was accepted and became a Federal Information Processing Standard (FIPS). An IRDS is critically different from CASE tools because it allows for the creation of its own meta-schemas. This singular characteristic allows the knowledge worker administrator the ability to define appropriate knowledge worker product storage environments.

When these environments are appropriately defined, and when they are distributed through conventional DBMS environments (the most common platform for an IRDS), user organizations will be able to define, propagate, and reuse the critical business semantics that form the basis of useful information systems through whatever end-user software or hardware interfaces may be appropriate at the time of their need. Achieved then will be:

Data: centralized semantic control with decentralized data storage:

* Data that is able to be consistently understood by multiple sites

* Controlled, concurrent processing of nonredundant data

* Single versions of *truth* in enterprise reports

* A feeling that individual needs are reflected in data values and usages

- Appropriate local control and ownership of data

- Common standards for definition and practice

- Accommodation of local data storage requirements

Process: centralized development control with decentralized data storage:

- Programs that are able to be developed locally and distributed as necessary

- Processes that are able to access data in different locations

- Common report formats and meanings

- A feeling that individual processing scenarios and user interfaces are accommodated

- Control over localized integrity requirements

- The deployment of standard, cost-effective programming practices that can be locally used

- Satisfaction of local processing needs

APPENDIX 1

Glossary

This appendix contains a glossary of terms contained in this book.

Action type

Action type identifies the types of actions that can take place:

- SELECT—viewing or reading data
- DELETE—removing data from the database
- INSERT—placing new data into the database
- UPDATE—change data from one value to another

Assertion

A set of independently defined pseudocode that when executed, must test true when no updating is occurring. An action that causes a violation to an assertion is rejected. An assertion is the same as a table constraint except that it is independently named and defined.

Business event

A named and described instance of a use of an information system. As business functions are accomplished and require services from an information system, the business event occurs and causes the execution of an information system.

Business event & information system

A table that represents the interrelationship between instances of the two entities on either side of the "&" sign.

Business function

A business function is a named set of activities that may involve other business functions and people. If data is actually transformed, it makes use of a business event that signals the execution of an information system.

Business function & business event

A table that represents the interrelationship between instances of the two entities on either side of the "&" sign.

Business function & document

A table that represents the interrelationship between instances of the two entities on either side of the "&" sign.

Business function & form

A table that represents the interrelationship between instances of the two entities on either side of the "&" sign.

Business organization

A unit within a business that has a charter to perform a certain class of business functions or activities.

Business process & database view

A table that represents the interrelationship between instances of the two entities on either side of the "&" sign.

Business process & external view

A table that represents the interrelationship between instances of the two entities on either side of the "&" sign.

Business term

A business term is a name that has a special meaning to the database system. The term may be subject matter or computer related. A subject matter related term might be, for example, remaining balance. A computer term would be DBMS, the abbreviation name for the database management system.

Column

A column is a data element that has been allocated to a table. The column may have a different or more localized name than the name of the data element. Further, the column may have a more restrictive set of editing and validation rules than the data element.

Column & DIR

A table that represents the interrelationship between instances of the two entities on either side of the "&" sign.

Communications link

A named and described link between two or more processing nodes.

Compound data element

Whenever a data element consists of subordinate data elements, it is called a compound data element, and each of the subordinate data elements is identified and referred back to the data element that defines it.

Compound data element & data element

A table that represents the interrelationship between instances of the two entities on either side of the "&" sign.

Data element

A distinct business fact represented through definite values. A data element may be single-valued, multivalued (vector), multi-dimensional, group, or repeating group.

All the values from a multivalued and multi-dimensional data element are of the same data type but represent different values of the same business fact. A data type denotes a specialized architecture of data values for a data element, for example, character or numeric. The DBMS typically enforces the rules implied by the specialized data element value architecture. For example, the double precision data type would automatically exclude alphabetic values.

If all the data values for the data element are defined to be the same length, then the data element is fixed length. If values are allowed to be different lengths, then the data elements are variable length.

If the data element is allowed to contain subordinate data elements, it is called a group. Each data element within the group may have a different data type. Each data element within the group represents a different subordinate business fact. The group might be profits, and the subordinate business facts could be the first through the fourth quarters.

If a group is multivalued, it is called a repeating group. A multivalued data element, or a single- or multivalued group is also known as a data aggregate. Each data model allows only certain types of data elements. A repeating group might be annual profits. The first subordinate business fact would be year, and the other four would be the quarters.

A DBMS may reserve the definition of some of the more physical characteristics of an element, such as length and type to the physical schema, leaving to the logical definition only the definition of the element name and a general type clause such as character and numeric.

Data element & derived data element

A table that represents the interrelationship between instances of the two entities on either side of the "&" sign.

Data element & DIR

A table that represents the interrelationship between instances of the two entities on either side of the "&" sign.

Data element domain

A collection of data from one data element. All the data are of the same data type, and fit within a prespecified range of values. Additionally, all the data is drawn from the same domain of business facts. For example, the data element domain, wages, would cover the data elements: yearly-salary, monthly-salary, and hourly-salary.

Data element domain & DIR

A table that represents the interrelationship between instances of the two entities on either side of the "&" sign.

Data integrity rule & database view element

A table that represents the interrelationship between instances of the two entities on either side of the "&" sign.

Data integrity rule & external view element

A table that represents the interrelationship between instances of the two entities on either side of the "&" sign.

Data integrity rule (DIR)

A data integrity rule is a statement that must test true when no database updating is taking place. A data integrity rule may relate to data elements within the same or different tables. A data integrity rule may also state a condition that must be true in a row instance before an action can take place, for example, all data elements must be valued before the row is accepted into the database.

A data integrity rule, acting as a referential integrity rule can dictate the action after a certain architecture of update is attempted. The two referential integrity actions are: [CASCADE] DELETE, and SET NULL (or SET DEFAULT). By implication if the conditions do not exist that permit either of those two actions to occur, then the initial action (ADD, DELETE, or MODIFY) is itself rejected. The types of match that are examined are: MATCH ALL or MATCH NONE.

While referential integrity is explicitly defined in ANSI/NDL and the ANSI/SQL, it also exists implicitly in varying forms in other data models. ANSI/NDL referential integrity exists through the use of the INSERTION and RETENTION clauses in the schema set clauses that are specified on behalf of a member table.

ANSI/SQL referential integrity exists through the specification of the REFERENCES clause within the definition of a "child" table. The clause identifies a column within the "child" table that is referred to as a "foreign key," and a table name and column name of another table that is acting as the "parent" of the referential action. If no parent row's column is specified, then its primary key is the default specification.

Database domain

The domain of a database represents a business policy based description of the data that is to be represented in the database.

Database domain & object

A table that represents the interrelationship between instances of the two entities on either side of the "&" sign.

Database process

A procedure that transforms the database from one value state to another. A database process may contain subordinate database processes. Database processes interface with the database through views.

Database view

A database view is a view that forms the interface between database processes and the database.

Database view element

A database view element is a column that has been identified to be employed in a view. A database view element may have a different name, but must contain the same semantics as a column.

Database view element & external view element

A table that represents the interrelationship between instances of the two entities on either side of the "&" sign.

DBMS column

A named unit of metadata within a DBMS table. For example, the first name column within the PERSON table might be PERSON_FIRST_NAME.

DBMS column & [database] column

A table that represents the interrelationship between instances of the two entities on either side of the "&" sign.

DBMS column constraint

A set of pseudocode that operates on only one column within the table to which it is associated that must test true when no updating is occurring. An action that causes a violation to the DBMS column constraint is rejected.

DBMS table

A named collection of columns of data that is under the control of a specific DBMS and that resides within a particular schema.

DBMS table & assertion

A table that represents the interrelationship between instances of the two entities on either side of the "&" sign.

DBMS table & stored procedure

A table that represents the interrelationship between instances of the two entities on either side of the "&" sign.

DBMS table & trigger

A table that represents the interrelationship between instances of the two entities on either side of the "&" sign.

DBMS table constraint

A set of pseudocode that operates on only the columns within the table to which it is associated and that must test true when no updating is occurring. An action that causes a violation to the DBMS table constraint is rejected.

DBMS view

The DBMS version of a view. That is, a view that conforms in both syntax and semantics to the requirements of the implementing DBMS.

DBMS view element

A column within a DBMS view.

Delivered product

A specific product about enterprise database that makes sense as a unit to the creator of a project. For example, the *logical database design* for a specific functional component such as human resources would contain a number of methodology work products such as entity relationship diagrams, object, tables, columns, and so forth.

Derived data element

A data element whose value is derived by a formula that is contained within the scope of the enterprise database.

Derived data element & compound data element

A table that represents the interrelationship between instances of the two entities on either side of the "&" sign.

Document

A document is a complex collection of business data that is usually published by some enterprise, e.g., a survey, or report of the U.S. Bureau of Census, and that is important to the enterprise. The document is typically decomposed and then some aspect of it is input into the database application. The analysis of the document produces a mapping between the cells of data on the document and the external view elements that represent those cells to the database application.

Document cell

A unit of a document that is of interest to enterprise database, usually as an input.

Edit table DIR

A type of data integrity rule. The types are table look up, valid and invalid values, and range values.

Encode-decode DIR

A list of codes and values employed to explain data that is contained in the database. For example, DC means District of Columbia.

Enterprise

The term used in this book for describing the corporation or business about which various database components are identified, specified, implemented, and maintained. The enterprise may be a university, a corporation (large or small), and it may be centralized or decentralized. For very small enterprises, many of the enterprise database components may be treated trivially. For large enterprises these very same components are treated robustly. The database components include architectures (data, database process, etc), models (specific designs for data, database process, etc), methodologies (work steps to effect architectures and models), and the repository (specialized database application for storage of all enterprise components).

External view

An external view is a view that acts as an interface between the database process and the external agent providing data to the database process. External agents are information systems, reports, files, documents, forms, internal processes, and screens.

External view element

An external view element is a business fact that is to be obtained from or provided to a report cell, a file element, or an input form cell. An external view element may have a different name and different semantics from a database view element, and in such a case, the business process that exchanges the data between the database and the external views must resolve these semantic differences.

External view element & DIR

A table that represents the interrelationship between instances of the two entities on either side of the "&" sign.

External view element & document cell

A table that represents the interrelationship between instances of the two entities on either side of the "&" sign.

External view element & file cell

A table that represents the interrelationship between instances of the two entities on either side of the "&" sign.

External view element & internal process input

A table that represents the interrelationship between instances of the two entities on either side of the "&" sign.

External view element & internal process output

A table that represents the interrelationship between instances of the two entities on either side of the "&" sign.

External view element & report cell

A table that represents the interrelationship between instances of the two entities on either side of the "&" sign.

External view element & screen element

A table that represents the interrelationship between instances of the two entities on either side of the "&" sign.

File

A collection of records known to the operating system under a single name, and that are accessed by a single O/S access method.

File & internal process

A table that represents the interrelationship between instances of the two entities on either side of the "&" sign.

File block

A self contained set of data/metadata that represents a coherent set of data from within a record of a file. For example, if a file contains personnel data, and if a record is for one employee, a file block would be the eduction data for the employee.

File cell

A discrete item of data with well defined semantics that occupies specific space within a record instance in a file.

File cell & DIR

A table that represents the interrelationship between instances of the two entities on either side of the "&" sign.

File cell & internal process

A table that represents the interrelationship between instances of the two entities on either side of the "&" sign.

Foreign Key

A foreign key is the designation of one or more columns within one table that act as the primary key of another table. The purpose of the foreign key is to represent a relationship between one row of the parent table to one or more rows of a dependent table and to imply automatic actions whenever foreign key data value changes occur.

Foreign key & column

A table that represents the interrelationship between instances of the two entities on either side of the "&" sign.

Form

A form is an organized set of business data that is input to the database application. The analysis of the form produces a mapping between the cells of data on the form and the external view elements that represent those cells to the database application.

Form cell

A specific unit of data that is to be contained on a form into which data is to be recorded.

Function key

A numbered key on a data entry keyboard, either of a PFn or a Fn designation. *PF* means program function, and *F* means function. Normally there are 12 PF/F keys. When each key is pressed, the described and named action is taken.

Implemented data model

The set of DBMS tables that represent the transformation of the technology independent specified data model into the specific design actually implemented by the DBMS. The implemented data model contains interrelationships between the other models.

Implemented process model

The set of DBMS tables that represent the transformation of the technology independent specified process model into the specific instances of the programs that accomplish the mission of the database and that interact with the DBMS. The implemented process model contains interrelationships between the other models.

Individual staff members

The names and skill descriptions of available workers for a project.

Information system

A named collection of data processing activities that may involve the use of internal processes, database processes, reports, files, and screens. The information system may have subordinate information systems. The contained logic is cast into information system control logic blocks and subordinate information system control logic blocks.

Information system control logic

An information system control logic block is a set of control logic that is specified in a standard pseudocode that controls the access to database processes, reports, files, screens, and internal processes.

Information system control logic & file

A table that represents the interrelationship between instances of the two entities on either side of the "&" sign.

Information system control logic & database process

A table that represents the interrelationship between instances of the two entities on either side of the "&" sign.

Information system control logic & internal process

A table that represents the interrelationship between instances of the two entities on either side of the "&" sign.

Information system control logic & screen

A table that represents the interrelationship between instances of the two entities on either side of the "&" sign.

Information system control logic & report

A table that represents the interrelationship between instances of the two entities on either side of the "&" sign.

Internal process

A procedure that is accomplished whenever called for the manipulation of some screen, file, report, or database process.

Internal process block

A self-contained unit of a process.

Internal process input & DIR

A table that represents the interrelationship between instances of the two entities on either side of the "&" sign.

Internal process input & external view element

A table that represents the interrelationship between instances of the two entities on either side of the "&" sign.

Internal process input message

An ASCII string that is to be sent back to the calling program of the internal process on behalf of a specific internal process input.

Internal process input

The named and described unit of data that is input to the internal process.

Internal process message

An ASCII string that is to be sent back to the calling program of the internal process.

Internal process output

The named and described unit of data that is output from the internal process.

Internal process output & DIR

A table that represents the interrelationship between instances of the two entities on either side of the "&" sign.

Involved methodology task

An involved methodology task is a methodology task that is required to accomplish a particular work task of a project.

Involved metric

The identification of the set of metrics involved in a particular methodology task. For example, a methodology task may involve analysis, design, presentation, review, and documentation. Each activity type may require a different skill mix and different metrics.

Job

A set of computer processing that executes as a unit.

Job unit

A self-contained component of a job.

Job unit & role

A table that represents the interrelationship between instances of the two entities on either side of the "&" sign.

Job unit, role & DBMS view

A table that represents the interrelationship between instances of the two entities on either side of the "&" sign. In this case, one of the entities is the set of valid pairs of job unit and role, while the other is DBMS view.

Job unit, role, DBMS view & action type

A table that represents the interrelationship between instances of the two entities on either side of the "&" sign. In this case, one of the entities is the set of valid triples of job unit, role, and DBMS view, while the other is action type.

Job unit, role, DBMS view, action type & organization

A table that represents the interrelationship between instances of the two entities on either side of the "&" sign. In this case, one of the entities is the set of valid quads of job unit, role, DBMS view, and action type, while the other is organization.

Job unit, role, DBMS view, action type, organization & user

A table that represents the interrelationship between instances of the two entities on either side of the "&" sign. In this case, one of the entities is the set of valid quints of job unit, role, DBMS view, action type, and organization, while the other is user.

Key Designator

The indication as to whether a column serves as a primary key, as a candidate key, or within one or more foreign keys.

Methodology task

An assembly of work activities that produce a specific methodology work product. A work product might be an entity relationship diagram. The methodology tasks provide the necessary and sufficient guidance for the production of the methodology work product.

Metric

An identified amount of staff hours required to perform a particular activity in support of a named methodology work product.

Mission description

The mission description hierarchically defines the goals and objectives of the enterprise in end-result, behavior-oriented language. For a large enterprise, the mission model can occupy from 25 to 35 pages of text in addition to the hierarchical diagrams. The mission does not detail what the business is doing, or who is doing it, or how it is done. That is traditional functional analysis, a technique that serves only to shine up tarnished functionality.

The mission description is the foundation of enterprise database. Upon it all other models are developed, implemented, and maintained; they act as the mission's realization.

Mission description & business function

A table that represents the interrelationship between instances of the two entities on either side of the "&" sign.

Mission description & business term

A table that represents the interrelationship between instances of the two entities on either side of the "&" sign.

Mission description & database domain

A table that represents the interrelationship between instances of the two entities on either side of the "&" sign.

Mission description model

The mission description model consists mission descriptions, business functions, database domains and objects, and business terms. Collectively, the mission description model is a high-level, defining model of the enterprise.

Object

An object is a named collection of policy homogeneous data and the database processes necessary to correctly transform the object from one valid business state to another, starting with the NULL state.

Business's commonly make decisions on the basis of objects. Objects are derived from database domains, but are defined nonredundantly.

The data structure component of an object results from a policy based analysis of discovered entities. Upon analysis, some entities, such as COMPANY and CONTRACT become objects. Other entities become data elements, which are stand-alone business facts, such as SALARY, TELEPHONE NUMBER, and START DATE. Finally, some entities become property classes within the context of an object, such as EDUCATION within EMPLOYEE, CRITICAL DATES within CONTRACT.

The data structure component of an object consists of its property classes along with the property classes's inferred data elements, all in the form of third normal form tables.

In addition to data structures, a fully defined object contains the appropriate set of database processes and DIRs to completely govern its complete set of state transformations.

Object & property class

A table that represents the interrelationship between instances of the two entities on either side of the "&" in the table name.

Operational data model

The set of tables that represent the physical attributes of the O/S files that represent the implemented database. The operational data model contains interrelationships between the other models.

Operational process model

The set of tables that represent the physical attributes of the run units that represent the implemented processes. The operational process model contains interrelationships between the other models.

Organization & business function

A table that represents the interrelationship between instances of the two entities on either side of the "&" sign.

Primary key

A primary key is the designation of one or more data elements that can be used to locate one row instance. Traditionally, the value set of a primary key is unique across all instances of a row.

Primitive data transformations

A primitive data transformation is the definition part of a mini-specification that is to be used for computer module development. Linked to the primitive data transformation through the business process are the involved views and the appropriate set of data integrity rules.

Processing node

A named and described unit of computing processing power. For example, a Sun SPARC station, a mainframe, a minicomputer, or a microcomputer.

Processing node & schema

A table that represents the interrelationship between instances of the two entities on either side of the "&" sign.

Processing unit & job

A table that represents the interrelationship between instances of the two entities on either side of the "&" sign.

Project

A named set of activities that are to accomplish a specific component of enterprise database. A project has a schedule and produces a named set of work products.

Property class

An inferred collection of policy-homogeneous data elements that is defined independently of objects, but is referenced by an object for inclusion. Examples of property classes are CRITICAL DATES, and BIBLIOGRAPHIC INFORMATION. The EMPLOYEE table would likely include the property class BIBLIOGRAPHIC INFORMATION, and the CONTRACT, ORDERS, and SHIPPING TICKET objects would likely include the CRITICAL DATES property class.

When a give property class is cited within multiple objects, the inferred setr of data elements may be different. For example, the inferred data elements for the property class CRITICAL DATES would be different for CONTRACT from those for PURCHASE ORDER.

Range value tables

An enumeration of those data element, column, or data element domain values that are a valid and/or invalid range of values within a domain of values. The enumeration may be range only, discrete and range, or finally collections of valid and invalid ranges.

Report

A report is a formatted output from an interrogation. The structure and the format of a report contains a heading, description, calculations, and view element references.

Report & internal process

A table that represents the interrelationship between instances of the two entities on either side of the "&" sign.

Report block

A self-contained unit of a report.

Report Cell

A column whose value becomes part of a report with or without transformation.

Report cell & DIR

A table that represents the interrelationship between instances of the two entities on either side of the "&" sign.

Report cell & internal process

A table that represents the interrelationship between instances of the two entities on either side of the "&" sign.

Report message

An ASCII string that is to be sent back to the report requestor.

Role

A named function that is performed by one or more users. For example, accounting clerk.

Schema

The collective name used for all the tables contained in a database. For example, the FINANCE schema name would mean all the tables associated with a particular database that contains finance information. While a schema may reside on multiple nodes, the same data may not. Distributed schemas are horizontally partitioned.

Screen & internal process

A table that represents the interrelationship between instances of the two entities on either side of the "&" sign.

Screen block

A self-contained unit of a screen.

Screen element

A named and described unit of data that is either displayed or is able to be input or changed.

Screen element & DIR

A table that represents the interrelationship between instances of the two entities on either side of the "&" sign.

Screen element & internal process

A table that represents the interrelationship between instances of the two entities on either side of the "&" sign.

Screen element message

An ASCII string that is to be sent back to the person viewing the screen immediately after an action is taken against a screen element.

Screen element security requirements

A statement of the type of security that is be enforced at the screen element level.

Screen message

An ASCII string that is to be sent back to the person viewing the screen.

Screen security requirements

A statement of the type of security that is be enforced at the screen level.

Specified data model

The set of DBMS tables that represent the technology independent specification of the database that is required to accomplish the database's mission and that is to be subsequently implemented by a DBMS. The specified data model contains interrelationships between the other models.

Specified process model

The set of DBMS tables that represent the technology independent specification of the processes that are required to accomplish the database's mission and that are to be subsequently implemented through various programming languages that interface with a DBMS. The specified process model contains interrelationships between the other models.

Stored procedure

A stored procedure is a process that is executed by the DBMS upon request by an end user program.

Subordinate business event

A business event that is contained within the business event that is designated as its parent.

Subordinate business function

A business process that is contained within the business process that is designated as its parent.

Subordinate business organization

A business organization that is contained within the business organization that is designated as its parent.

Subordinate compound data element

A compound data element that is contained within the compound data element that is designated as its parent.

Subordinate database domain

A database domain that is contained within the database domain that is designated as its parent.

Subordinate document

A document that is contained within the document that is designated as its parent.

Subordinate form

A form that is contained within the form that is designated as its parent.

Subordinate information system control logic

An information system control logic block that is contained within the information system control logic block that is designated as its parent.

Subordinate job unit

A job unit that is contained within the job unit that is designated as its parent.

Subordinate methodology task

A methodology task that is contained within the methodology task that is designated as its parent.

Subordinate mission description

A mission description that is contained within the mission description that is designated as its parent.

Subordinate process block

A process block that is contained within the process block that is designated as its parent.

Subordinate report block

A report block that is contained within the report block that is designated as its parent.

Subordinate screen block

A screen block that is contained within the screen block that is designated as its parent.

Subordinate work task

A work task that is contained within the work task that is designated as its parent.

Table

A table is a policy homogeneous collection of assigned data elements that has a name and description. A data element that has been assigned to a table is called a column. A table is derived from the merger of objects and the data elements appropriate for representation through the object's property classes. The data that represents a specific instance of all the elements is called a row.

Once data elements are assigned to a table, one or more of the data elements must serve as the table's primary key. Optionally, one or more of the data elements may serve as candidate key, and foreign key.

Task effort estimate

A task effort estimate is the quantity of staff hours of each different type that is required to accomplish the quantity of work products required by a methodology task in support of a work task of a particular project.

Time charges

The actual quantity of hours along with the quantity of work products that were performed during a particular work period.

Trigger

A set of pseudocode that automatically executes either before or after an insert, delete, or modify operation takes place.

User & job

A table that represents the interrelationship between instances of the two entities on either side of the "&" sign.

User

A name most commonly applied to a person who causes the execution of a job unit.

View

A view is a linguistic expression of the syntax and semantics of the interface between a database and a run unit. The run unit may be programmed in a 3GL (e.g., COBOL, FORTRAN, or C) or 4GL (e.g., FOCUS, CLARION, Oracle, or Sybase)

The view represents a logical partitioning of the database for the run unit's access. A view's components, which collectively are called the select clause consist of: columns from tables, where clauses, and intertable relationship expressions. When a view is executed, that is, when the database is accessed through the view, the result is a set of rows consisting of single-valued elements called view elements. When views are derived from other views, they are called nested.

The main benefit of a view is that it prevents the run unit from having to contain detailed database selection and navigation logic. Because of this mutual independence, the run unit can use FIND, GET, DELETE, STORE, or MODIFY to access view rows.

Valid, invalid, and range value tables

An enumeration of those data element, column, or data element domain values that are either valid or invalid, or are a valid and/or invalid range of values within a domain of values. The enumeration may be valid only, invalid only, discrete only, range only, discrete and range, or finally collections of valid and invalid values. In any of the combination cases, the IRDS must contain a processor to identify conflicts.

Work factor

A work factor is a work effort multiplier that most often raises the nominal quantity of staff hours required to produce a methodology work product. The work factors address staff skill assessments, familiarity and prior experience, tools and equipment, work environment, and customer reviews.

Work period

A fixed span of time during which work is performed.

Work task

A work task is a specific unit of work that produces a particular product.

APPENDIX 2

High-Level WBS for Enterprise Database

This appendix is a high-level work breakdown structure listing of the enterprise database project methodology. The actual task listing is over 100 pages.

1	Preliminary analysis
1.01	Form project team, plan phase, & estimate project
1.02	Create initial database project requirements description
1.02.01	Request and review documentation of prior related database efforts
1.02.02	Conduct broad interviews with user management to determine business objectives for database project
1.02.03	Perform preliminary data analysis
1.02.04	Formulate list of business objectives that are to be achieved
1.02.05	Formulate reasonable list of mechanisms to evaluate project success
1.02.06	Reach consensus on objectives and evaluation mechanisms
1.03	Specify initial mission descriptions, mission description diagram, database domains, & construct database domain diagrams
1.04	Merge initial database domain diagrams
1.05	Create high-level business function diagram
1.06	Create preliminary analysis phase report
1.07	Create business and technical terms glossary, and organize in learning order
1.08	Create preliminary analysis presentation
1.09	Conduct phase review
2	Conceptual specification
2.01	Form project team, plan phase, and revise project plan
2.02	Create logical database of business requirements
2.02.01	Perform detailed data analysis
2.02.02	Perform detailed data analysis for data transfer and conversion
2.02.03	Update project mission descriptions, mission description diagram, database domains & construct database domain diagrams
2.02.04	Define data integrity model
2.02.05	Specify data integrity rules
2.02.06	Verify data integrity model
2.02.07	Create logical database specification report
2.02.08	Create logical database presentation
2.02.09	Conduct subphase review
2.03	Specify physical database requirements
2.03.01	Specify database process model
2.03.02	Specify information systems model

2.03.03	Create business event model
2.03.04	Create business function model
2.03.05	Estimate database size
2.03.06	Evaluate requirements for backup
2.03.07	Specify database integrity subsystem
2.03.08	Consolidate logical database changes to accommodate physical database
2.03.09	Prepare physical database requirements specification
2.03.10	Create physical database presentation
2.03.11	Conduct subphase review
2.04	Analyze interrogation requirements
2.04.01	Identify, name, and then create information system process diagram for each specialized report subsystem
2.04.02	Analyze standard report requirements
2.04.03	Analyze ad hoc report requirements
2.04.04	Prepare interrogation requirements report
2.04.05	Analyze data transfer and data conversion reporting requirements
2.04.06	Create interrogation presentation
2.04.07	Conduct subphase review
2.05	Specify system control requirements
2.05.01	Specify audit trail needs
2.05.02	Specify backup & recovery needs
2.05.03	Specify concurrent operation requirements
2.05.04	Specify security & privacy requirements
2.05.05	Specify reorganization requirements
2.05.06	Specify multiple database requirements
2.05.07	Prepare system control requirement report
2.05.08	Create system control presentation
2.05.09	Conduct subphase review
2.06	Validate cross-product of data integrity and data transformation models
2.07	Create cross-product validation presentation
2.08	Conduct subphase review
2.11	Create conceptual specification phase report
2.12	Create conceptual specification phase presentation
2.13	Conduct phase review

3	Binding	
3.01		Form project team, plan phase, and revise project plan
3.02		Review conceptual specification phase for completeness and revise as necessary
3.03		Remedy any data availability and quality problems determined during conceptual specification phase
3.04		Determine impact on enterprise model

3.05   *Evaluate, select, and/or procure DBMS packages*[29]
3.06   Determine Implementation Strategy
3.07   Prepare binding phase report
3.08   Create binding phase presentation
3.09   Conduct phase review

4   Implementation
4.01   Form project team, plan phase, and revise project plan
4.02   *Create or revise logical database*
4.03   *Create or revise physical database*
4.04   *Create or revise critical interrogation subsystems*
4.05   *System control implementation*
4.06   *Develop or revise ancillary supports*
4.07   Plan and conduct system quality tests (SQT)
4.08   Create implementation phase report
4.09   Create implementation phase presentation
4.10   Conduct phase review

5   Conversion and deployment
5.01   Form project team, plan phase, and revise project plan
5.02   Review prior phase for completeness and revise as necessary
5.03   Secure, install, and test all equipment
5.04   Conduct all training
5.05   Convert all data

6   Production and administration
6.01   Form project team, plan phase, and revise project plan
6.02   Database system production
6.02.01   Commence database system
6.02.02   Conduct ongoing database system production
6.02.03   Develop and maintain specified and implemented views as necessary
6.03   Develop interrogation subsystems
6.04   Determine database system maintenance policy
6.05   Perform standard system maintenance
6.06   Perform emergency maintenance
6.07   Accomplish database system revision
6.08   Perform system acceptance test

---

[29] This task and the tasks in italics below are not required for a COTS procurement.

APPENDIX 3

DBMS Selection and Evaluation Category List

This appendix is a listing of the categories of questions that are asked in the DBMS Selection and Evaluation Questionnaire.

2.   The logical database
2.1   Requirements
2.2   Database schema
2.2.1   IRDS utilization
2.2.2   Naming
2.3   Tables
2.3.1   Table description IRDS utilization
2.3.2   Table description naming
2.3.3   Table integrity
2.4   Columns
2.4.1   IRDS utilization
2.4.2   Column descriptions
2.4.3   Column data types
2.4.4   Column editing and validation
2.4.5   Column use types
2.4.5.1   Primary keys
2.4.5.2   Candidate keys
2.4.5.3   Secondary keys
2.4.5.4   Foreign keys
2.4.5.5   Multi-value elements use designators
2.4.5.6   Multi-use designators
2.5   Schema relationships
2.5.1   Schema relationship description
2.5.2   Schema relationship types
2.5.3   Schema relationship procedures
2.5.4   Schema relationship referential integrity
2.5.4.1   Non-value-based referential integrity
2.5.4.2   Value-based referential integrity
2.6   Logical schema definition language
2.7   Schema maintenance
2.7.1   Table maintenance
2.7.2   Column maintenance
2.7.3   Schema relationship maintenance
2.7.4   Referential integrity maintenance
2.7.4.1   Referential integrity ambiguity detection

349

5.9.6.1   Logical database development
5.9.6.2   Logical database maintenance
5.9.6.3   Access strategy routines
5.9.6.4   Operating system access methods
5.9.6.5   HLI routines
5.9.6.6   Query-update language routines
5.9.6.7   Report writer routines
5.9.6.8   System control routines
5.9.7   TP monitor region restrictions
5.9.7.1   Logical database development
5.9.7.2   Logical database maintenance
5.9.7.3   Access strategy routines
5.9.7.4   Operating system access methods
5.9.7.5   HLI routines
5.9.7.6   Query-update language routines
5.9.7.7   Report writer routines
5.9.7.8   System control routines
5.10   Application optimization

6.   Documentation
6.1   IRDS
6.1.1   End user documentation
6.1.2   Design documentation
6.2   DBMS
6.2.1   Logical database creation and maintenance
6.2.1.1   End user documentation
6.2.1.2   Design documentation
6.2.2   Physical database creation and maintenance
6.2.2.1   End user documentation
6.2.2.2   Design documentation
6.2.3   Interrogation language usage
6.2.3.1   Host language interface
6.2.3.1.1 End user documentation
6.2.3.1.2 Design documentation
6.2.3.2   Procedure-oriented language
6.2.3.2.1 End user documentation
6.2.3.2.2 Design documentation
6.2.3.3   Report writer
6.2.3.3.1 End user documentation
6.2.3.3.2 Design documentation
6.2.3.4   Query-update language
6.2.3.4.1 End user documentation
6.2.3.4.2 Design documentation
6.2.4   System control
6.2.4.1   End user documentation

APPENDIX 4

Repository Selection and Evaluation Category List

This appendix is a listing of the categories of questions that are asked in the Repository Selection and Evaluation Questionnaire.

1   Repository naming and control

2   Mission description model
2.1 Mission descriptions
2.2 Business terms
2.3 External documents

3   Data modelling components
3.1 Database domains
3.2 Data integrity rules
3.3 Data elements
3.3.1   Data element naming
3.3.2   Data element structure
3.3.3   Data element data types
3.3.4   Data element editing and validation
3.4 Data records
3.5 Data record elements
3.5.1   Data record element naming
3.5.2   Data record element use designators
3.5.2.1 Primary key use designators
3.5.2.2 Secondary key use designators
3.5.2.3 Candidate key use designators
3.5.2.4 Foreign key use designators
3.5.2.5 Multi-value data record elements
3.5.2.6 Multiple use designators
3.6 Data element domains
3.6.1   Types of data element domains
3.6.2   Domain operations and restrictions
3.6.3   DBA-defined data element domains
3.7 Data element encode/decode tables
3.8 Objects
3.9 Valid, invalid, and range value tables

4   Process modelling components
4.1 Business events

17   Repository costs
17.1   Standalone PC costs
17.2   Multiple user (LAN) costs
17.3   Mainframe use costs
17.4   Repository maintenance costs
17.5   Repository training costs
17.6   Repository documentation costs

APPENDIX 5

Questionnaire Respondent Directions

This appendix contains the set of directions for responding to either the DBMS or the repository questionnaire.

1.1 Response Format

The response to each question must conform to the following format:

<response>::= <answer><comma><release><comma><reference>

<answer>::=<three hyphens><affirmation>

<comma>::= ,

<three hyphens>::= ---

<affirmation>::=<Y> ¦ <N> ¦ <R> ¦ <U>

Where,

    <Y>::= Means that a feature or capability is provided, or

    <N>::= Means that a feature or capability is not provided, or

    <R>::= Means that, in answer to a question that solicits acknowledgment of a restriction, for example, the number of the data elements in a record type, a specific restriction is imposed, or

    <U>::= Means that in answer to a question that solicits acknowledgment of a restriction, for example, the number of the data elements in a record type, no restriction is imposed.

<release>::=<G> ¦ <B> ¦ <A> ¦ <S> ¦ <X>

Where,

<G>::= Generally released to all users without cautions of any kind, or

<B>::= Beta released to certain users for a "final" round of testing; but not yet (G)enerally released, or

<A>::= Alpha testing, that is, in the final stages of testing within the DBMS vendor's own facility, but not yet released for (B)eta testing, or

<S>::= Scheduled facility that is finished specification, in development, possibly through unit testing, but not yet in (A)lpha testing, or

<X>::= A feature that has been identified and documented, but is not yet (S)cheduled.

<reference>::= {<document number><,><page number>}...

The document numbers can be either abbreviated, or indirectly referenced so long as a legend of referenced document numbers is provided. The documentation referenced must be official, published as part of a DBMS's version or release, and be publicly available documents. If there are multiple references, they should be separated by semicolons (;). If a reference is not provided for answers as required above, or if the referenced material is determined not to support the answer, credit will not be awarded. If any question is left unanswered, credit will also not be awarded.

1.2 Response Examples

1.2.1 Example 1

QUESTION: 3.   Can a database schema contain an author.---N

The answer means that an author cannot be supplied to the clause that defines a schema.

1.2.2 Example 2

QUESTION: 3.   Can a database schema contain an author.---Y,B, Ref 17, page 108.

The answer means that an author can be supplied in the BETA release of the software, implying that the feature is not currently available in the general release. The material is documented in document number 17, page 108.

1.2.3 Example 3

QUESTION: 10. Are there any restrictions on the number of schema record elements that can be defined in a schema record type.---R,G, Ref 24, page 22.

This answer would mean that there is a restriction on the number of data elements that can participate in a schema record type, and that the restriction is imposed in the general release of the system. The facility is documented on page 22 of reference 24.

Note: If the restriction is documented elsewhere, then a reference to the location of the restriction must also be provided.

1.2.4 Example 4

QUESTION: 2. Are the procurement costs for acquiring multiple copies of a multiple user optional DBMS component provided.---Y, Ref 108, page 75

The answer indicates that the material is provided and is contained in reference 108, page 75.

1.3 Alternative Answers

If a capability is not available, but the vendor has an alternative approach that should be considered, then that material or justification should be referenced. Upon evaluation, the proposed alternative may be awarded credit.

Bibliography

Agrios, Potochnik. *Practical Considerations for Distributed Databases*, paper 300. Redwood Shores, CA: Oracle International Users Conference, 1992.

Andleigh, Gretzinger. *Distributed Object-Oriented Data-Systems Design*. Englewood Cliffs, NJ: Prentice Hall, 1992.

Atre, Shaku. *Distributed Databases, Cooperative Processing, & Networking*. New York, NY: McGraw Hill, 1992.

Berson, Alex. *Client/Server Architecture*. New York, NY: McGraw-Hill Series on Computer Communications, 1992.

Boar, Bernard H. *Implementing Client/Server Computing*. New York, NY: McGraw Hill, 1993.

Coad, Nicola. *Object-Oriented Programming*. Englewood Cliffs, NJ: Yourdon Press Computing Series, 1993.

Coad, Yourdon. *Object-Oriented Analysis*. Englewood Cliffs, NJ: Yourdon Press Computing Series, 1991.

Coad, Yourdon. *Object-Oriented Design*. Englewood Cliffs, NJ: Yourdon Press Computing Series, 1991.

DeMarco, Tom. *Controlling Software Projects*. Yourdon Press Computing Series, 1982.

Feuerlicht, Blair. *Management of Replicated Data in a Distributed Oracle Environment*, paper 820. Redwood Shores, CA: Oracle International Users Conference, 1992.

Freedman, Weinberg. *Handbook of Walkthroughs, Inspections, and Technical Reviews*. New York, NY: Dorset House Publishing, 1990.

Gause, Weinberg. *Are Your Lights On?*. New York, NY: Dorset House Publishing, 1990.

Gorman, Michael M. *Database Management Systems: Understanding and Applying Database Technology*. Wellesley, MA. QED Information Sciences, Inc., 1991.

Humphrey, Watts S. *Managing the Software Process*. Reading, MA: Addison Wesley, 1990.

Inmon, W. H. *Advanced Topics in Information Engineering*. Wellesley, MA: QED Information Sciences, Inc., 1989.

Martin, Chapman and Leben. *Systems Application Architecture*. Englewood Cliffs, NJ: Prentice Hall., 1992.

Page-Jones, Meilir. *The Practical Guide to Structures Systems Design*. Englewood Cliffs, NJ: Yourdon Press Computing Series, 1988.

Page-Jones, Meilir. *Practical Project Management*. New York, NY: Dorset House Publishing, 1985.

Perry, William E. *Managing Systems Maintenance*. Wellesley, MA: QED Information Science, Inc., 1981.

Schnaidt, Patricia. *Enterprise-Wide Networking*. Carmel, IN: Sams Publishing, 1992.

Smith, Patrick. *Client/Server Computing*. Carmel, IN: Sams Publishing, 1992.

Walsh, Mike. *Productivity Sand Traps & Tar Pits*. New York, NY: Dorset House Publishing, 1991.

Yourdon, Edward. *Modern Structured Analysis*. Englewood Cliffs, NJ: Yourdon Press Computing Series, 1989.

Zells, Lois. *Managing Software Projects*. Wellesley, MA: QED Information Science, Inc., 1990.

Index *

* Note: Commonly used words like DBMS and project were not indexed as those indexes would not provide a discriminating alternative to a table of contents.